PARIS HOLLYWOOD

Writings on Film

—◆—

PETER WOLLEN

VERSO

London • New York

First published by Verso 2002
© Peter Wollen 2002
All rights reserved

1 3 5 7 9 10 8 6 4 2

Verso
UK: 6 Meard Street, London W1F 0EG
USA: 180 Varick Street, New York, NY 10014–4606
www.versobooks.com

Verso is the imprint of New Left Books

ISBN 1–85984–671–8 ✓
ISBN 1–85984–391–3 (pbk)

British Library Cataloguing in Publication Data
A catalogue record for this book is available from the British Library

Library of Congress Cataloging-in-Publication Data
A catalog record for this book is available from the Library of Congress

Typeset in 10/12pt Baskerville by SetSystems Ltd, Saffron Walden, Essex
Printed and bound in the UK by Biddles Ltd, Guildford and King's Lynn
www.biddles.co.uk

CONTENTS

PART III: THEMES AND STYLES

15 The Canon   216

16 Time in Film and Video Art   233

17 Mismatches (& *Acousmètres*)   242

18 *Back* to the Future   255

19 Speed and the Cinema   264

    Notes   275

    Film-makers/Directors Index   297

    Filmography   300

    General Index   305

I

AN ALPHABET OF CINEMA[1]

I am going to begin at the beginning, with A. Perhaps with the collaborative film *A & B in Ontario* that Joyce Wieland made with Hollis Frampton, and completed after his death—in which each film-maker in turn shot a segment of their own for the other to respond to, like a game of tag, or a cinematic dialogue? No,

A is going to be for Aristotle. This may seem a strange choice, but I believe that Aristotle can be seen, convincingly enough, as the first theorist of film. Certainly he was the first theorist of narrative and, in his *Poetics*, written or recorded in the fourth century BC, he wrote about tragic drama as an art-form that had six components plot, character, dialogue or screenplay (counting both as content, or signi-fieds—what Aristotle called 'thought'—and as form, or signifiers, what Aristotle called 'diction'), music and spectacle. These are also, of course, the basic constituents of the cinema and so it becomes relatively simple to transpose Aristotle's theory of tragic drama into a theory of film. Aristotle's approach was marked by his own experience of life, the social and political context in which he lived. His father was a court physician, serving the King of Macedon (Philip, the father of Alexander the Great), and, all his life, Aristotle was inevitably involved with Macedonian politics. He served as tutor for a while to the young Alexander, before he became king, and he remained on close terms with the authorities after the Macedonians went on to conquer Greece itself.

Aristotle's life was far from calm. He lived through an extraordinary period of history, one during which Alexander extended his empire far to the East, to what is now Pakistan. It was also an extremely bloody and destructive period. Struggles for power were customarily settled by one family member assassinating another. Aristotle's protector during his period of exile in Asia Minor, his wife's uncle, was betrayed by the Macedonians to the Persians and killed. Aristotle's hometown of Stageira was razed to the ground and its inhabitants slaughtered. His nephew was cruelly murdered by Alexander. When Aristotle himself left Athens, shortly before his death, the column erected in his honour was torn down by angry Athenian nationalists, who seem to have regarded him as a Macedonian agent. In effect, his life was marked by a torrent of unexpected and appalling reversals of fortune—peripeteias, as he called them—by fatal misunderstandings and miscalculations, and by bloody struggles within the ruling family to which he was connected. In this sense, Aristotle's view of Greek tragedy as an imitation of life was perfectly plausible. It portrayed events which, however horrific, must have seemed quite normal to him—the Oedipus story, the troubles of the ruling House of Thebes. More than once, Aristotle received unexpected word of some terrible event that would change the course of his life.

I think we can see the cinema as reflecting, in the same kind of way, the bloody and tragic twentieth century. This may seem strange for an art-form created largely in America, where whole cities have never been levelled to the ground, but it is not so hard to understand in the rest of the world—in Europe, Africa or Asia. Like Greek tragedy, cinema has continuously echoed the violence and terror of the twentieth century. At the same time, it has distanced itself from them. As Aristotle argued, narrative—or emplotment—distances art from the history it mirrors. It focuses on the ways in which actions are caused and have effects, so that the spectator can learn from them, can gain an understanding of events which may at first seem simply meaningless and arbitrary; and thus gather the practical wisdom necessary to survive and cope in turbulent times. My own reading of Aristotle is not so much that he thought tragedy purged the emotions—he mentions the word 'catharsis' just once in passing—but that he thought it enabled us to learn about history and how it works, even—especially—in its most frightening and overwhelming aspects: the fateful moments when hidden truths are revealed, when families and dynasties fall apart and the passions destroy public order. Narrative is interwoven with the shocks and peripeteias of fortune.

Paradoxically, I began to read Aristotle in order to understand the writings of his great antagonist, Bertolt Brecht. Brecht himself directly attacked the idea of an Aristotelian theatre, seeking to replace it with what he named 'epic' theatre, but I now think his polemic was based on a common misunderstanding. Aristotle's idea of tragedy was very far from the kind of psychologically involving theatre that Brecht attacked. Like his fiercest critic, Aristotle saw tragedy as essentially didactic and political. Brecht's tragic vision of history, a vision shaped by world war, by successful and failed revolution, by the civil strife of the Weimar period and the rise to power of Hitler, was not so very distant from that of Aristotle, shaped by Alexander of Macedon and the crisis of the Athenian *polis*. For Daney, cinema—true cinema—began with *Hiroshima, Mon Amour*, a film about our personal response to an immense historic tragedy. Resnais's film became the measure against which all others were judged. It was in their relation to *Hiroshima, Mon Amour* that Daney came to see Rossellini and Godard as the great moral film-directors of our time, an epoch marked by the Holocaust, by the use and proliferation of weapons of unimaginable destruction, by endless episodes of violence and terror—in Algeria, in Cambodia, in France itself. As time went on, the historical and political context of the cinema became increasingly central to Daney's writing about film, as he turned Godard's maxim that travelling shots (*mise en scène*) are always a matter of morality into the touchstone of his critical reflection. Later, I shall have a little more to say about travelling shots.

B is not for Brecht, although of course it could be. Or even for B-movies, much as I always loved them. It is for *Bambi*. *Bambi* was the first film I ever saw and it left, no doubt, a deep mark on me, even a traumatic one. After seeing it, I repressed it, I put it out of my mind—until one day, on the outskirts of Santa Barbara, California, I was driving down the road with friends, sitting in the back of an open car, when I looked up and suddenly had a vision of my terrifying childhood memory, right there: the forest fire in *Bambi*. At first I couldn't grasp what I had seen but, as I recovered from the shock, I realized that there was a huge drive-in movie screen right across the road and we had happened to drive past it precisely at my traumatic moment. Horror and pity—Aristotle's categories—had stayed with me, more or less suppressed, for years which, increasingly, I spent in the cinema, without ever thinking back to the trauma. When I did, after my Santa Barbara 'return of the repressed', I started to realize that the horror and pity were not simply explicable in terms of the little Disney deer. There was something else at stake. *Bambi* was made during the war and, in a hidden sense, it was a war film. In fact, it was released in August 1942, at the onset of the Battle of Stalingrad.

My own memories of the war—a little later, when I lived in a small industrial town in the North of England, just south of Manchester— were of air raids: what has become generically known as the Blitz. I remember the sirens, when I had to get out of bed and go down into the closet under the stairs, or crouch under the table in the larder, listening to the buzz of the rocket bombs overhead, aimed at Manchester, but often straying off-course to fall on Macclesfield. Looked at this way, it is easy to interpret *Bambi* as a war film, with the hunters as the Nazis, the forest fire as the Blitz, the father as missing, away at the front, and the mother as a casualty of war. Aristotle again—the horror stems essentially from political conflict and barbarism. I still think, secretly, that *Bambi* is one of the great films. *Snow White* is more admired by connoisseurs but, in an un-Aristotelian way, it has a happy end—in his terms, it is a comedy, and therefore a lower form. From an artistic point of view, *Three Caballeros* is the most adventurous, less overwhelmed by kitsch than the grandiose *Fantasia*. But *Bambi* is the Aristotelian tragedy, the film about trauma. Serge Daney notes, in the very first sentence of his book *Persévérance*, that he had never seen *Bambi*—or, indeed, he boasts, any other Disney film, ever.[2] Instead, he remembers quite a different film— Charles Laughton's *Night of the Hunter*, which he saw when he was twelve, the age of the boy in the film, persecuted by Robert Mitchum's terrifying preacher. The films we remember best from our childhood always seem somehow autobiographical, always seem to be about ourselves in an especially strong sense. But Daney's flight from Disney has another explanation—Disney represents for him the limit of cinephilia, the point where it becomes complicit with the Society of the Spectacle. Obviously, I can't entirely agree with him. *Bambi* has a different meaning for me. It was the source of my cinephilia.

C, then, is for Cinephilia. I remember reading an article by Susan Sontag in which she argued that cinephilia was dead, even in Paris.[3] I hope not. I am not convinced. By 'cinephilia' I mean an obsessive infatuation with film, to the point of letting it dominate your life. To Serge Daney, looking back, cinephilia seemed a 'sickness', a malady which became a duty, almost a religious duty, a form of clandestine self-immolation in the darkness, a voluntary exclusion from social life. At the same time, a sickness that brought immense pleasure, moments which, much later, you recognized had changed your life. I see it differently, not as a sickness, but as the symprom of a desire to remain within the child's view of the world, always outside, always fascinated by a mysterious parental drama, always seeking to master one's anxiety by compulsive repetition. Much more than just another leisure activity.

For a number of years, I used to watch around ten to twenty films a week, week in, week out. I used to buy *What's On*, then the listings magazine for London, and mark all the films I had not yet seen—not the new releases but the old movies shown in repertory in doomed cinemas like the Imperial, the Essoldo, the Tolmer, the Ben Hur, the Starlight Club. Daney's equivalents in Paris were the Cinéphone, the Cyrano, the Lux, the Magic, the Artistic. When these decrepit, run-down cinemas closed, classic cinema ended with them. I would underline each film after I had seen it—in my battered copy of Coursodon and Boisset's *Twenty Years of American Cinema*, a compendium of Hollywood film in which the films were listed by director, from Aldrich to Zinnemann, with a little introductory sketch of each.[4] This was not long after the time when the 'auteur theory' was formulated in Paris—the theory that the dominant artistic personality in the cinema was that of the director, at least in any film worth watching. So each week, with my friends, I would plot our course round London, calculating the time it would take to get from one cinema to another, without missing the end of one film, *Run of the Arrow*, perhaps, in the Imperial (now the Electric) or the beginning of the next, *The Tall T*, in the Ben Hur, on the other side of town. Often we drove in Oswald Stack's Citroën DS. Later I published his interview book on Pasolini.

This option of an obsessive cinephilia was imported to London from Paris, from the film culture of the French critics, from Serge Daney's culture. Just at that time, critics became film-makers: Truffaut, Godard, Chabrol, Rohmer, Rivette. Cinephilia takes us back, once again, to the war when American films were banned under the German occupation. The first cinephiles gathered in clandestinity, in secret cine-clubs, to watch forbidden films from the pre-war days. Then, after the Liberation, there was a sudden influx of Hollywood films, unseen since the fall of France—a backlog that generated excited reverence for *Citizen Kane* and for *film noir*, seen as a cinema of Liberation, soon to be followed by a new generation of film-makers—Nicholas Ray, Otto Preminger, Frank Tashlin—and the late films of the 'Old Masters', Hawks, Hitchcock, Lang. Within France, American cinema remained a guilty pleasure, defiantly upheld. In England, it was French theory that was a guilty pleasure— Hollywood films were refracted through French culture. *Movie* magazine defiantly followed a MacMahonist line, the same line as Daney. My circle was more interested in Boetticher, Fuller and, among the classics, Douglas Sirk. In fact, it was Serge Daney who first drew our attention to Sirk, when he interviewed him for *Cahiers du Cinéma* on his return to Munich in 1964. Yet Sirk never figured prominently in Daney's own canon—he was simply another veteran director to be caught on the tape-recorder, along with Cukor, McCarey or Sternberg, an investment in the past which mutated into an investment in the future.

D must certainly be for Daney, but it is also for Dance—Vincente Minnelli and Gene Kelly. Looking back on the dance film now, having written a whole book on *Singin' in the Rain*, I know that the trajectory of the MGM musical is not at all simple—the two stars of the Freed Unit, Kelly and Minnelli, had very different tastes and temperaments. Minnelli was formed by the 1920s, by the revival in smart circles of the Eighteen-Nineties, aestheticism and the Decadence. He revered Freud and Aubrey Beardsley. Gene Kelly was formed by the 1930s, by the Depression and the Popular Front. Minnelli saw himself as part of the fashionable art world—he was influenced by Surrealism and brought a dream-like delirium to the musical. Kelly was part of the down-market dance world: brought up in the world of tap-dancing and working men's clubs, the world of vaudeville, but aspiring to the world of ballet, to the world of high art. For me, Kelly was one of the few great geniuses of Hollywood. With *On the Town*, he took the musical out of the studio, onto the streets of New York, into everyday life. With *Singin' in the Rain*, he perfected his invention of what we might call 'cine-choreography', his combination into one person of dancer, choreographer and film-maker, so that each dance was conceived and executed together with camera-angle and movement. Dance was no longer 'filmed' from outside. It merged with film. Kelly broke down the distinction between off-stage and on-stage, between narrative and spectacle. He dramatized dance, choreographed action. It was tragic that, after *Singin' in the Rain*, Kelly was forced to leave America because of the Blacklist, the witch-hunt, like Chaplin and Welles. By the time he returned, Hollywood had changed and he had aged as a dancer.

E, it follows, is for Eisenstein, another ruined film-maker, an image-maker 'haunted by writing' (Daney's phrase), by the shot as ideogram, obsessed with the synchronization of sound, movement and image. Eisenstein became world-famous during the days of silent film and, like so many other directors of that period, he had mixed feelings about the coming of sound. He feared that cinema—which had established itself as an autonomous art during the silent period—would be recolonized, so to speak, by theatre and by scripted dialogue. So he set out to formulate a completely different project for sound cinema, one that was based on synchronization of the senses, the auditory and the visual, in which the soundtrack would interact with the image, as music interacts with dance. Eisenstein studied Disney's early sound animation films—especially his Mickey Mouse films—in which gesture and editing were synchronized with the musical score. In *Alexander Nevsky*, he worked with his composer, Prokofiev, in the same kind of way, to create a kind of integrated audio-visual spectacle. When Soviet tyranny prevented Eisenstein from fulfilling his plans in the cinema, he hoped to realize them in opera. He produced Wagner for the stage, turning to the great nineteenth-century theorist of the integration of the performing arts (drama, spectacle and music) not as a hierarchy, as in the *Poetics*, but on strictly equal terms.

Daney took the opposite, Brechtian view—sound and image should be in conflict. In his review of Straub and Huillet's Schoenberg films, *Einleitung* and *Moses and Aaron*, he praises them for their disjunction of sound and image, their insistent heterogeneity. Sound and image, Daney puns, were 'not reconciled'. Like Daney, I was a great admirer of Straub and Huillet, with their Brechtian distaste for unities of any kind. It was the example I followed in my own films. Yet, for me, the most significant aspect of Eisenstein's response to the coming of sound lay not so much in his specific teaching as in his strategic turn towards theory in general. Partly this was because, out of favour with the communist establishment, and unable to direct, he was employed as a teacher in the Moscow Film School. But, fundamentally, it was because he was trying to formulate a new aesthetic, to understand a new medium, sound film, which he saw as completely different from silent cinema—to break with the fetish of silence, just as Straub wanted to break with the fetish of synchronization. Eisenstein's attempt to combine film theory with film practice made an enormous impact on me. It was linked in my mind to the transition of Jean-Luc Godard from theory to practice, from writing about film to writing with film, as he tried once again to think through the relationship of sound and image in a new way, just as Eisenstein did.

I still cling to the idea that theory and practice belong together. I don't see my books or my lectures as separate activities from my screenwriting or my film-making. In my essays on counter-cinema, I tried to lay the groundwork for an experimental cinema which would be oppositional in both form and content, both signifier and signified. With Laura Mulvey, I began to make films, experimental films—as Serge Daney put it, in another context, Eisenstein rather than Pudovkin. In the aftermath of May 1968, it seems that Daney too might have ended up as an avant-garde film-maker, making a very similar kind of film—he was one of the group of Parisian film-makers that gathered around Silvina Boissonas, a group that included Philippe Garrel, who Daney judges to have been 'the best'. I don't agree. I think that Jackie Raynal was a much more significant film-maker, a pioneer of the unedited long take, and I prefer

Boissonas's own work to Garrel's. Sadly, Daney gave up film-making for travel, for becoming, as he puts it, the unknown star of a solipsistic film which nobody but himself would ever see, which could only be glimpsed through the postcards he sent back home to his friends, as it were from location. Daney saw Straub–Huillet and Godard–Miéville as the exemplary film-makers of his generation, and struggled, in his writings, to prevent them from being marginalized. He was looking for a model which was neither that of the Industry nor, as it evolved, that of the Festival, however important festivals had become—increasingly so, since the days of Antonioni and the New Wave. He understood, of course, that Wenders (whose work he liked) was the quintessential festival director, yet he was not himself what you might call a festival critic.

F—you have probably guessed—is for Festival. Film festivals began in the 1930s when the Venice Festival was founded by Mussolini as part of his effort to make Italy the centre for a European cinema. After the war Cannes began to play a similar kind of role. Then came Berlin and Moscow and Edinburgh and Toronto and Pesaro and Tunis and Quaga-dougou and Telluride and Sundance and the Midnight Sun Festival in Finland, north of the Arctic Circle. The number of festivals began to stretch out towards infinity. Recently, when I was in Brazil, the Brazilian artist and videomaker Artur Omar told me his theory that there was a whole new genre of films—the festival film genre. Films in this genre were specially made according to their own rules and traditions in order to win prizes at festivals. They were immediately recognizable as festival films by juries, critics and audiences alike. They had become integrated into the institution of cinema.

The festival film is hard to separate from the idea of a 'New Wave'. After the French New Wave came the new cinemas of Italy and Germany—Bertolucci, Pasolini, Fassbinder, Wenders, Syberberg. In fact, support for 'Young German Cinema' was consciously organized by Alexander Kluge and Volker Schlöndorff on the model of the French New Wave, very successfully. Gradually 'New Waves' spread outside Europe—there was the Brazilian Cinema Novo, under the leadership of Glauber Rocha, director of *Black God, White Devil* and *Antonio Das Mortes*, which fused the idea of a European New Wave with the traditional

Brazilian project, dating back to Cavalcanti, of creating a 'Cinema of the North-East', of the backlands. Later came the discovery of the Chinese New Wave, the Australian New Wave, the Taiwanese New Wave, the Iranian New Wave. In effect, 'New Wave' began to fuse with 'National Cinema'. It no longer represented a revolution, but a tradition.

G—in contrast—is for Godard, for anti-tradition. Godard was the most extraordinary artist to emerge from within the original French New Wave. I was in Paris when *A Bout de Souffle* (*Breathless*) first came out and I saw it every day for a week. At the time, people commented on the way it broke the traditional rules of film-making—its use of jump-cuts, its interpolation of *cinéma-vérité* techniques into narrative film. Recently, when I saw it again, in a beautiful new 35mm print, it seemed almost classical. Its strangeness had been eroded by time. Godard himself never really fitted into the festival genre. By the end of the sixties he had moved decisively into the avant-garde. For him, the 'New Wave' was more like an escape-hatch from the grip of Hitchcocko–Hawksianism—

H is for Hitchcocko–Hawksianism—and a pathway towards avant-garde film. Godard was formed by *Cahiers du Cinéma*, but rather than Hitchcock and Hawks, who became the twin idols of one wing of the *Cahiers*, I feel it was Nicholas Ray who had the biggest impact on him. I don't really agree with Godard about Ray as far as Hollywood was concerned: I always saw Hitchcock as much more of an experimental film-maker than Ray. I revered Hitchcock, not only for the way in which he put his own unmistakable stamp on every Hollywood film he made but, most of all, for having the courage to make an experimental feature film such as *Rope*, all shot in ten-minute takes, despite the presence of stars like James Stewart and Farley Granger. The *Cahiers* position, however, offered another, alternative model of the way films were made in the industry, one which fitted Ray much better—that of the *film maudit*, the 'accursed' or 'doomed film', the film whose qualities shone through its ruins. *Cahiers* was founded partly as a result of the Festival du Film Maudit, presided over by Jean Cocteau, himself a kind of doomed film-maker, and this model of doom already implied that the conflict between artist and industry was fundamentally irreconcilable. Godard simply proved this to himself by his own example, making his own equivalents of *Johnny Guitar*, before following Nicholas Ray out of the industry and into the counter-culture. It is these threads that Wenders picked up and wove back into the fabric of the mainstream cinema, via the festival film.

I, by contrast, is for Industry and, more specifically, for Ince. Thomas Ince was the director and producer who should get the main credit, if that's the word, rather than D. W. Griffith, for creating the institution of Hollywood, for laying the foundations of the industry. It was Ince, at his own studio, who realized that the script was not just a dramatic story told in dialogue, but the template of the entire film, which could be broken down, scene by scene, to determine the estimated cost of production, the shooting schedule, the requirements that would be made of each department (sets, costumes, effects) and so on. Even today, the costume designer and the cinematographer and the props person carry annotated versions of the script, setting out what will be needed from them in each successive scene. Viewed in this light, the script is not so much an artistic product as an organizational tool, the fundamental prerequisite for the creation of Hollywood as an industry. It is the conceptual assembly line on which industrial production is based. It is also the opposite of Improvisation, the opposite of Godard. Blame or credit should go to Thomas Ince.

J is for Japan, the other country, besides America, that is universally recognized as having produced great artists within a commercial and genre-based industry—Kurosawa, Mizoguchi, Ozu. This system collapsed in the sixties, when the careers of Mizoguchi and Ozu were already over, although Kurosawa, after a nervous breakdown and a survived suicide attempt, was able to continue working precariously in international co-productions. I remember how it was mandatory for cinephiles, nearly forty years ago, to choose between the three of them. Kurosawa was the festival success. Ozu was the traditionalist whose work could be read, paradoxically, as avant-garde because of its extreme formalism. Mizoguchi was the specialist in women's films and what is now known as melodrama. I chose Mizoguchi and denounced the others, stupidly it now seems to me. Among cinephiles, there was a fierce spirit of exclusion, the inevitable result of their basic project of completely rewriting the canon. For Daney, Mizoguchi always remained the great master, although, much later, he wrote a vigorous defence of Kurosawa's comeback film, *Dodes-kaden*, one of the great films of all time, seeing there—and especially in *Dersou Uzala*—an unusually complex play of on-screen and off-screen space, an organization of visuality that refused to favour either extreme, the exclusiveness of the framing edge or the inclusiveness of the moving lens, the travelling shot.

K is for *Kane*, the *film maudit* par excellence. In formal terms, it is plainly an Aristotelian tragedy, with its pyramidal rise, its climax or peripeteia, its downfall and its tragic end. It is also an inventive, even an experimental film, especially in its narrative structure and its use of sound. Welles brought into cinema all the expertise with sound he had acquired in radio. In a way, he was able to solve Eisenstein's dilemma, to find means of using recorded speech creatively. Symbolically, *Citizen Kane* represents the rebirth of American film, the beginnings of modernity, the break with nineteenth-century conventions, with the mildewed stagecraft Griffith had brought to Hollywood from Broadway. Welles was the only American theatre director Brecht admired.

L and M take us to the middle of the alphabet, but to the beginning of cinema, to its legendary founders—Lumière standing for 'realism' and Méliès for fantasy, for *The Trip to the Moon*. But the Lumière brothers also made the first narrative film—*The Waterer Watered*—based on a story derived from a comic strip. It's a simple trickster story, hinged on a practical joke, but it's the microscopic seed of all the narrative cinema that followed, the cinema Welles modernized.

N, there's no doubt about it, has to be for Narrative. Essentially the history of early cinema is the history of the development of a 'film language' that would facilitate story-telling on film. It has been argued that verbal languages develop in the same kind of way—from simple pragmatic procedures, then on through a stage of 'grammaticalization', and finally to a fully fledged syntactic structure. We can see the process at work in children's acquisition of language and in the phenomenon of 'creolization', through which pidgins must pass on their way to becoming new languages. I believe much the same process occurred with film language, as 'grammaticalized' features such as cross-cutting, the point-of-view shot, the flashback, etc., were gradually introduced and diffused, until they were accepted automatically by the audience. Film never developed into a complex language like English or Japanese. It remains a largely pragmatic discourse, with only the nascent features of a grammar. But, perhaps, at some stage in the evolution of the medium, it will develop further. As with dialogue and conversation in verbal language, interactivity would probably be the precondition for this. This reminds us that N is also for New Media, before we move on to our next letter.

O is for Online. Strictly speaking, we are moving away from cinema now, yet the cinema itself is clearly mutating into a digital art, with its dependence on special effects and its potential for home delivery and interactivity. Digital technology is changing the whole nature of image-capture, allowing images to be changed, combined and appropriated. When cinema goes online, we will be able to download films and simultaneously summon up clips from other films for comparison, background information from research libraries and archives, even out-takes that we can use privately to make our own revised versions of sequences. Film-studies seminars will be global events with participants in distance-learning classrooms, watching and discussing the same films. I used to think that film would become an extinct art—like stained glass or tapestry—but I believe now that film as a collective spectacle will continue, just as the theatre has continued, despite the coming of cinema. Cinemas will remain, lovingly maintained by a new breed of retrocinephiles, just as theatres have remained and even flourished. Technology has always been part of the history of film. The Lumière brothers were inventors who put their expertise with still photography together with the intermittent motion of the sewing machine to produce the moving-picture camera. Until recently, we could say nothing much had happened since Christmas 1895 in the technology of cinematography, except for some improvements to lens and film-stock. That is no longer true. Cinema is finally being recreated, or perhaps I should say re-engineered.

P is personal—for *The Passenger*, a film directed by Antonioni, which I wrote with my script-writing partner Mark Peploe in the early 1970s. I was going to say something about its innovative use of technology and the use of a remote-controlled camera in the great penultimate shot, but I changed my mind. I want to tell a story, which is really a story about story-telling, a story about narrative. Quite recently I was asked by a screen-writing student about the role of coincidence in story construction—could it ever be justified? By way of an answer, I told the story then. Some years ago I was making a television documentary in Britain, a film about Tatlin's Tower, an enormous spiral structure, designed to straddle the River Neva in Petrograd, with revolving floors on each level. I wanted to compare it to the Globe Tower, planned for the Coney Island amusement park in Brooklyn, a little earlier historically. The Globe Tower was also meant to revolve—although neither structure was ever actually built. I had read about the Tower in Rem Koolhaas's amazing book *Delirious New York*, which contained a long section on Coney Island and reproduced an image from a contemporary postcard which showed what the Globe Tower would have looked like.[5] Somehow I managed to trace Rem Koolhaas, who began as a script-writer himself, but now, of course, is a world-famous architect. To my surprise he had an apartment in London, although he is Dutch, still based in Rotterdam, I believe, and so I telephoned and arranged to go round and see him. He produced a huge battered suitcase full of old postcards of New York, and there, sure enough, were a set of images of the Globe Tower. After I had found them, I began chatting with him about the film and suddenly he said, 'You know, I once met Mark Peploe. It was quite a strange situation. I was on the train from Paris to Rotterdam . . .' and I said, 'I think I know this story. Mark already told me about it.'

Some time earlier—quite a few years earlier, in fact—Mark Peploe had told me the story of how he had once got on the train in Paris in order to travel to the Netherlands on business. After a while, he had gone to the restaurant car to get something to eat. He had just finished his meal and was having coffee when a stranger appeared and asked if he could share the table—just like Eve Kendall in *North by Northwest*. Mark said, 'Of course' and after that, there wasn't any further conversation— Mark just finished his meal and sat there reading his newspaper—when, suddenly, as they began to approach the station for Rotterdam, the stranger in the other seat leaned forward and asked him, 'Excuse me, but are you perhaps Mark Peploe?' Mark was stunned. He said yes, he was, and then, as the train drew into the station, the stranger got up, apologized for interrupting, picked up his bag and left.

Rem Koolhaas confirmed to me that, yes, of course, this was the very same story that he was going to tell, but from his point of view, from the other side of the encounter. I mentioned that Mark had never been able to understand how a complete stranger could possibly have guessed who he was, so Rem Koolhaas tried to explain, with words to this effect: 'Well, really, it just occurred to me. I could see he was reading an English newspaper, so I thought he was probably English—and I noticed he seemed to be reading the film page very closely. And then, quite recently, I had been to see *The Passenger* and I knew that the writers were both English. I had seen a photograph of you somewhere, and so I knew it wasn't you. That meant it might be Mark Peploe, so I asked him if he was.' I said, 'But why? There must have been more to it than that.' He paused, and then he said, 'Well, in a way, there was There *was* something else. I had gone to see *The Passenger* with some friends and, afterwards, we had argued about it. They liked the film, but I didn't. I had a problem with the script. I thought that the story line depended far too much on a series of coincidences, and then, sitting there in the train, wondering who I was looking at, it crossed my mind, wouldn't it be a strange coincidence if that was Mark Peploe.' So—coincidence validated. Aristotle would have approved. Serge Daney mentions *The Passenger*, unexpectedly, in a discussion on documentary. He praises the moment when an African seizes the camera from the European journalist who is filming him and reverses its gaze. Not just chance, not just coincidence— a shared vision of cinema, springing from 1968.

Q is for *Qu'est-ce que le cinéma?*—*What is cinema?*—the title of the four pocket-size books of collected essays written by the great critic and theorist André Bazin, founder, first editor and intellectual godfather of *Cahiers du Cinéma*.[6] So what is cinema? For Bazin's generation, it was *Citizen Kane* and Roberto Rossellini's *Rome, Open City* and Jean Renoir's *La Règle du Jeu* (*Rules of the Game*). The Welles and the Renoir are still the top two films on the Critics' Poll that the British film journal *Sight and Sound* conducts every ten years—in fact, they have been ever since the 1960s.

R, as chance would have it, is not only for Roberto Rossellini and *Rome, Open City*, but also for Renoir and *Rules of the Game*. Renoir's film, like Welles's, is about modernity—its hero is an aviator, a kind of Lindbergh or Saint-Exupéry, who has achieved fame through the radio, the modern medium of its time, the medium that formed Welles's attitude to sound. André Jurieu is a modern public figure, an avatar of a media-dominated society, of a new, shrinking world. His fatal flaw is that he can't help speaking the truth, whereas everyone else lives in a 'modern' world in which words have become devalorized. Serge Daney scarcely mentions Bazin—instead, he sees the *Cahiers* through the lens of Jean Douchet, who (like Barthes) combined dandyism with a commitment to hermeneutics, to interpretation. In London, we dug back, down to ontology and phenomenology, back to Bazin. Bazin described *Rules of the Game* as a realist film, largely because of its use of location shooting and depth of field in the cinematography, which he saw as analogous to Greg Toland's use of deep focus in *Citizen Kane*. Like *Kane*, it was a *film maudit*, butchered by its distributor, reconstructed and re-released under Bazin's supervision ten years after it was made. 1941, when *Kane* came out, was also the year of Renoir's first American film, *Swamp Water*. Renoir had been forced to leave France after the German invasion and had managed to get on a boat from Lisbon to New York. And 1941 was the year—if you will forgive the coincidence—in which Sternberg made *Shanghai Gesture*.

S, then, is for Sternberg, *Shanghai Gesture* and Surrealism. The surrealists in Paris sent round a questionnaire to their members after viewing, or re-viewing, *Shanghai Gesture*. There is a scene in the film where Doctor Omar—'Doctor of What?' he is asked, and he replies 'Doctor of Nothing'—where Doctor Omar (played by Victor Mature) gives Poppy, the heroine (played by Gene Tierney), a mysterious box, which is never opened. Perhaps I imagined this. In any case, in my dream, the surrealists were asked what they thought was in the box. They imagined a host of strange, bizarre dream-like objects, in keeping with the mysterious and delirious world of Sternberg's movie, set in a crazed bordello and gambling hell in pre-war Shanghai, run by the sinister Mother Gin Sling. My suggestion is much more mundane, but just as magical. I think that the box contained a pair of red-and-green glasses for watching three-dimensional films.

When I was thirteen years old I went to the Festival of Britain, a kind of World's Fair which was held in London (in 1951) to celebrate the Hundredth Anniversary of the Great Exhibition of Victorian times, for which they built the Crystal Palace. At the Festival of Britain, among the other attractions, was the Telecinema, so

T is for Telecinema and Third Dimension. It is for Television, too, cinema's domestic sibling, its rival which offers us, as Daney once complained, a 'haemorrhaging of images', lacking a true aesthetic and the power to change us as 'subjects', as human beings. The Telecinema was the first theatre specially built to project television onto a large screen—as you sat waiting for the films to come, you watched the rest of the audience as they were televised entering the theatre and ascending the escalator to their seats. The main programme consisted of specially made 3D films for which you had to put on polarizing glasses, with one lens red and the other green. There were two animation films in the programme, made by Norman McLaren, and a demonstration film of the London Zoo. For me, the great moment was when the giraffes stretched their necks out from the screen and high over the audience, as though you could stretch up towards them and touch them. The Telecinema was my first introduction to the idea of experimental film, the search for new possibilities—both animated abstraction, with the McLaren dance of cathode ray patterns, and technical experiment, with the Pathé film of the zoo.

T is also for Technology. When the Lumière brothers and Méliès made their first films, the audience went for the spectacle—to see what the new medium was like, to experience the technology of cinema itself. The cinema has constantly reconstructed itself through waves of technological innovation—sound, colour, wide-screen, 3D, Dolby, Imax, digital editing, new media. Experimental film-makers, on the other hand, have exploited its technical resources in their own subversive way, misusing (or travestying) them even, not to submit them to the law of narrative, but to develop new forms of film-making, to create new beginnings for the art of film.

U is for Underground Film—the name given to marginal film-making in the 1960s, spread across North America and Europe by the Film Co-op movement. Underground film-making was an attempt to get back to a kind of primitive innocence, to recreate the time of Lumière, to re-enter the unspoiled visual Paradise of film—unspoiled, that is, by the serpent of narrative. Notoriously, Andy Warhol just switched the camera on and shot whatever was in front of it until the reel ran out. In his film *Empire*, he filmed the Empire State Building for eight hours, without a single movement of the camera or a single visible cut. Other films subverted the technical and material sub-structure of cinema—flicker films, films which showed the dust-particles and scratches that are part of every film's destiny, films that blew up the image by refilming it until the spectator became aware of the grains of silver embedded in the celluloid—whose tarnishing from light to dark still remains the essential physical precondition of cinema. These films were seen, of course, as perverse, aberrant, but they mark the moment when film became conscious of itself purely as film, when film artists dedicated themselves to revealing the concealed foundations of their art, exploring its neglected potential. Not innocent exactly—but certainly against the grain.

Strangely, Serge Daney neglected experimental film, perhaps because the Co-op movement never really flourished in France. In the 1970s I wrote a piece distinguishing two avant-gardes—one based on the Co-ops, the other an avant-garde within the feature-film format. Daney only recognized this second avant-garde, the cinema of Akerman, Duras, Garrel, Straub and Godard. He argued that experimental films, the films of the first avant-garde, defied critical interpretation because they dealt directly with the primary processes, with pure signifiers, whereas avant-garde narrative was concerned not only with visual perception but also with meaning—'elements of thought, of the signified'. In some ways, his distinction between these two types of film mirrors my own dichotomy in 'The Two Avant-Gardes', and yet it completely misses the subversive 'conceptual' dimension of the Co-op tradition, as opposed to the 'perceptual'. Now we have reached the verge of what theorists have come to call 'gaze theory', the analysis of the cinematic 'look', the televisual 'glance'. The camera's look always has a meaning beyond the perceptual mapping of space. It relates to power, surveillance and gender, however pure it may seem at first. I could not help noticing that although Daney writes about the feminine in its relation to the voice (as in Godard's films, for instance), his theory of the spectator's gaze is ungendered.

V is for Voyeurism—the perversion of the look, of the visual, which lies at the heart of the cinema. One of the very first cinematic devices was the Keyhole mask. V is for *Vertigo* and *Now Voyager*. In her essay on 'Visual Pleasure and Narrative Cinema', Laura Mulvey traced the way in which voyeurism (or scopophilia) links together narrative and spectacle through the point-of-view shot, especially in Hitchcock's films, as in *Vertigo*.[7] The point-of-view shot aligns the three looks of the cinema— camera's look, character's look and spectator's look—so that all three are directed at the same object of the gaze. Typically, Laura Mulvey argues, this object is gendered as female and that gaze is male, as it is in both *Vertigo* and *Now Voyager*. These two films are also 'make-over' films, in which the male hero recreates for his gaze the image of the woman he desires. In Cukor's *The Women*, however, a film with an all-woman cast, the 'looks' in the dress salon are female, looks of rivalrous assessment rather than authority and power. In the fashion insert, the look can be gendered as female—scopophilia reflects a different economy of desire.

W is for *Wavelength*, Michael Snow's great experimental film, the masterpiece of the disembodied look, of 'pure perception', made in 1967. In Snow's own words,

> The film is a continuous zoom which takes 45 minutes to go from its widest field to its smallest and final field. It was shot with a fixed camera from one end of an 80-foot loft, shooting the other end, a row of windows and the street. This, the setting, and the action which takes place there are cosmically equivalent. The room (and the zoom) are interrupted by four human events (including a death).

In fact, the dead body, stretched out on the floor, soon falls visually out of the frame as the zoom inexorably advances, and is simply forgotten. The camera finally reaches its destination in a photograph of choppy waves pinned up on the far wall of the loft. It moves into this photographic space within a space, glides slowly forward over the surface of the water towards the horizon and then stops. In effect, *Wavelength* is one extended, concentrated, unrelenting gaze—the camera's gaze reduced to its essence, mechanical and uninterested in event or narrative, simply observing and moving on. Narrative—or the possibility of narrative—is registered, discarded and forgotten. It is the narrative look that entails gender.

X is a difficult one. It is for experiment, but I have already covered that. It is for Roger Corman's *The Man with the X-Ray Eyes*, but that would take us too far down a backwater. X stands for an unknown quantity—for the strange fascination that makes us remember a particular shot or a particular camera movement. It is what the early French theorists of silent film called *photogénie*, the photogenic—an effect of light and shadow, playing over significant forms, revealing and concealing something we don't quite understand. Garbo's face. It is an interruption of narrative by a moment when time freezes and we are fascinated by the image in front of us. Barthes tried to find a name for it—the symbolic, the third meaning, the punctum. Let's call it X.

Y is for *Les Yeux sans Visage*, Franju's *Eyes without a Face*, the look de-humanized. In another form, it is Vertov's camera-eye, the camera that comes alive like a robot, stalks through the city, hides beneath the tracks to film the train roaring overhead, sails through the air to film the torrent below, hurls itself at the audience, filming the spectator, reversing the gaze, as in *The Passenger*, as Vertov had required in his idea of the *kinok*, the utopian idea of a communal cinema made by the public rather than by specialists, all filming each other, dissolving the look into reciprocity.

Z is the final frame of the zoom shot. Z is for *Zorn's Lemma*, Hollis Frampton's masterpiece, a film made by following a predetermined set of rules, based, axiomatically, on the significance of the number 24 as, coincidentally, both the number of letters in the Latin alphabet and the number of frames projected per second, using the statistical frequency of English words beginning with each letter to determine the film's underlying structure. A cinematic algorithm, whose computational procedures ensured the solution of a filmic problem. And, finally, Z is for Zero—*Zero for Conduct*, zero visibility and Godard's slogan, 'Back to Zero'. As we enter the age of new media, the cinema is reinventing itself. We need to see that reinvention in radical as well as mainstream terms, to try and reimagine the cinema as it might have been and as, potentially, it still could be—an experimental art, constantly renewing itself, as a counter-cinema, as 'cinema haunted by writing'. Back to zero. Begin again. A is for Avant-Garde.

PART I

Directors and Film-Makers

2

GUERRILLA CONDITIONS:
THE CINEMA OF
WILLIAM SEWARD BURROUGHS[1]

Between 1960 and 1966 William Burroughs and his close associates
Brion Gysin, Ian Sommerville and Anthony Balch—worked on a number of film projects, two of which eventually reached the London
cinema. *Towers Open Fire* opened at the Paris Pullman on Draycott
Gardens in 1964, as the supporting short film to Tod Browning's
Freaks. *The Cut-Ups* was screened in 1966 at the Cinephone in Oxford
Street. The unreleased film *Bill and Tony* was a kind of 'expanded
cinema' project, involving portrait films designed to be projected onto
the bodies of subjects themselves, so that one person's image was superimposed on the body of another. These three short film projects were
each a strange mixture of avant-garde art, home movie, science fiction
and audio-visual experiment, reflecting Burroughs's preoccupations at
the time, copiously laced with the master's own do-it-yourself semiotic
theory and his anarcho-visionary commitment to idiosyncratic forms of
political resistance and insurgency. Burroughs himself was predomi-
nantly responsible for the driving ideas behind the films, although many
of these had their source in Gysin's work as a painter and his excited
discovery of the 'Cut-Up' method in the autumn of 1959. Ian Sommerville, a Cambridge science graduate, provided technical expertise—he
invented the 'dream machine' which figures in the films and he took
charge of the complicated sound mixes which Burroughs required—and
Anthony Balch, who came out of the film world, took charge of the

cinematography and what might loosely be called the direction of the films.

Burroughs had known Gysin distantly in Tangier in the mid-fifties, remembering him suspiciously as a 'paranoid bitch-on-wheels' as well as proprietor of the 1001 Nights restaurant.[2] However, he reversed his view completely after getting to know him much more closely in the autumn of 1958, when Gysin arrived in Paris and moved into the 'Beat Hotel' at 9 Rue Git Le Coeur, where Burroughs was already ensconced. Ian Sommerville came into Burroughs's orbit about a year later, August 1959, when he was introduced to him as a young man who could look after the ailing writer during his detoxification. In 1960, Burroughs also met Anthony Balch in Paris, through the Brion Gysin circle. Their collaborative film-making began in 1961 when Balch embarked on shooting footage for a film then envisaged as *Guerrilla Conditions*, which consisted, more or less, of home-movie footage featuring Burroughs and associates at home and in the streets of Paris, Tangier and New York. In the end most of this footage ended up cannibalized into *Towers Open Fire*, which went into serious production in London towards the end of 1962, and *The Cut-Ups*, which succeeded it in 1964 and was also created in London. The ideas behind *Bill and Tony* were based on an old Burroughs routine and had been worked out by Gysin and Sommerville back in the summer of 1961, but the project was never prioritized and it gradually faded away, although Anthony Balch made the effort to revive it ten years or so later. During this time, it should be noted, Burroughs was also busy at work on his trilogy, *The Soft Machine*, *The Ticket that Exploded* and *Nova Express*, as well as producing *Dead Fingers Talk* and a number of shorter but no less important works, such as *Time*, 'a book of words and pictures'.[3]

In fact, it is impossible to think about the films without situating them in the context of Burroughs's multifarious other projects—not only his published works but also the personal scrapbooks, the tape-recording obsession and a variety of other word–image experiments. In many ways, the films not only reflected what was in the books, but were part of an expanding spectrum of audio-visual interests which themselves fed into the books, perhaps even inspired them. *The Ticket that Exploded*, published in 1962, explicitly acknowledged Burroughs's debt to Sommerville for pointing out 'the use and significance of spliced tape and all the other tape recorder experiments suggested in the book' and to Anthony Balch for 'the film experiments suggested', as well as thanking Gysin for 'the closing message'. In fact, the underlying debt to Gysin was much more extensive than that, considering the impact on Burroughs of Gysin's own earlier experiments with cut-ups, calligraphy and pictographic texts, as well as his discovery of jajouka ritual music, with its insistent drum rhythms, contrasting pipe tones and jazz-like improvisation style. All of these elements resurface not only in Burroughs's printed words, but also in his fold-ins and scrapbooks, his photographic projects and, of course, in the films, which introduced movement and sound to supplement the still image. Essentially, Burroughs should be viewed as a multi-media artist, whose obsessions and fascinations ranged across the whole field of the audio-visual—image, painting, glyph, written word, spoken word, sound effect, music.

The relationship between word and image was fundamental to Burroughs's thinking at this time. While it is often difficult to follow the precise thread of his discourse, veering as it does between the paranoid, the fantastic and the frankly incredible, all the while claiming allegiance to an anti-Aristotelian 'factualism', it seems clear that Burroughs became obsessed, during this period, by the whole question of the relationship between word, sound and image as they functioned in control systems. Perhaps I can put it this way: based on his experience as a heroin addict, Burroughs reached the conclusion that human beings are extremely vulnerable to control by forces introduced into their minds and bodies from outside. While drugs provide an obvious instance of this kind of destructive and externally generated control system, Burroughs also saw analogous systems working through viruses—in fact, he feared that kicking a drug habit might lead simply to greater susceptibility to damaging viruses. By analogy, Burroughs saw words and images as working in a similar way to viruses—entering consciousness from outside and then shaping and controlling thought and behaviour. As he succinctly put it, 'Word authority more habit-forming than heroin' in a world populated by 'orders addicts'. Burroughs had studied Mexican archaeology at university, and from early on in his career as a writer he had developed a consuming interest in the ways in which, as he came to believe, pre-Columbian priest-rulers had ruthlessly controlled the Mayan peoples of Central America through a system of calendar glyphs. Over time, this early vision of totalitarian control gradually mutated into the science-fiction world of the trilogy, in which glyphs were reformulated as the 'word and image locks' which control our minds, just as drugs, viruses and sexual desires control our bodies.

During 1959, Burroughs was introduced to Scientology by Gysin and became fascinated by the movement's use of questionnaires combined with tape-recording, followed by the repeated playback of answers, in order, it was claimed, to clear the mind of unwanted memories. Burroughs came to see the technique as a control mechanism, but one which could be turned against controllers by rebel forces if it could be reformulated in the right way. This quest for an effective de-controlling device was the source of the elaborate tape experiments which Burroughs conducted, with the help of Sommerville's technical expertise. By manipulating spoken words, repeating them and permutating them, as in his cut-ups of newspapers and magazines, Burroughs hoped to de-couple them from their rigid correlation with specific mental images and create instead what he called 'association blocks' of randomized word-to-image links, somewhat along the lines of the randomized word-to-word links created by cut-ups. The same logic applied, by extension, to the cut-ups of image sequences which Burroughs and Balch used in their films. In fact, in the Nova mythology he developed, Burroughs had already postulated the idea that control was exercised in the 'Reality Studios' where addictive illusions were manufactured out of word and image banks, along the lines of those accumulated by *Time*, *Life* and *Fortune*, a control system 'more effective' than the Mayan system. (Bill Gates was yet to come.) He also came up with the idea that controllers modelled human behaviour through a 'biologic film'. As Jennie Skerl has summarized, in relation to *The Soft Machine*, 'the "machine" of the narrative fantasy is a word-and-image system: reality is a film, identity a script, and the body is behaviouristically programmed through visual and auditory stimuli. Revolt is achieved by turning the machine against itself through newspaper cut-ups, film cut-ups, photomontage, and synaesthesia.'[4]

In *The Ticket that Exploded* Burroughs writes,

The film stock issued now isn't worth the celluloid it's printed on. There is nothing to back it up. The film bank is empty. To conceal the bankruptcy of the reality studio it is essential that no one should be in a position to set up another reality set. The reality film has now become a weapon and instrument of monopoly. The full weight of the film is directed against anyone who calls the film in question with particular attention to writers and artists. Work for the reality studio or else.[5]

Nonetheless, intrepid partisans storm the reality studios, disconnect the control machine, capture the 'board books' whose symbols refer to the association locks that limit our freedom to think and imagine creatively. Instead 'plays on stage with permutating sections moved through each other, Shakespeare, ancient Greek, ballet—Movies mix on screen half one half the other—plays in front of movie screen synchronized so that horses charge in and out of old Westerns—characters move in and out of the screen flickering different films on and off . . .' The fall of the studio leads to a carnivalesque breakdown of boundaries and an unlimited mixing of diverse identities.

Towers Open Fire begins with a board meeting in a room furnished with film cans, presumably a version of the 'grey room' which, according to Burroughs (in *Nova Express*), is the control-and-command centre of the evil system, eventually to be overrun by rebels who have succeeded in 'breaking through to the grey room'. Questioned about this key item in his mythology by a *Paris Review* interviewer in 1965, he commented,

I see that as very much like the photographic darkroom where the reality photographs are actually produced. Implicit in *Nova Express* is a theory that what we call reality is actually a movie. It's a film, what I call a biologic film. What has happened is that the underground and also the Nova police [led by Inspector Lee, a Burroughs persona and a 'good policeman', as he described the role played by apomorphine in the body's war against heroin addiction] have made a breakthrough past the guards and gotten into the darkroom where the films are processed, where they're in a position to expose negatives and prevent events from occurring.[6]

In *Towers Open Fire*, the grey room becomes the boardroom where the 'board books' are kept, artworks whose illuminated pages were created for the film by Anthony Balch—in the absence of Brion Gysin, who

Balch felt should really have done the job. On their way to besiege the grey room, the rebels cause a stock market crash (recycled newsreel footage) by selling stock at arbitrary intervals and stare into Sommerville and Gysin's dream machine while jajouka music plays on the sound-track—'anything that can be done chemically can be done in other ways'.

The film ends with Mikey Portman dancing a soft-shoe routine in homage to *Singin' in the Rain*. The dramatic finale, however, comes immediately before, when a group of masked commandos storm the British Film Institute's board room and strafe a display of photographic images with 'orgasm guns'. Hand-painted dots and slashes fill the screen and the pages of the 'board books', covered with glyphs based on the ancient Egyptian Book of the Dead, are scattered to the winds, floating down into the Street of the Dogs, where they settle on the roadway only to be driven over by passing cars. This apocalyptic ending contains clear echoes of two crucial sections in *The Ticket that Exploded*, 'Will Hollywood Never Learn?' and especially, of course, of the eponymous 'Towers Open Fire'. The first of these begins with the berserk Time Machine, a kind of computerized Mayan calendar, issuing 'insane orders and counter orders' as 'governments fall with a whole civilization and ruling class into streets of total fear' and ends with a jubilant invocation of victory. Immediately afterwards come the commands ' "*Focus.*" "*Did it.*" "*Towers, open fire*—"' and the storming of the grey room, 'Place Of the Board Books And The Death Dwarfs', until finally a message of victory goes out from the rebel force's technician:

—*Installations shattered—Personnel decimated—Board Books destroyed—Electric waves of resistance sweeping through mind screens of the earth—The message of Total Resistance on short waves of the world—This is war to extermination—Shift linguals—Cut word lines—Vibrate tourists—Free doorways—Photo falling—Word falling—Break through in grey room—Calling Partisans of all nations—Towers, open fire—.*

Given their shortage of resources, the film-makers had some difficulty in living up to their spectacular source of inspiration—the rebels' weaponry came from Hamley's toy store and fired ping-pong balls—but *Towers Open Fire* contained the first pioneering experiments with image cut-ups and tape montage, much of it mixed by Burroughs himself on his Grundig recorder. Gysin's prototype dream machine, made for exhibition in Paris, played a central role in the film, often accompanied by Moroccan music, doubling the flicker of 'machine-gun editing' with its own strobo-scopic visual effects. Another passage showed superimpositions of faces as Burroughs intoned a ritual curse in his most icily malignant and metallic tones. *Towers Open Fire* was not a completely successful film, partly because its low-budget amateurism shone disconcertingly through at crucial moments, and some of the innovative things Burroughs and Gysin were saying still 'hadn't really sunk in', as Balch later admitted. Yet, in its own idiosyncratic way, the film carried the message of resistance in form as well as content, launching a tightly targeted assault on the image totalitarian-ism of Hollywood and the boardbooks of mainstream cinema.

The Cut-Ups, which followed only two years after *Towers Open Fire*, was a much more accomplished film. There was no longer any attempt to tell a coherent story, simply an all-out sound and image assault on the standard cinematic conventions of continuity and entertainment. The film consists of four basic sections, shot by Balch, corresponding to the four locations in which the film was shot (Paris, Tangier, London and New York). Each of these sections was then edited down, also by Anthony Balch, into a series of shots, all exactly one foot of film in length. The anonymous negative cutter was then instructed to edit the four sets of one-foot modules together, head to tail, alternating them according to a preordained system of permutations. When the image track was completed Sommerville and Burroughs then mixed an independent soundtrack to coincide exactly with its final length—twenty minutes and four seconds. As in *Towers Open Fire*, Burroughs plays the leading role, supported by Mikey Portman and, this time, Brion Gysin rather than Anthony Balch, who stayed behind the camera. We see Burroughs in a series of seedy hotel rooms and city street scenes, punctuated by shots of the dream machine, Gysin painting, erasing and overpainting a canvas on a roller, stretched out on the floor, and producing a series of sheets of calligraphy rotated to create an illegible palimpsest, written over and across in different directions. Besides calligraphic script, these ink drawings also contain a typically laconic Burroughs text—'Guerrilla Conditions—Army Needs Base—Enemy Cannot Reach Our Area—Poetry Creates Myth—Enemy Cannot Enter Because—' and so on and so on.

In the hotel room scenes, Burroughs conducts a medical examination, involving an anonymous youth, and a financial transaction, involving a suitcase of money. A number of topical newspaper headlines were also filmed—such as 'TARGET SET FOR 3 PM' and '23 DIE AS BOMB RIPS U.S. EMBASSY'. In the street, Burroughs stops to make a telephone call, looks up at a series of advertising hoardings and, in a relatively long (and therefore recurring) sequence, passes what appears to be a Vietnamese man, walking towards him in the opposite direction. At one point shots are superimposed and at another Burroughs goes into negative—otherwise there is simply the relentless rhythm of the cross-cutting. The powerful impact of the film derives from its editing strategy, the tension between the repeated intake of new information and the frustration when it is cut arbitrarily short, the constant cross-referencing demanded as the image moves back and forth between different locations and different sequences. At the same time, the rhythm of the images often seems subordinated to the hypnotic rhythm of the sound, with snatches of dialogue repeated over and over, phrased as if they were part of an interrogation. In fact, the dialogue was modelled on Scientology interview scripts, which followed a rigid questionnaire format: 'Look at that picture. Does it seem to be persisting? Good. Thank you. How does it seem to you now?' Towards the end of the film the soundtrack is dominated by the insistent repetition of one phrase, 'Yes! Hello', superimposed on itself and time-shifted, as if it were being 'inched' back and forth over the sound head. The film finally ends with the sign-off phrase, 'Very good. Thank you', as though an interrogation was now concluded—phantasmatically, an interrogation of the unresponding spectator. The relentless soundtrack and editing protocols can seem to give the film an authoritarian aspect, as if the viewer were undergoing some kind of ordeal, although we also know that what is really going on is the rewrite operation in the grey room, by virtue of which insurgent guerrilla forces finally destroy the Nova Mob's audio-visual control systems and liberate the world from sound and image addiction.

On one level, *The Cut-Ups*, like *Towers Open Fire*, has to be seen as a political film, although its political message is carried implicitly through its formal strategies rather than explicitly through its content, where it is only sporadically hinted at. At the same time, looked at aesthetically, *The Cut-Ups* can be seen as a breakthrough experimental film, although it has never been fully accepted into the avant-garde canon. In the years between 1960 and 1963, Burroughs, Gysin and Sommerville put on a number of multi-media performance shows which brought them into contact both with Lettrists and with Fluxus. These began with Brion Gysin reading permutated poems for the BBC, but Sommerville's experiments with epidiascope and slide projector soon led to the production of much more elaborate pieces. These proto-cinematic performances began at Cambridge University (Sommerville's alma mater) with a tape-slide piece in which images of Burroughs were projected onto the body and face of Gysin while he mouthed a taped text spoken by Burroughs—the direct forerunner of *Bill and Tony*. After a performance at the Institute of Contemporary Arts in London, the trio were invited to participate in a series of performances organized at the American Center in Paris by the Lettrist poet Bernard Heidsieck. These took place under the umbrella of *Domaine Poétique* and were much more technically sophisticated, featuring the projection of paintings, collages and photographic images, complete with fades and dissolves. As a result of these shows, information about the *Domaine Poétique* performances was relayed back to Fluxus HQ in New York. George Maciunas subsequently included *Domaine Poétique* in his schematic chart of the contemporary avant-garde, bracketing the performances with 'Extended' and 'Expanded Cinema'.

Despite all these new connections, the Balch–Burroughs films (like Samuel Beckett's film work) were never incorporated into the standard histories of underground or avant-garde film, which were largely constructed around the taste of the New York Film-Makers' Co-op led by Jonas Mekas. As Brion Gysin recalled, in an interview for *Cantrill's Filmnotes* conducted in 1984,

> The whole New York art establishment, including Jonas Mekas, didn't want us, right from the start. We arrived with a very heavy aura of reputation which nobody wanted to have anything to do with. They found it too heavy and I think they found it competitive. They were trying to be very heavy themselves—Mekas, Warhol. Up to this day, I've never met Mekas or Warhol.[7]

Of course, Gysin, like Burroughs, was somewhat given to paranoia but his complaint is comprehensible. The films made by the Burroughs group never fitted comfortably into the dominant narrative of avant-garde film as it was formulated by the leading New York curators and critics and subsequently taken up by their followers in Europe and on the West Coast. In film terms, they were a group of oddballs, situated outsided the main experimental film circuits. Balch, in particular, came out of the commercial world of Wardour Street, where he had worked in advertising, subtitling and distribution, putting together trailers and organizing publicity. The films he made with Burroughs were screened in West End cinemas rather than alternative venues such as the Co-op. Burroughs was seen as a literary figure, part of the Beat Generation, and there was undoubtedly some scepticism about his attempted crossover into film— something Warhol, as a visual artist, never suffered from.

Looking back on the films now, over thirty years later, we can see them as part of a complex cultural movement running right across conventional artistic boundaries. The cut-up technique, in itself, developed from the heritage of Dada and Surrealism. There were also obvious affinities with Lettrism, which itself took dadaist techniques into film, as Gysin must have been aware. The period when the films were made coincides, in Paris, with the rise of *musique concrète* and, in the United States, with John Cage's use of the tape mix and, in the visual arts, the development of assemblage by Johns and Rauschenberg. In 1959, Al Hansen launched his New York Audio-Visual Group and, in 1960, his *Projections* mixed a collage of film and slides together with performance and dance, a path followed by George Whitman, Carolee Schneeman and Yvonne Rainer, among others. In the field of film, the Burroughs–Balch films coincide with Godard's *Les Carabiniers*, *Masculin Féminin* and *Made in USA*, as well as Guy Debord's situationist film *Critique de la Séparation* and the collage books which he composed with Asger Jorn in the late fifties. All these works have a political dimension and all of them use a collage of words and images in a way which loosely parallels Burroughs's contemporaneous films, scrapbooks and cut-ups—for example, in their use of newspapers and advertisements. However, we are talking now about work which was created in the same cultural climate, rather than work which exerted a direct influence.

Balch and Burroughs had, however, seen some early experimental films—by 1964, at least, when Jeff Nuttall went to visit them in

Bayswater, they had seen both Jack Smith's 1963 *Flaming Creatures* and a Brakhage film, almost certainly *Window Water Baby Moving* (1959). According to Nuttall, they were not impressed by the Jack Smith film but intrigued by the Brakhage because of its direct impact on the nervous system and its dislocation or redirection of the 'neuro-psychological complex'.[8] We can hazard a guess that *Flaming Creatures* was somewhat too camp for Burroughs's austere taste, as well as being much less innovative formally than Brakhage's film, to which he responded much more sympathetically, given its subliminal imagery, erratic editing and multiple superimpositions. Nonetheless, when I look at *The Cut-Ups*, I am reminded of experimental films as yet unmade, rather than either Smith or Brakhage—film such as Paul Sharits's single-frame flicker films, Andrew Noren's found footage films and Hollis Frampton's *Zorn's Lemma* (1970). Flicker films have a clear affinity with Sommerville and Gysin's dream machine—they both make use of the stroboscopic effect of rapid changes of light and darkness. Paul Sharits began his experiments with flicker while he was attached to the Fluxus group but, like Gysin and Burroughs, he tended to give a mystical spin to his preoccupation with perception, as well as adopting an aggressive attitude towards the viewer, explicitly expressed through his use of violent scissor images.

Hollis Frampton's film resembles *The Cut-Ups* in a very different way—in its use of the grid format, which provided a frame for the permutation of a series of modules, each of identical length, following a preordained algorithm. *The Cut-Ups* could easily be categorized as an unusually early example of both the flicker film and the structural film or some hybrid of the two. The stroboscopic dream machine dates back to 1960, when Sommerville first proposed it, and permutation was used as a compositional principle for written texts in The *The Exterminator*, published later the same year.[9] At the same time Burroughs was experimenting not only with cut-ups but also with the fold-in technique, folding a newspaper and realigning the folded sections—a process which led naturally to the grid format that he later adopted in his scrapbooks and for the collage compositions, juxtaposing print, calligraphy and photographic imagery, which he later worked on with Brion Gysin. The mathematical procedures necessary for more complex forms of permutation were left to Sommerville to work out—Sommerville also developed a complex grid format for still photography, which he explained in a 1964 issue of *Gnaoua*: 'Imagine a two-dimensional plane covered with a rectangular grid. Further imagine that each pair of rectangles which have a side in common are such that each of the pair is a mirror image of the other, being reflected across their common side.'[10] Following this procedure to its limit, Sommerville aimed to come up with a recursive structure so that an entire collection of photographs could be reduced to a single image 'wherein each rectangle is a collage of photographs which are in turn collages of photographs etc.'

Sommerville later went on to work for a computer company and his interest in randomization, algorithms and recursive structures plainly anticipates later work with digital media, involving cellular automata, fractals and so on, as Robert Sobieszek has pointed out.[11] In this sense, too, *The Cut-Ups* can be seen as a premonitory work, an early blaze on the trail that led eventually to computer art. In 1965, after all, Burroughs had observed that 'there's going to be more and more merging of art and science . . . I think the whole line between art and science will break down and that scientists, I hope, will become more creative and writers more scientific.'[12] The grid structure also anticipates many of the favourite strategies of Conceptual Art, such as those used by Sol LeWitt, whose wall drawings were typically created according to the same basic principles, following an algorithm to create a series of permutations within a grid. Arguably, Sommerville's interest in sound, which was essentially a sidetrack in the development of electronic music as it advanced towards digital editing, combined with Burroughs's own word and image obsessions to produce a new type of electronic spoken-word composition. This new genre of tape mix then merged, in turn, with the grid structure of Burroughs's cut-ups and photo-collages to create a unique and hitherto unprecedented form of film. It is very unlikely that this could have happened if it had not been for the collective nature of its creation—the conjunction of writer, artist, sound composer and filmmaker. Both the collectivism and the technicist bias brought to the group by Burroughs and Sommerville ran quite contrary to the individualistic ethos of much experimental film, with its underpinning of romantic self-expression.

Burroughs took for granted the inherently collective and technological form of film as a mode of production, a bias which fitted both with Balch's formative experiences in the film business and with Sommerville's mathematical and technical approach to art as an arena for problem-solving. In fact, Burroughs's dominant model of cinema was plainly that of Hollywood, the audio-visual control system par excellence, and his strategy involved turning Hollywood back on itself by subverting and reconfiguring its own medium. The traces of an old fascination with Hollywood can clearly be seen in both *Towers Open Fire* and *The Cut-Ups*. They come through in both narrative and character, especially in the presentation by Burroughs of his own meticulously crafted persona. Balch too was steeped in Hollywood genre and cult films. The dominant influences at work were those of the gangster movie, *film noir*, the horror film and the science-fiction film, just as they were in Burroughs's literary texts. It comes as no surprise that, when Burroughs wrote a more or less conventional script, it should be *The Last Days of Dutch Schultz* or that Anthony Balch's favourite movies should include, not only *Peeping Tom* and *Shock Corridor*, but also just about all of Bela Lugosi's films as well as Jack Arnold's shamelessly low budget *It Came from Outer Space*. The bricolage mentality and the weirdly paranoid vision so typical of Balch and Burroughs were already something of a Hollywood B-movie speciality.

In the end the compliment was returned and Burroughs himself had his life and equanimity disturbed, but his prestige and fame and bank balance enhanced, by the outriders of Hollywood—Hopper, Cammell and Roeg, Van Sant, Cronenberg. The last time I talked to him before he died was at a crowded film world gathering, with Theresa Russell and Anjelica Huston at one end of the rather small room and Bernardo Bertolucci, Michael Herr and John Malkovich at the other. Burroughs was sitting on the sofa eating quail's eggs, which he had never encountered before, and, as he sat shelling them, he started reminiscing to me, running through a litany of mutual acquaintances from the days when I first knew him. 'Graham Wallis is dead, isn't he?' 'Yes, Bill, he's dead.' 'And Ian Sommerville's dead? And Mikey Portman's dead? And Tara Browne?'—'Yes, Bill, they are.' He wasn't dead though, not yet. There seemed to be a certain wry satisfaction that he was still around to remember them all. It was an eerie moment, as he sat there surrounded by smiling, successful people, casting his mind back to those long-ago days in Earl's Court, Bayswater and St James. There was a logic to it, though. Those times in London, I thought, from the end of the fifties through into the sixties were really the high-point of his life, the years of unmatched productivity—the books, the collages, the tapes, the mixed media, the films. *Naked Lunch* safely behind him now, he became more than a great writer. He became a crossover artist in the true sense of the word, with film as the ultimate crossover form. Sad to remember, but the best of days. Those were the days he stormed the reality studios and took the grey room.

3

VIKING EGGELING[1]

The story begins in Sweden, in the city of Lund. It was here that Viking Eggeling was born, over a hundred years ago, in 1880 (on 21 October). His father, Fredrik Eggeling, had a music store in the market square, right in the centre of town, and was himself an accomplished musician— a virtuoso on the clarinet, a teacher of music and singing, a composer and arranger for the military band in which he also played, the publisher of *Eggeling's Song Book*. Viking was one of twelve children, and their father formed them into a family choir. Here, of course, are the roots of Viking Eggeling's later work, in its musical dimension—his *Thorough-Bass for Painting*, his *Horizontal-Vertical Orchestra* and, of course, his *Diagonal Symphony*. Eggeling, it is perhaps worth noting, was a poor student while at the Cathedral School in his native Lund, but he did receive good marks both for music and for penmanship, the two pillars of his later achievement.

In 1897, Eggeling left Lund for Germany to study as a book-keeper, an occupation perhaps suggested by his distinction in penmanship. It seems that it was not until after he left Sweden that he began to be seriously interested in visual art. From Germany he moved on to Switzerland and thence to Milan, where he attended art classes, before returning to Switzerland in 1907 to take up a post as book-keeper at a Swiss business college. This post was really a pretext for his teaching an art class on the side and was thus Eggeling's first professional involvement with art. By the time he left Switzerland, probably in 1911, and arrived in Paris to pursue an independent career as an artist, he was already in his thirties. As far as I could discover, he did not show any of his work in a public exhibition until February 1916, when he exhibited at the Cabaret Voltaire in Zurich, the founding site of Dadaism. Thus his public career as an artist lasted for less than ten years, up to the time of his death in 1924. Almost all of it was dedicated to one single, ongoing, herculean task—the conceptualization, elaboration and creation first of his *Thorough-Bass for Painting* sequence of drawings, then his *Horizontal-Vertical Orchestra* scrolls and finally his extremely time-consuming film, *Diagonal Symphony*. In effect, these three works were three stages of one single, vastly ambitious project, whose realization posthumously assured Eggeling of a secure place in the history of film as art.

During his years as an independent artist, Eggeling lived first in Paris, then in Switzerland, principally in Ascona and Zurich, and finally in Germany, in the city of Berlin and in the family house of his friend and collaborator Hans Richter, located about 100 kilometres to the south-east of the city. These three separate milieux can be characterized briefly as follows: in Paris, Eggeling was part of the poor artists' world of Montparnasse, a cosmopolitan group of struggling young painters, in whose works the cubist revolution was still being consolidated. In Switzerland, Eggeling was one of an equally cosmopolitan group, created not by the artistic attractions of Switzerland but by its neutrality in the 1914–18 war. First he joined the established counter-cultural community (as we might call it today) at Ascona, a lakeside village in the Italian-speaking south of Switzerland. Later he moved to Zurich, where recently arrived exiles from many countries had created a community around the Cabaret Voltaire, the cradle of Dada and a beacon of opposition to the war. Finally, after the war ended, Eggeling left Switzerland for Germany, where he was often isolated and totally consumed by his work, but retained contacts with old Zurich friends who now formed part of the Berlin Dada group, as well as making new friends in the world of international Constructivism. He began to make contacts on a European scale, which put him in touch with artists as well known as Fernand Léger in Paris, Theo Van Doesburg from the Netherlands, Laszlo Moholy-Nagy from Hungary and El Lissitsky from Russia. At the time of his too early death, Eggeling was clearly on the point of moving into the forefront of a new pan-European avant-garde.

In Paris, we hear of Eggeling in two contexts. First, there were his living quarters on the Boulevard Raspail, where he shared a house with a number of other artists, the best known of whom was the Italian painter Modigliani. Second, there was Madame Vassilieff's canteen, a few blocks west, which had been opened by a Russian artist to accommodate the poor but hungry artists who lived in the area. Here a group of Swedish painters and musicians congregated and we can presume that Eggeling, who had a fine singing voice, enlivened many festive evenings. The most important friend he met in Paris was Hans Arp, who encountered him at the artists' house on the Boulevard Raspail, and described him later as more interested in talking about his theories of art than actually painting. In fact, Eggeling's interest in theory was a life-long trait and, as it turned out in the end, a great asset which gave his work a rigour that others lacked.

The most important thing to bear in mind, however, about Eggeling's stay in Paris was that, in age, he fitted exactly into the heroic generation which created twentieth-century modernism. Braque was born in 1882, Picasso, Léger and Gleizes in 1881, Eggeling in 1880. Apollinaire, Cendrars, Joyce, Kafka, Pound, Stravinsky and Webern were all of the same generation. It was crucial to his development that he was in Paris at exactly the right time, during the breakthrough of Cubism. In particular, this was a period when music and musical instruments were particularly important in cubist design. In thinking about Eggeling's formal vocabulary—the musical vocabulary of parallel black and white bars, serried ranks of lines, florid curves and S-shapes—it is intriguing to recall the use of clef signs, sheet music, guitar strings and frets, violin and mandolin forms, in the work of Braque, Gris and Picasso. Braque's 1912 *Homage to J. S. Bach*, for example, is particularly suggestive. The origins of Eggeling's correlation of music and graphic design may lie in pre-war Parisian Cubism.

Ascona, a village, scarcely a small town, nestling under the mountains on the shores of Lago Maggiore, brought quite new experiences and influences to Eggeling. It was here that he must have begun to work on his all-consuming project. In many ways, Ascona, so long overlooked, now seems central to the birth of modernism, not so much because of its art-historical role, but because it was the source of what we would now call the counter-culture. Anarchists were the first wave of outsiders and free-thinkers to come to Ascona: Bakunin, Kropotkin, Muhsam and the local Swiss anarchist Brupbacher. Next came the simple-lifers, the vegetarians, nudists, theosophists, occultists and translators of the *Tao Te Ching*, who established a colony on Monte Verità, in the hills overlooking the town. The third wave was that of the dancers—Rudolf Laban brought his dance school to Ascona from Munich for the first time in 1913 and moved there permanently after the war broke out. Here, through Laban and his students, such as Mary Wigman, modern European dance was nurtured. Next came the artists, among them Eggeling and Arp and his future wife, Sophie Tauber, and, at the same time, thinkers and writers such as Hermann Hesse, Martin Buber and Otto Gross, prophets preaching mysticism and peaceful anarchism and the new enterprise of psychoanalysis. Eventually the Eranos circle came to be based in Ascona, bringing Gross's analyst, Carl Gustav Jung, and Dr Suzuki, the interpreter of Zen Buddhism. In the end, Monte Verità was transformed into a health spa—and finally, after the artists, came the tourists.

During the war, while Eggeling was there, Ascona was closely linked to Zurich and the Cabaret Voltaire, serving as a kind of back-to-nature retreat for exhausted urban bohemians. Eggeling's principal channel of contact with the Swiss art world was through Hans Arp, whom he had known in Paris and who had also moved to Ascona after the war broke out. Arp, indeed, was himself Swiss, although he had spent much time travelling abroad. He was six years younger than Eggeling, but already more successful and better connected. Through Arp, or perhaps through Emil Szittya, a Swiss writer he knew in Paris, Eggeling began to make contacts in Zurich and meet the group whose activities were focused on the Cabaret Voltaire, founded in 1916. Arp too was closely involved with the Cabaret and his wife, Sophie Tauber, a student at the Laban dance school, also performed there, as did many other Laban dancers. It seems that Arp was Eggeling's principal sponsor in Zurich, one of a group which also included Otto and Adya Van Rees, who had also moved from Paris to Ascona to Zurich, as well as Marcel Janco and Arthur Segal, two of the Rumanian phalanx in Zurich who were crucial, particularly through Tristan Tzara, to the eventual triumph of Dada.

Arp had been decisively influenced by the Russian painter Kandinsky whom he had met on a pilgrimage to his Munich studio in 1912. It was Kandinsky who pushed him towards non-figurative art, exhibited his work in the second *Blue Rider* show and published it in the *Blue Rider Almanac*. Kandinsky was also the mentor of Hugo Ball, the founder and organizer of the Cabaret Voltaire. Ball, a playwright and dramaturge, had been deeply impressed by Kandinsky's views on the need for a synthesis of the arts, a new avant-garde *Gesamtkunstwerk*, and he had been on the point of taking over the management of the Munich Artists' Theatre, with the aim of putting Kandinsky's ideas into practice, when war broke out and he fled to Zurich. In many ways, the Cabaret Voltaire can be seen as an extension of the Munich art world, a kind of improvised offshoot of the Munich Artists' Theatre, with the same programme of bringing all the advanced arts together under one roof, pushing onward towards a new art for a new spiritual epoch, and seeking to capture the true 'inner sound' of words and images, uncontaminated by the practical and conventional language of a discredited culture.

Through Arp, and the other refugees from the Munich art world who had come to Switzerland at the outbreak of war and gathered together in Ascona and Zurich, Eggeling must have absorbed Kandinsky's programmatic ideas about art. In particular, Kandinsky believed in a world of correspondences between sounds and images, music and painting. He himself carried out experiments in synaesthesia and struck up a friendship with Schoenberg, whom he saw as his counterpart in the world of music. He was particularly impressed by the fact that coming, so to speak, from the other side, from the world of music, Schoenberg had reached similar conclusions to his own and had even composed an opera, *The Lucky Hand*, with a near-abstract stage design and a score for coloured lights which would complement the music. I think we can assume that Eggeling, with his own musical background, must have been further inspired by Kandinsky's writings—and by the followers of Kandinsky he met—to develop his own ideas on visual music. With its roots in French Symbolism, the idea of a visual art based on an analogy with music was widespread at the beginning of the century—we find it in the colour music of the brothers Corra in Italy, the light-box scroll of Duncan Grant in England, the experiments of Leopold Survage in Paris—but there is no doubt that Kandinsky was the single most influential art-world figure to advocate visual–musical correspondence as the theoretical basis for a truly modern art.

For example, in his essay 'On the Question of Form' published in the *Blaue Reiter Almanac* in 1912 and reprinted in 1914, Kandinsky wrote about his idea of a 'science for art', the elaboration of rules 'which will soon lead to a thorough-bass of painting'—the underlying bass line foundation of a symphony or concerto.[2] (This was the same *Almanac* in which Arp's work was reproduced.) Later Eggeling himself explicitly took up this idea of the 'coming thorough-bass', based on a speculative 'science for art', and began his own series of drawings titled precisely *Thorough-Bass for Painting*. Much of his experimental and theoretical work was an attempt to elaborate just such a thorough-bass, a 'simple composition', in Kandinsky's terms, which would run continuously through a symphonic work (or complex visual composition) and provide the foundation for its harmonic structure. In 1924, a German journalist, explaining Eggeling's work, referred to the idea of a 'thorough-bass for painting' as the key to understanding it, presumably on Eggeling's own instigation. I have sometimes wondered whether Eggeling first restricted himself to black and white because he saw the register of black and white as somehow equivalent to the bass line, the basso continuo, to which subsequent colour harmonies could potentially be keyed. Here Eggeling would differ from Kandinsky, who saw black simply as representing silence and white as pure sound.

During this period, however, Eggeling came across another source for his musical theorizing—in the work of Ferruccio Busoni. Busoni was a virtuoso concert pianist, best known for his performances of Bach, whose music he himself had edited, so that the pieces he played were often referred to as Bach–Busoni. Busoni was also a composer in his own right, one of the founders of modern music, as well as a tireless essayist and theorist. Eggeling had clearly read Busoni's *Outline for a New Musical Aesthetics*, first published by a small Trieste publishing house in 1906 but reissued by Insel-Verlag in Leipzig in 1916.[3] This book, dedicated to the poet Rilke, sketches out a utopian vision of a new music, described by one critic as committed to 'abstract sound, unrestricted technique and complete absence of tonal boundaries'. Busoni suggested dismantling the traditional octave with its major and minor keys and substituting in its stead a system of 113 scales based upon seven tones, enriched by third tones and sixth tones, in addition to the orthodox semitone. He wanted to base composition on contrapuntal rather than harmonic principles, with Bach as his primary historical inspiration. Busoni was later attacked for his 'musical Futurism'—and indeed he was a friend of the futurist painter Boccioni—but his audacity must have appealed to Eggeling. Eggeling, with his Asconan anarchist sympathies, would surely have responded to Busoni's attack on the reactionary 'law-givers' who held back free musical development.

Moreover, Busoni, who prided himself on his internationalism, had come to live in Zurich during the First World War, and we know that he attended performances at the Cabaret Voltaire. Eggeling's friend and collaborator, Hans Richter, remembers meeting and talking to Busoni about counterpoint as the composer held court by the fountain in the square outside the railway station. James Joyce, another musical exile in Zurich, also talked with Busoni by the same fountain—every day Busoni would enjoy his evening meal in the station restaurant from where, in melancholy mood, he could watch the trains depart, north to Germany and south to Italy, before descending to the square to sit and talk. Perhaps it is also relevant, at least as far as Eggeling is concerned, that Busoni's wife, Gerda Sjostrand, was herself Swedish. Unlike Kandinsky, who stressed harmony, Busoni advocated polyphony and counterpoint.

Later Marcel Janco, Eggeling's Rumanian friend, recalled how, based on his conversations with Busoni, Eggeling had developed a theory of 'visual counterpoint'.[4] He speculated that Eggeling was inspired to begin his compositions as a direct result of his talks with Busoni. Perhaps it is more likely that, just as Kandinsky's ideas are visible in the *Thorough-Bass for Painting* series, Busoni's ideas come to the fore in the *Horizontal-Vertical Orchestra* series, which are more complex and more serial. Indeed the *Horizontal-Vertical Orchestra* drawings appear to have developed first by spatially extending the *Thorough-Bass* motifs, then by transposing spatial extension into temporal series. In his later work, as Eggeling explained to Raoul Haussmann in Berlin, the 'counterpoint of forms' became his guiding principle.

Although Eggeling explained his graphic compositions primarily by analogy with music, there was another way in which he conceptualized his work. Eggeling often referred to it as an attempt to create a universal—an Adamic or Edenic—language, a prehistoric paradise language. Eggeling and other writers who knew him well—Richter and Van Doesburg, for instance—frequently talk about his efforts to create an alphabet or a lexicon of graphic forms which would constitute the basis for a new kind of visual language. The pamphlet which Eggeling and Richter wrote jointly in Germany in order to seek funding for their projects was actually entitled *Universal Language*.[5] Of course, both music and cinema were often envisaged as just such a universal means of communication, transcending verbal language barriers, but it seems that Eggeling had a deeper commitment to the idea. One strand in his thought was his longing for a universal humanism and internationalism, especially salient, of course, during the dreadful 1914–18 war. A universal language must have seemed a necessity within Eggeling's utopian vision of a world in which national conflicts would be superseded. It also relates to the experiments in new modes of language which dominated the poetry performances at the Cabaret Voltaire. The poems written and read by Hugo Ball, Tristan Tzara, Richard Huelsenbeck and others were themselves written in a kind of 'transnational' language. Take, for instance, Ball's poem 'Sea-Horses and Flying Fish', which runs as follows:

> tressli bessli nebogen leila
> flusch kata
> ballubasch
> zack hitti zopp
>
> zack hitti zopp
> hitti betzli betzli
> prusch kata
> ballubasch
> fasch kitti bimm

zitti kittilabi billabi billabi
zikko di zakkobam
fisch kitti bisch

bumbalo bumbalo bumbalo
zitti kittilabi
zack hitti zopp

tressli bessli nebogen grugru
blaulala violabimini bisch
violabimini bisch bisch

fusch kata
ballubasch
zick hitti zopp

It might be argued that this poem is based on German in some way, just as Joyce's *Finnegans Wake* is based in some way on English or Khlebnikov's *zaum* poetry is based in some way on Russian, but Ball's intention was plainly to try and create a radically new language, without any national associations. Ball prided himself on the internationalism of the Cabaret Voltaire, which brought together French, Germans, Rumanians, Italians, Russians, Spaniards and, of course, its solitary Swede. The famous simultaneous poem 'The Admiral Is Looking for a House to Let', performed by Huelsenbeck, Janco and Tzara, was composed in three separate languages, German, English and French—the languages of nations at war with each other—read simultaneously, with repeated interruptions of roaring, whistling and outbursts in an invented transnational language.

Simultaneist poems of this kind also involved a kind of counterpoint or polyphony in their performance. The dadaist interest in simultaneism derived originally from the poems of Henri Barzun, but the Dada circle must surely also have been aware of the early simultaneist work of Blaise Cendrars. Cendrars, Swiss in origin, was a close friend of Eggeling's friend Emil Szittya, and he knew Ascona well, principally through the renegade psychoanalyst Otto Gross, the model for the hero of his novel *Moravagine*. Cendrars was also a key figure in the circle around Apollinaire, Picasso and Delaunay, and later became a close friend of Fernand

Léger, playing a crucial role in his turn towards film. In 1912, Cendrars produced a pioneering simultaneist work with Delaunay's wife, Sonia Terk. This consisted of a single scroll, more than two metres in length, with Cendrars's poem 'La Prose du Trans-Sibérien' printed down one side in avant-garde typography, and an abstract colour painting by Terk down the other side, to create, in Apollinaire's words, correspondences like 'musical chords' between word and image.[6] It is in this tradition that Eggeling later began to compose his own musical-graphic scrolls. He surely knew the Terk–Cendrars scroll, although he would have been unaware of other models, such as Duncan Grant's 1914 *Abstract Kinetic Painting with Collages*, a scroll several yards in length, to be unrolled through a light-box in time with music by Bach.

Dada poetry is often perceived as nonsense, but the ideas behind it were much more positive and much more complex than that. First, it was a political gesture—a protest against the nationalism implied by national language. Second, it was an attempt to move towards abstraction, on the model of the visual arts, seeking the 'inner sound' of words which, in Kandinsky's view, was the intuitive core of all meaning. This could involve a direct musical analogy, as in Kurt Schwitters's Dada *Primal Sonata* (*Ur-Sonate*). Third, it was an attempt to rediscover, in Hugo Ball's term, the 'paradise language' spoken before the Fall, as yet uncontaminated by what he saw as the catastrophe of European civilization, brought to crisis by the war. And fourth, it was an attempt to create a new language for a new, spiritually more developed and unified humanity, also along the lines suggested by Kandinsky, albeit with a utopian anarchist or socialist tilt.

I think that these same impulses were at work in Eggeling's attempt to create a universal graphic language which would be both musical and visual—and eventually the filmic unity of the two. In this sense, there are comparisons which we could make between Eggeling and Joyce, Khlebnikov and Schwitters, all of whom sought to create new transnational or primal languages, appearing, to the untutored listener, as vehicles for pure sound or image rather than conventional meaning, but nonetheless designed to have a deep intuitive sense, as the layers of linguistic convention were peeled away. Joyce, we know, was interested in Esperanto, Khlebnikov in the primal roots of words (like Heidegger later), Schwitters and Eggeling in the analogy between language and music. Others, such as Walter Neurath and Gerd Arntz, set out to create a new graphic language whose basic signs were called isotypes, in order to facilitate effective international communication and to display information in a form which could be grasped conceptually through direct vision. This language of isotypes, developed during the 1920s, was the ancestor of the international language of graphic signs and ideographs which we find today in airports and other such cosmopolitan places.

Eggeling's universal graphic language was unusual in that it was a form of notation, based ultimately on musical notation, but designed to be looked at rather than listened to. It is related indirectly to a series of historical attempts to create graphic conceptual languages on the model of stenographic notes, ciphers or pictographs—a project which eventually led to Boole's systematization of symbolic logic. When Hans Arp first saw Eggeling's compositions, he saw them 'as a kind of hieratic writing', like ancient Egyptian writing, just as Hugo Ball's compositions were a kind of hieratic sound poetry, ritualistically enunciated by a masked figure like a shaman. Another point of comparison would be the dance notation devised by Rudolf Laban (now known as Labanotation). Already in Ascona while Eggeling was there, Laban was working on an early system of dance notation which involved framing and tracing movement in a geometrical figure—a dodecahedron which represented the spatial limits of bodily extension.

Eggeling's own attempts to create a universal alphabet seem to have been based on abstraction from nature, governed by a conceptual system based on polarities and analogies. He seems to have seen, in the work of Cézanne and the cubists—and particularly that of Derain, his favourite modern painter—a model of abstraction from nature in order to create a series of geometrical forms which could then be varied according to a set of rules, based on formal analogies and antinomies. In his few surviving notebooks we find not only examples of abstraction from nature but also a number of pages which illustrate his conceptual system, showing how abstract forms can both concur and contrast with each other in pairs of oppositions, such as empty:full, extended:contracted, high:low, horizontal:vertical, straight:curved, closed:open, heavy:light, simple: complex, regular:irregular, single:multiple, vigorous:weak, large:small, geometrical:ungeometrical, and so on.

A similar approach can be found in Arp's theory of abstraction, which was also based on organic forms, particularly plant forms, which themselves are already abstract and geometrical in their basic structure. Arp described Eggeling's work, when he first saw it, as plant-like—growing, intertwining, separating, dying and reappearing. Kandinsky also wrote about abstraction from nature, describing in the *Almanac* how children's art 'occasionally is raised to the level of the purely schematic', even though it is realist in intent.[7] Folk art too can have the same quality— and here we might recall Eggeling's father's interest in folk forms— songs, games and dances. Cubism, in Kandinsky's view, was searching for abstract relationships but used an excessively limited vocabulary of 'triangles and similar geometrical forms' with too much regularity. In contrast, Kandinsky cited the Douanier Rousseau as a model of the child-like painter, able to 'succeed in reaching the inner sound of things'.

Music and language are, of course, both time-based forms. Eggeling's movement towards film, as a time-based graphic form, seems to have passed through four stages. First, he created series of separate drawings, representing motifs and developments of motifs. Then he put the separate drawings in sequence together on a scroll. Next, as Marcel Janco relates, he used a bound sequence of drawings like a large flip-book.

> I still remember one night in 1919. I met Eggeling in the street. He was smiling, which was quite unusual and gave me something of a surprise: he took a thick notebook out of his pocket, about 8 cm by 20, and stood in front of a window where there was more light. Then, with a glorious gesture, he riffled through, say, 40 to 60 pages in rapid succession. The thick paper notebook made a kind of arc and with a movement of his index finger he skilfully made the drawings flip through after each other at great speed. Then he looked up at me and he could see how impressed and surprised I was. I had the illusion of a sequence of images miraculously superimposed on each other like at the cinema.

The fourth stage, of course, was to move into film itself.

The move to film was made possible by Eggeling's collaboration with a younger artist, Hans Richter, whom he had met in Dada circles, through Tristan Tzara, in 1918. Like Eggeling, Richter identified with the Hans Arp wing of Dadaism, which was mainly concerned with abstract art. At first, his work followed faithfully in the steps of Eggeling, as he produced his own scroll paintings, titled *Prelude* or *Fugue*, with a basic vocabulary of forms clearly modelled on those developed by his mentor. He was inspired too by Hugo Ball's question, 'Is the language of signs the actual paradise language?'—a formulation which transferred the vanguard role from poets to painters. Richter was also influenced by Arp in his view of art as an attempt to find a balance between the 'law of chance' and the 'law of rule', the 'combination of the spontaneous with the planned'. Arp, like Ball, was interested in children's art, where we might encounter the same tension between chance and rule in its pure form. As a result of Sophie Tauber's influence, Arp began to abandon the dynamic diagonals of his earlier work, derived, as he admits, from Futurism, and move towards more static, horizontal–vertical forms. At the same time, he would use chance methods, introducing spontaneity into the compositions and judging by eye rather than by rule. Eggeling, meanwhile, persevered with his own logical system of composition, which was even more stringent than Sophie Tauber's.

In 1921, after the war ended and Zurich Dada consequently broke up, Eggeling and Richter moved to Germany, where Eggeling, poverty-stricken as always, stayed as a house-guest at the home of Richter's parents. While they were there, a banker friend and neighbour of Richter's family offered the two artists 10,000 Deutschmarks to make films from their sketches and scrolls. They felt that this was still not enough money to do the job and decided instead to produce a pamphlet which they could use to raise public support for their ideas. They sent a copy to Albert Einstein, for instance, and received a letter back from him commending their work. They were then able—or at least the more entrepreneurial Richter was then able—to persuade UFA, the giant German film corporation, that there was enough interest in their ideas to warrant giving them facilities and technical help at their studio in Berlin. In fact, only Richter completed an actual film—*Rhythmus 21*. To do this, in the face of greater difficulties than they had imagined and an unhelpful technician, he had to give up his original idea of making a film of his

entire six-metre scroll *Prelude*, and was forced instead to simplify it
drastically, making a much cruder, although still effective, work using
papiers collés: rectangles and squares advancing, retreating, overlapping,
entering and crossing the frame. Eggeling, however, was not willing to
compromise and, after UFA withdrew their support, struggled on to
complete his *Diagonal Symphony* with his companion, Erna Niemeyer, as
his helper. Eventually he quarrelled with Richter—apparently because
Richter's parents' patience as hosts had reached its limit and they
confiscated a supposed Giorgione painting which Eggeling had somehow
acquired, claiming it in lieu of rent. Eggeling left in a fury and Richter
felt bound to support his parents. Soon afterwards, Eggeling went back
to Sweden and managed to persuade one of his sisters to advance him the
money to assemble a simple animation stand, so that he could continue
the work at his own home.

Eggeling's move to film was the logical conclusion of his project, not
simply as the obvious strategy for an artist increasingly preoccupied with
problems of time (he had been reading Bergson assiduously) but also, I
think, as part of a deeper reaction against the whole tradition of oil
painting. Here too I believe Arp was a mentor. Arp later noted that,
back in 1916, 'Sophie Tauber and I had decided to renounce completely
the use of oil colours in our compositions. We wanted to avoid any
reference to the paintings which seemed to us characteristic of a pretentious and ostentatious world.' It is interesting, in this context, to note
that Tauber and Adya Van Rees, both women artists, had been educated
in a craft rather than a fine art school, and worked primarily with
tapestries and embroidery. The same year, 1916, Hugo Ball recorded in
his diary a conversation in which Arp recommended abstraction and
plane geometry, attacking the ostentation and bombast of oil painting.
'He is in favour of the use of unequivocal (preferably printed) colours
(bright papers and fabrics); and he is especially in favour of the inclusion
of mechanical exactness.'[8] Ball was suspicious—it reminded him of 'Kant
and Prussia' who, 'in the drill yard and in logic, are in favour of the
geometrical division of spaces'. Arp saw it differently—as a battle against
ostentation and bombast, against 'unhealthy egotism' and the cult of
personality. In cutting his printed, coloured paper, he preferred to use a
guillotine rather than scissors, which might still betray the artist's hand,

and he also argued in favour of collaboration between artists, a stance which does something to explain Eggeling's turn to geometry, his development of a precise logical system, his move from drawing by hand to the more impersonal and mechanically exact form of film and his collaborations, first with Richter and then with Niemeyer.

Eggeling finally completed the film version of his *Diagonal Symphony* in the autumn of 1924 (three years after he had exhibited it privately as a series of scrolls). The labour of drawing the whole thing frame by frame, then cutting the forms in tinfoil and filming them frame by frame with primitive equipment, was finally over. On 5 November he held a private screening attended, among others, by Laszlo Moholy-Nagy, El Lissitsky, Werner Graeff and many artists and critics who were to become prominent in the world of avant-garde film. By now Eggeling was in touch with Theo Van Doesburg, who wrote enthusiastically about his project, and Fernand Léger, whom he visited on a trip to Paris. Like Arp or Léger, Eggeling can now be seen not so much as a dadaist, but as a slightly unorthodox figure in the world of international Constructivism, committed to geometrical abstraction and interested, like the others, in the cinema and modern technology. His next (unrealized) scheme was a system for the projection of light onto the clouds at night, based on the still-to-be-developed theory of 'Eidodynamics'.

On 3 May 1925 the first public screening of Eggeling's work took place at the UFA Palast theatre in downtown Berlin. The programme consisted of Hirschfeld-Mack's *Colour Sonatas*, Richter's *Rhythmus*, Eggeling's *Symphonie Diagonale*, Walter Ruttmann's *Opus, 2, 3 and 4*, Léger and Murphy's *Ballet Mécanique* and Picabia and Clair's *Entr'acte*. In effect, this was all the best work available in avant-garde film at the time: an astonishing programme which laid the foundations of a new film aesthetic. Just sixteen days later, on 19 May, Viking Eggeling died.

Today Viking Eggeling is usually seen, quite rightly, as an outstanding pioneer of abstract film—anticipated perhaps by Richter and Ruttmann, but only because his project, which he embarked on long before they began theirs, was so much more elaborate and difficult to realize. I would like to make a still bolder claim for Eggeling, one which throws into question the traditional division between fine art and film, whereby artists in each are confined to quite separate histories and systems of evaluation. Eggeling should be seen not simply in terms of film and music, but as a central member of a group of painters, all associated with the Cabaret Voltaire, who had tried to escape from the oil painting tradition into other kinds of abstraction. I am thinking of Viking Eggeling, Hans Arp, Sophie Tauber, Otto and Adya Van Rees, Marcel Janco and Arthur Segal. Hans Richter was also associated with this group towards the end. They all exhibited together and issued joint statements together, as dadaists and dissident dadaists. After the war, the group split up. Eggeling died. Janco returned to Rumania. Arthur Segal had gone with Eggeling and Richter to Berlin and then, after 1933, to Spain and finally to England. Always an idiosyncratic artist, Segal developed a kind of narrative painting, rather like a cinematic storyboard, and later a strange, premature photo-realism. The Van Reeses went back to the Netherlands, returning every summer to Ascona (to which Arp too returned in the end). Hans Richter pursued twin careers as an international constructivist and an experimental film-maker. Sophie Tauber and Hans Arp travelled widely, becoming involved with *Abstraction-Création*, *Cercle et Carré* and finally, in Jean Arp's case, Surrealism.

This diversity of their post-war careers has obscured the original connection between all these artists, an oversight made worse by the tendency of art historians to see Zurich Dada in very limited terms. Art historians have read its history backwards from the vantage-point of subsequent Paris or Berlin Dadaism, through the very different activities Tzara and Huelsenbeck promoted after the war. The orthodox version stresses the irrationalism and nihilism of the Dada poets, rather than the constructive utopianism of the Dada painters. Of course, Ball himself belonged primarily to the literary side of the movement, but it was absolutely central to his vision of Dada that the Cabaret Voltaire should be a place where all the arts met, where painters gathered alongside performers and poets. These undervalued visual artists all need to be restored to their rightful place in history. Among them, I am glad to pay special tribute to Viking Eggeling, not simply as a pioneer film-maker but, in more general terms, as a visionary committed to a synthesis of the arts (music, poetry, painting, dance) for which film provided a dynamic, technological vehicle, much as experimental artists today are drawn towards the new digital media.

4

WHO THE HELL IS
HOWARD HAWKS?

There is an interesting story concerning Howard Hawks to be found in
Barbara Leaming's Avon biography of Katharine Hepburn. In this book,
Leaming tells the story of Hepburn's romance with John Ford, which
began, apparently, during the filming of *Mary of Scotland*. The following
year, she was to make *Bringing Up Baby* with Howard Hawks. The
screenplay was written by Dudley Nichols and, according to Leaming,
Hawks wanted it tailored for Hepburn, whose relationship with Ford was
already well known to Nichols. In fact, Hawks's set was full of what
Leaming calls 'members of the Ford group'—Ford cronies such as Ward
Bond, Barry FitzGerald and D'Arcy Corrigan were all in the cast and the
associate producer, once again, was Cliff Reid. Ford himself visited the
set a couple of times. The relationship between Susan (Hepburn) and
David (Cary Grant) in Hawks's film, Leaming argues, was based on
Hepburn's relationship with Ford, whose dignity she was forever punc-
turing and who, in Leaming's words, possessed an 'exasperating ambiva-
lence; he [Ford] is the sort of man who says, "I love you, I think."'
Howard Hawks, Leaming also points out, 'gave Cary Grant, who played
David, the small round glasses that were Ford's trademark'.[1] Also, it
might be added, Harold Lloyd's.

It is a fascinating anecdote, not least because it underlines Hawks's
liking for scenes which mirrored or even parodied the behaviour of people
he personally knew or knew of, their own mannerisms and relationships

or just odd things that had happened to them, whether they were film people or aviation people or whoever. In the same way, Lauren Bacall's performance in *To Have and Have Not*, made soon afterwards, was clearly modelled on Hawks's own new wife, 'Slim'. Hawks would direct actors by asking them how they would deliver a line if they were in the same situation, asking them to be themselves rather than the characters, to relive episodes from their own lives, even the most embarrassing and humiliating (and therefore the funniest), like the time Cary Grant somehow managed to get the dress of the wife of the head of the Metropolitan Museum caught in the zip of his flies (in a theatre, of all places) so that, in Todd McCarthy's words, 'they had to lockstep to the manager's office in order to find a pair of pliers'.

This parasitism on real life was fundamental to Hawks's whole modus operandi as a director. It is why his films veer towards a strange kind of *cinéma vérité*, as Bogart and Bacall fall in love or Montgomery Clift learns to respect John Wayne. He also relied shamelessly on scenes and situations borrowed from both his own and other people's movies, for whose memory of which the screen-writer Jules Furthman was especially prized—thus explaining, perhaps, Hawks's many echoes of Sternberg. At the same time, Hawks was always inventing self-aggrandizing stories about his own exploits—how he told Sternberg how to dress Marlene Dietrich, for example, or how he gave the original idea for *Casablanca* to Michael Curtiz, a particularly audacious claim, since he himself had blatantly borrowed from *Casablanca* in making *To Have and Have Not*. Yet, in a way, Hawks's compulsion for purloining, collecting, mix-and-match and tall story-telling may have been his strongest quality as a director, the one that made his films look like the very essence of Hollywood.

On the other hand, in making films which looked like the essence of Hollywood rather than like original works of art, Hawks also made it difficult for dubious critics to accept him as an artist, an innovator or a director with a clear personal agenda. Hawks's style turned out to be no-nonsense studio professionalism, salted with a kind of Robert Altman talent for improvisation on the set. Notoriously, Hawks worked in almost all the genres, treating them pretty much the same—the group could be cow-punchers or pilots delivering the mail or Free French patriots—it didn't much matter as long as there was danger and loyalty and sacrifice and a romance, salted with wisecracks and gimmicks, or, in the case of a comedy, plagued by humiliation, misunderstanding and descent into chaos. Tragedy and comedy were the two complementary faces of fun— the fun that involved life-threatening danger and the fun that involved a cascade of embarrassing mishaps. Given all this, it is not hard to see why Hawks's reputation rode on such a roller-coaster—how he could appear the constructivist of film (Henri Langlois), the master of pulp, operetta and action (Manny Farber), the French classicist, the Corneille (Jacques Rivette), the Greek tragedian, the Sophocles (Andrew Sarris), the serious moralist (Robin Wood), the bard of the male group (Peter Wollen) or of the Hawksian woman (Molly Haskell).[2]

It is because of this polyvalence and confusion about Hawks, of course, that he entered the canon so late in his career and that his promotion created so much controversy. Canons are created through a confluence of devious paths: (1) the archival and curatorial path; (2) the cinephile and cultist path; (3) the critical and theoretical path; and finally (4) the path bringing tribute and homage from a future generation of film-makers. For directors to enter the canon, the very first prerequisite is that their films should be available. They should be preserved in archives and screened in retrospectives. In Hawks's case this was all the more important because he was not recognized as a great film-maker when his films first came out, despite the commercial success of most of his work. In fact, the construction of Hawks's subsequent reputation depended primarily on the efforts of one man, the enthusiasm of Henri Langlois, director of the French Cinémathèque in Paris after the Second World War.

Langlois had first been struck with admiration for Hawks in 1928— in the silent days, the antiquity of film—when, at the age of fifteen, he saw Louise Brooks at the Ursulines cinema in *A Girl in Every Port*. He remembered the film vividly all his life, even if his main attraction was to Brooks and his life-long respect for Howard Hawks could almost seem a kind of by-product, praise for the man who launched Brooks's career. *A Girl in Every Port* was apparently something of a cult film in Paris when released in 1928. The novelist, poet (and film editor) Blaise Cendrars described it as marking 'the first appearance of contemporary cinema', and the critic Jean-Georges Auriol praised it, in *La Revue du Cinéma*, as signalling the transfer of artistic leadership in film from France to America, thanks to Howard Hawks, 'a veritable magician', a director whose 'simplifying style' underlay the 'astonishing seductiveness of his images'.[3] Looking back on *A Girl in Every Port* many years later, Langlois still saw it as the first truly modern film. He celebrated Hawks as the consummate professional, the engineer and the contemporary man, comparing his film to a Manhattan skyscraper. 'Hawks, like Gropius', he wrote, 'conceived his films as one might conceive a typewriter, a motor or a bridge.'[4] *Ceiling Zero*, Langlois later observed, was 'assembled as a motor is assembled'—Hawks avoided pretentious trick-work and used, in his own words, 'the simplest camera in the world'.[5]

Seven years after his epiphany at the Ursulines, Henri Langlois founded the French Cinémathèque, both an archive to collect lost films and a show-place to screen them at the Cercle du Cinéma. Soon afterwards, of course, screenings were interrupted by the Second World War and it was not until after the Liberation that the Cercle du Cinéma was revived. Throughout the post-war forties and fifties, Langlois regularly showed Hawks films—his own favourites were *A Girl in Every Port*, of course, and then *Dawn Patrol*, *Ceiling Zero*, *Only Angels Have Wings* (what we might call the 'aviation trilogy') together with *Twentieth Century*, *Bringing Up Baby* and *His Girl Friday* (the 'screwball comedy trilogy'), followed by *To Have and Have Not* and *The Big Sleep* (Hawks and *film noir*). It was at Langlois's makeshift little cinema in the Rue de Messine that the group of young cultists who wrote for *Cahiers du Cinéma* (and eventually launched Hitchcocko-Hawksianism upon a bemused public) first saw Hawks's work—Truffaut, Godard, Rohmer, Rivette, Chabrol, the new cinephile generation of critics, a group known teasingly as 'the godchildren of Henri Langlois'.

Despite the *Cahiers* group's reverence for André Bazin, it was really Langlois who nurtured their taste and shaped their research into the history of the art they loved. Indeed, as Richard Roud has pointed out, 'their limited knowledge of English made them uniquely equipped to appreciate cinematic style: the American films often had no subtitles, thereby inviting a closer look at how movement is expressed through visual texture, composition, camera movement and editing'.[6] It was due to the *Cahiers* group's cultist enthusiasm, combined with their taste for rankings, that the *politique des auteurs* (or 'auteur theory') was launched and Hawks was placed in the forefront of a polemical new film canon. In 1953 Rivette published 'The Genius of Howard Hawks' and Rohmer his glowing review of *The Big Sky*, in 1954 Rohmer reviewed *Gentlemen Prefer Blondes*, and in 1955 André Bazin dubiously asked, 'How Could You Be a Hitchcocko-Hawksian?', while a much sharper counterblast, 'Some Over-Rated Directors', came from the rival and more political journal *Positif*.[7] Then, in 1956, Howard Hawks himself arrived in Paris, en route to the land of the Pharaohs with William Faulkner, and was interviewed in depth for the *Cahiers* by an eager Jacques Rivette and François Truffaut.[8]

Outside France, however, there was still a very long way to go. In his book, *'You Ain't Heard Nothing Yet'*, the American cinephile Andrew Sarris—also author of *Confessions of a Cultist*—describes how he received a letter from his friend and mentor Eugene Archer, asking plaintively, 'Who the hell is Howard Hawks?' Archer was a reviewer for the *New York Times*, now in Paris on a Fulbright scholarship and spending much of his time studying the new *Cahiers du Cinéma* and queueing up for screenings at the Cinémathèque, which had now moved on to larger premises, in the Rue d'Ulm on the Left Bank. Sarris writes:

> In the Paris of 1957, Archer had been shocked to discover that the *Cahiers* critics were unimpressed by Ford, Huston, Kazan, Stevens, Wyler and Zinneman, up against their sacred cows, Howard Hawks and Alfred Hitchcock. Archer and I thought we knew all about Hitchcock. He was supposed to be fun, but not entirely serious. But Hawks? Who was he? And why were the French taking him seriously?[9]

The progressive internationalization of the cult of Howard Hawks now began, with Archer and Sarris's search for an answer to that question.

One year later, in 1958, as a sideshow to the Brussels World's Fair, a poll was taken of 117 critics from around the world, each asked to name the ten greatest films in the history of cinema. Among American directors, 107 votes went to films by Ford, 44 to Vidor, 30 to Wyler, 22 to Milestone, 19 to Capra, 16 to John Huston. Only eight went to Hawks, seven for *Scarface*, one for *Only Angels Have Wings*. The underlying problem, for a fledgling auteurist, was that Hawks's films were largely unavailable. The ageing prints that Manny Farber had seen at the old 'Lyric-Pix-Victory' theatres and written about in *Underground Films* were dropping out of circulation—films from the thirties and early forties, from *Scarface* to *The Big Sleep*. It was not until 1961 that Archer (now back in New York), Sarris and Peter Bogdanovich drew up a list of Hawks films they especially wanted to see (or re-see) and took it to Dan Talbot, who ran the New Yorker theatre, persuading him to launch a 'Forgotten Film' season, screening twenty-eight classics, eleven of them by Hawks. 'I saw all the Hawks films and was blown away,' Bogdanovich later reminisced. 'One Saturday we showed *The Big Sleep* and *To Have and Have Not*, and we had lines round the block.' Hawksianism was on the road at last!

Hawks fitted well into an aesthetic schema built on the foundation of personal enthusiasms. His body of work—as many critics have shown— was astonishingly coherent, given the length of his career and the fact that he never claimed to be anything but a professional entertainer, rather than a Huston or a Kazan, albeit one whose personality dominated his career. Sarris never specified his criteria in making his evaluations, never really *theorized* them in any serious way. Questions of value are notoriously difficult to theorize and Sarris was quite unashamed in trusting his own taste. In many ways, the underlying function of the *politique des auteurs* was to serve as a polemical instrument for revising the film canon. In fact, Sarris was not quite as extreme as he appeared to his opponents. If we study the fate of the 'Brussels favourites', we find that John Ford stayed in the forefront of Sarris's pantheon, as did a number of directors from the silent era, alongside the *Cahiers'* new favourites, such as Hawks, Hitchcock, Welles, Ophuls and Renoir. On the other hand, Huston, Milestone and Wyler, the conventional favourites, were all judged over-rated and unceremoniously dumped as showing 'Less Than Meets The Eye'.

As a result of Eugene Archer's Fulbright, Hawks had become the rallying-point for a new generation of cultists turned critics, who quickly grasped that one of Hawks's most significant characteristics as a director was that he worked in almost all the available genres (even including science fiction). Consequently, his strengths could be attributed only to his mastery over cinema as such, rather than any particular type of film. He was not an Anthony Mann who specialized in westerns or a Vincente Minnelli who specialized in musicals. As the saying went, he transcended genre. In fact, once Sarris had grasped the thinking that lay behind the Hawksianism of the *Cahiers* critics, he began to frame his aesthetic judgements within the context of what he now called, shamelessly, the 'auteur theory'. He began to applaud directors' style rather than content, to show a preference for 'popular' as opposed to 'serious' art.

Following the success of the New Yorker's Hawks screenings, Bogdanovich suggested to the Museum of Modern Art that they should now put on a full-scale retrospective. As it turned out, Hawks was then releasing his new film *Hatari*, and Richard Griffith, at the Museum, agreed to hold a retrospective if Bogdanovich could get Paramount to pay for it as a part of their launch campaign. Bogdanovich proved persuasive and the retrospective took place in 1962, with a monograph prepared by Bogdanovich.[10] It then travelled across the Atlantic to both Paris and London, where it stimulated a special issue of *Cahiers du Cinéma* and a Hawks issue of *Movie* magazine, containing a crucial article by Robin Wood to which Lee Russell subsequently responded in *New Left Review*.[11] My own Hawks-based attempt to turn the 'auteur theory' into a genuine theory followed in 1968 when *Signs and Meaning in the Cinema* was published.[12] In fact, my own interest in Hawks stemmed originally from Paris, through my friend Patrick Bauchau, who knew both Archer and Sarris well and formed a crucial link between cinephiles in Paris, New York and London. (For those interested, he appears with Eugene Archer in Eric Rohmer's film *La Collectioneuse*.) It was under their influence that I frequented the Cinémathèque in the Rue d'Ulm after leaving university, and began to develop from cultist to critic to theorist.

Returning once more to Paris, if we look again at Jacques Rivette's pivotal essay, 'The Genius of Howard Hawks', we find that many of Sarris's criteria were already in use—Rivette discusses the Hawksian *oeuvre* as a whole, while noting that it was divided between two reciprocally related elements, madcap comedy and action drama. Laughter, Rivette points out, is inextricably bound up with a foreboding of danger and imminent tragedy. As he brusquely put it, 'Scarface's secretary speaks comically garbled English, but that doesn't prevent him getting shot.'[13]

In fact, he observed, many of the films that Hawks presented as comedies—*Monkey Business* or *I Was a Male War Bride*—are also cruel, tilted towards degradation, debasement and demoralization. Hawks, in fact, emerges from Rivette's account as a somewhat sinister artist, whose positive values of community, responsibility, bravery and tenacity are constantly undercut by an intransigent sense of bitterness, loss and the cruelty of life. Rivette appeals to the authority of Corneille and classical tragedy in defence of 'his' Hawks, but I can never avoid the thought that the genius Rivette describes is basically a genius for black comedy.

Seen in this way, Hawks suddenly seems very much closer to Hitchcock, with his own mix of cruelty and farce, and the *Cahiers* doctrine of 'Hitchcocko-Hawksianism', as Bazin dubbed it, begins to look more coherent and persuasive. In fact, it suggests to me that the elevation of Hawks within the canon, initiated as it was in France, bears a close relationship to the simultaneous elevation of his old friend and collaborator William Faulkner, whose own nihilistic mingling of comedy with tragedy has frequently been noted. Hawks worked with Faulkner on repeated occasions from 1932 onwards and the two men became close friends, discovering that they shared many interests—hunting, fishing, flying, drinking and, of course, tall story-telling. The more I learn about the relationship between Faulkner and Hawks, the more I am struck by the way their professional partnership developed out of a fundamental bond of shared character traits, tastes, concerns and obsessions. I began to think that Faulkner and Hawks were first recognized as masters of their respective arts in Europe (and specifically in France) for essentially the same reasons, because of qualities that their novels and films had in common.

The crucial period for the establishment of their reputation came at roughly the same time—in the immediate post-war period. In 1944, when Malcolm Cowley began the research for his project of publishing *The Portable Faulkner* (which eventually appeared in 1946), Faulkner had only one novel still in print—*Sanctuary*, which was originally published in 1931, the year in which Hawks made his own most famous film, *Scarface*. Cowley, a long-time admirer of Faulkner, wanted to redress what he felt was the critics' patronizing indifference to the writer's true worth. The American literary establishment as a whole had never fully accepted

Faulkner's work—the one positive defender was another writer, Conrad Aiken—and the most favourable and serious evaluations of Faulkner came, not from his own country, but in fact from France, where Malraux wrote the French preface for *Sanctuary* and Sartre published a celebrated essay on *The Sound and the Fury*, concentrating on Faulkner's literary techniques and especially his treatment of time, an essay which, as we shall see, André Bazin later cited in his own reconsideration of Hawks.[14]

Cowley worked hard to change Faulkner's image in America, but the *Portable*, which came out just after the war ended, was neither a commercial nor even a critical success. However, it did remind the critics of Faulkner's existence and the situation began to change as American intellectuals started to take stock of America's own changed relationship to the rest of the world. America was not simply a victorious power but, in military, political and economic terms, it was plainly the only power which could defend the newly liberated countries of Western Europe against a resurgent Soviet Union. To succeed in the battle of minds and ideas, intellectuals concluded, the United States must be recognized as a cultural power, one whose espousal of a free market in ideas was more successful and more attractive than the rival policy of the strictly regimented Soviet system. The time had come for foregrounding the achievements of writers—like Faulkner—whose work had previously been regarded as intense, violent, alienated, challenging, gothic and experimental, but who were already, as in Faulkner's case, well respected in Europe, and enthusiastically so in France.

In this context, Faulkner began to look very like Jackson Pollock. Indeed, Lawrence Schwartz, in his book *Creating Faulkner's Reputation: The Politics of Modern Literary Criticism*, acknowledges that his assessment of Faulkner's career strikes many of the same chords as Serge Guilbaut's assessment of Pollock's simultaneous rise to world fame, in his classic *How New York Stole the Idea of Modern Art*.[15] I believe Hawks's reputation benefited in exactly the same kind of way from the new political dispensation, except that the impetus for the re-evaluation of both Faulkner and Hawks came directly from Europe and specifically from France. As Schwartz noted, 'one of the first attempts to explain, in general terms, the new international importance of contemporary American literature appeared in the summer of 1947. It was an essay written by a Yale French professor, Henri Peyre: "American Literature through French Eyes".' In this essay Peyre argued, as Schwartz notes, that 'the best French critics (Sartre, Camus, Claude-Edmonde Magny, Maurice Blanchot) had devoted careful attention to such writers as Hemingway, Faulkner, Steinbeck and Dos Passos—attention not given by American critics'.[16] In fact, Magny actually linked Faulkner with film, commenting in her book on the *cinematic* quality and technique of Faulkner's writing.[17]

The campaign which led to the apotheosis of Howard Hawks as one of the great film-makers was also launched in France after the end of the Second World War, although Hawks himself had been active in Holly-wood since the pre-sound days, cinema's antiquity, having directed no fewer than eight silent films. In his classic essay, 'How Could You Be a Hitchcocko-Hawksian?', Bazin argued that, properly understood, the new *Cahiers* position should be interpreted as one which saw style as inher-ently embodying a world-view, so that, while we should not altogether discount the 'triviality' of Hawks's subject-matter, at least in his recent comedies, his approach to film-making, his formal 'intelligence' as a director, as Bazin put it, actually masked his 'intelligence, full stop' and that, as Sartre had argued, in direct reference to Faulkner, 'every technique refers back to a metaphysics'. Bazin not only compared Hawks to Faulkner but used precisely the same argument to validate Hawks that Sartre had employed to justify Faulkner.

Last, a word about the final stage of canonization—homage from a new generation of film-makers. As we might expect, we find such tributes earliest in the work of French directors—Godard's description of *A Bout de Souffle* as a remake of *Scarface*, his invocation of the noir Bogart of *The Big Sleep* and prominent display of a poster for *Hatari* in *Contempt* (*Le Mépris*), soon followed by Bogdanovich's remake of *Bringing Up Baby* as *What's Up Doc?*, John Carpenter's remake of *Rio Bravo* as *Assault on Precinct 13* and Martin Scorsese's *Who's That Knocking on My Door?*, in which the two leads exit a revival of *Rio Bravo*, discussing the role of Feathers. The tribute I still await is the movie version of Meta Carpenter Wilde's memoir, *A Loving Gentleman*, the story of her long affair with William Faulkner while *she* was Hawks's script-girl and personal assistant and *he*, of course, was helping Howard to sharpen structure, dream up situations and flesh out the dialogue. The Faulkner book their affair inspired was *The Wild Palms*, itself an influence on such French directors as Agnès Varda and Alain Resnais. Oddly enough, a script of *The Wild Palms* was my own very first screen-writing job. It was commissioned by none other than Gene Archer and its vicissitudes can be followed in Truffaut's caustic letters to Helen Scott. I am still sad he never made the film, although, knowing what I do now, I would write it very differently today.

5

HITCH: A TALE OF TWO CITIES
(LONDON and LOS ANGELES)

This chapter is written against compartmentalization—specifically, the national compartmentalization of Hitchcock into 'English' and 'American'. Hitchcock began his film career in 1919 when, after showing some samples of his work as a title card designer, he was hired by the new Famous Players-Lasky studio in Islington, a district in north London. This was an American-owned and managed studio and in his first three years of employment Hitchcock designed the titles and worked in other capacities for no less than eleven films. Just as it seemed that he might be able to make the transfer to direction, however, the American owners pulled out. The empty studio was rented to independent producers, this time actually English, one of whom, Michael Balcon, eventually launched Hitch on his long career as a director. Hitchcock subsequently made five pictures at Islington for Balcon and Gainsborough, still working, however, with then-famous American stars such as Virginia Valli, Carmelita Geraghty and Nita Naldi. Thus, from the very start, Hitchcock, although based in his native London, with excursions to Germany, was closely connected to Los Angeles, first through his American employers and then through the presence of Hollywood stars on the set of his 'English' films.

His time with Balcon was followed by nine years working for John Maxwell and British International at Elstree, another London suburb. It was during this period that Hitchcock triumphantly negotiated the transition to sound with his 1929 film *Blackmail*. He continued working for Maxwell until 1932 before he returned to Balcon to make the first version of *The Man Who Knew Too Much*, which he remade twenty years later for Paramount as an American film. The second Balcon period secured Hitchcock's place as Britain's leading director, as he successfully completed a string of hits for Gaumont-British, culminating in *The 39 Steps* and *Sabotage*, the first classic Hitchcock thrillers, which established him as the 'master of suspense'. His very last picture for Balcon, *The Lady Vanishes*, further developed the mix of spy film and screwball comedy on which Hitch had built his reputation. Soon afterwards he was invited to Los Angeles where, basically, he recycled the same genre mix for his new Hollywood producers, eventually working with Cary Grant (rather than Robert Donat) as the star of *North by Northwest*. Grant—also, of course, from England—quickly became his preferred Hollywood actor.

We tend to think of Hitchcock's Englishness in terms of his childhood in Leytonstone, his rise upward through the class structure to Shamley Green in Surrey, his bullying 'little man' sense of the world, his old-fashioned music hall sense of humour, his smirking taste for double entendre, his keen attention to social embarrassment, his Orwellian view of murder as one of the fine arts, and his fascination with sexuality as forbidden fruit. No doubt these are qualities rooted in his childhood as the son of a Catholic shopkeeper, as he nurtured aspirations to become a sophisticated man of the world in a merciless English social scene to which he felt fundamentally unfitted by his class and his cultural background, his private fears and his all too public rotundity and weight. But it was in England too that Hitchcock, so staunchly middle-brow in so many of his tastes, also acquired his cultivated interest in modern art, his perfectionism, his willingness to experiment and his fascination with new techniques, to which he always turned with immediate enthusiasm. It was another side of England, the artistic sophistication that Hitchcock acquired through his social superiors at the London Film Society, which stimulated his abiding interest in experiment, and led him towards the dream sequences in *Spellbound* and *Vertigo*, the rolling camera in *Rope*, the virtuoso montage in *Psycho*, the use of the Kuleshov Effect in *Rear Window*, the electronic soundtrack in *The Birds* and the unachieved collaboration with Len Lye on *The Secret Agent*.

Hitchcock became an American citizen in 1955, sixteen years after he had embarked for New York on the *Queen Mary* together with his wife Alma (whom he met at Famous Players-Lasky), their daughter Pat, their cook, their maid and his indispensable personal assistant Joan Harrison, who had been intimately involved in all his projects since 1935, the year he had first hired her as a secretary. Harrison stayed with Hitch when he left for the United States, working on his films right through to *Shadow of a Doubt*. Although she did leave in the late 1940s in order to pursue her own independent career, she returned again to the fold in the 1960s, to take charge of the nostalgically named Shamley Productions, where she was responsible for organizing Hitch's extremely successful television series, *Alfred Hitchcock Presents*. Shamley Green, it is worth noting, was Hitchcock's last address in England, a lovingly restored Tudor cottage set in the countryside on the outskirts of London, which he reluctantly had to give up following the deaths of his mother and brother since it was impractical to leave it empty.

For a long period after his arrival in America, Hitchcock was continually moving back and forth across the Atlantic—to make short films for the war effort, stung by taunts that he had fled Britain in its hour of need, then back to Hollywood before returning again to shoot *Under Capricorn* for the independent production company Transatlantic Pictures, which he had set up with Sidney Bernstein, an old friend from Film Society days, in order to escape the clutches of the monomaniacal Hollywood producer David Selznick. In 1955, Hitchcock was back in London again, where he was introduced to Charlie Chaplin by Bernstein. Chaplin explained that he considered himself to be a citizen of the world and consequently saw no particular point in changing the nationality that he had arbitrarily acquired at his birth. Hitchcock argued that as an American tax-payer, he felt that he was under a moral responsibility to become a citizen of his adopted country. However, as John Russell Taylor points out, the very next film he made was *The Trouble with Harry*, a quintessentially English project, albeit transposed into an American setting—New England, of course.[1]

If we look back at Hitchcock's very first English picture, *Pleasure Garden*—actually Anglo-German—we find a film in which the two leading parts were both played by American female stars. When his English producer, Michael Balcon, saw the finished film, he commented that it seemed completely American in its lighting and style. Hitch responded that this was only to be expected, since the bulk of his cinematic experience, both in the industry and as a film-goer, had actually been of American films. He wanted, in fact, to combine a view of the world that was quintessentially English with a professionalism and an overall look that were basically American. The stories that appealed most to Hitchcock, even when he was in America, were very English, both in style and atmosphere—du Maurier, for instance, or the spy thriller—and when they had American sources he anglicized them through his own detailed work on the script and through his choice of collaborators who understood and tolerated his predilections. On the other hand, he also wanted the gloss, sophistication and technical polish of Hollywood. He wanted both London and Los Angeles.

When we recall the earlier 'English' Hitchcock we think of black-and-white films that were typically based on West End stage hits, although the later Pinewood films were already veering towards the melodramatic thriller (Buchan, Maugham, Conrad, du Maurier). When we think of 'American' Hitchcock we think of films in colour, largely based on short stories or slim and fast-paced novels (Highsmith, Woolrich, Boileau and Narcejac, Bloch). In comparison, English Hitchcock can look awkwardly dated and confined—'disjointed, like a Nevinson painting, all jagged, angular', to use a phrase of Hitchcock's—while the later American Hitchcock seems more streamlined, more expansive, more hypnotic. But, in the last analysis, English Hitchcock was always already striving to be American, and Hollywood Hitchcock was always already drawing on a whirlpool of paranoia, sadism, voyeurism and schizophrenia triggered by the very English obsessions and fears that he brought with him from Leytonstone and Shamley Green to Bel Air and Scotts Valley.

In retrospect, it is striking how many of Hitchcock's American studio projects were set in Britain or based on British source material. *Rebecca* was adapted from a du Maurier story, *Foreign Correspondent* was set in London, *Suspicion* was based on a book by Francis Iles, the story idea for *Saboteur* was credited to Hitchcock himself, *Rope* came from a Patrick Hamilton play, *The Man Who Knew Too Much* was a remake of the earlier English version, *North by Northwest* recycled *The 39 Steps*, and so on, via J. Trevor Story's *The Trouble with Harry*, right through to *The Birds*, which came from another Daphne du Maurier short story, *Marnie*, a Winston Graham novel originally set in Devon, and *Frenzy*, a thriller set in London, adapted from a novel by La Bern, a favourite author for directors of English spiv films and crime thrillers. Similarly, Hitchcock's most successful source for television was the work of Roald Dahl. Working closely on these and other projects were Hitchcock himself, Alma (of course), Joan Harrison, Angus MacPhail, Charles Bennett, Raymond Chandler, Keith Waterhouse and Willis Hall.

One further footnote—perhaps most significant of all—Hitchcock, shortly after his arrival in Los Angeles, repaid the debt he owed from Islington days to both Jane Novak (star of *The Blackguard*, written by Hitch, directed by Graham Cutts) and Betty Compson (star of *Woman to Woman*, directed by Cutts, with Hitchcock as assistant director) by giving them each small parts in, respectively, *Foreign Correspondent* and *Mr and Mrs Smith*. Thus Hitchcock began his career as an English director in Hollywood by making an explicit connection to the American beginnings of his London career. The truth is that Hitchcock made every effort to Americanize himself professionally while he was still in England and then defiantly stuck to his English habits once he was ensconced in America.

There is a tell-tale story which Hitchcock recounted to John Russell Taylor. Towards the end of his career, he embarked on *The Torn Curtain*, a project inspired by a very English spy story, but he was prevailed upon by the studio, Universal, to cast Paul Newman opposite Julie Andrews— who was, at least, English. Newman, however, posed a serious problem. First, he was a method-influenced actor and Hitchcock loathed, not so much actors as such, but method actors as a particularly troublesome category. Hitch never forgot the horrors of his earlier experience with Montgomery Clift. Second, and much more unforgivably, Newman flaunted his shamelessly laddish Americanness. John Russell Taylor tells the story as follows:

> The first real social encounter between Hitch and Newman got them off on the wrong foot. Hitch invited Newman home to a small dinner party. The first thing Newman did was to take off his jacket at table and drape it over the back of his chair. Then he refused Hitchcock's carefully chosen

vintage wine and asked for beer instead. And, to make matters worse, he insisted on going and getting it himself out of the refrigerator and drinking it from the can.[2]

As Taylor notes, 'the whole of the shooting was overshadowed by the judgements reached that evening'.

Lurking beneath this story, of course, was the question of social class. Hitchcock had acquired fame and wealth and, with them, he had cultivated an idealized upper-class life-style. Although he came from a by no means poor background—his father was a shopkeeper whose successful business was eventually incorporated into the nation-wide chain store Mac Fisheries—he was still fascinated, from his earliest years, by the social style and mores of the traditional British upper class. His enthusiastic attendance at London Film Society screenings had given him an entrée into the more sophisticated world whose values he envied, the world of Ivor Montagu and Adrian Brunel. In a way, his interest in Murnau or Eisenstein or vintage René Clair was related to his taste for champagne and Parisian cuisine. At the same time, he developed an ambivalent fascination with upper-class women. The problem with English actresses, he told an interviewer in 1935, was that 'it is always their desire to appear a lady and, in doing so, they become cold and lifeless. Nothing pleases me more than to knock the ladylikeness out of chorus girls.'[3] In comparison, he thought, 'many of the American stars have come from the poorest of homes. They have had the common touch, and they have never lost it.'

In fact, Hitchcock took these attitudes with him on the ship to America. His favoured male alter egos—Farley Granger, James Stewart or Cary Grant—always appeared as sophisticates, whatever their real origins may have been, whereas when the women were dressed up as ladies they were then tormented for it, just as Madeleine Carroll was in *The 39 Steps*. In fact, long before he got to America, Hitch had fantasies of humiliating female American stars:

If I were directing Claudette Colbert (whom I consider one of the loveliest women in American films), I should first show her as a mannequin. She would slink through the showroom in her elegant, French way, wearing gorgeous gowns as only such a woman can. She would be perfectly coiffured, perfectly made-up. Then I would show her backstage. As she disappeared through the curtains, I'd make her suck down a piece of toffee or chewing gum which she had kept in her mouth all the time she was looking so beautiful.[4]

Of course, this particular fantasy, which Hitch justified as 'a touch of realism', was nothing to what he was able to do when he actually got to Hollywood. Nor did he ever get the chance to direct Claudette Colbert, although she was his first choice for the female lead in *Foreign Correspondent*.

Shortly after Hitch's marriage to Alma (at the fashionable Brompton Oratory) and his honeymoon in fashionable Saint Moritz, Michael Balcon suggested to Hitchcock that he might move to Mayfair, traditionally the 'society' core of central London. Hitchcock rejected the idea, explaining 'I never felt any desire to move out of my own class'. Instead he moved into a maisonette, at the top of ninety-two stairs—no lift—in a nondescript stretch of the Cromwell Road. After he arrived in Los Angeles, however, Hitchcock acquired a house in fashionable Bel Air, albeit a 'snug little house' (in his words) rather than a grandiose residence—John Russell Taylor describes it as 'an English-style cottage (or what passed locally for one)'.[5] There he read the English papers, 'sometimes weeks out of date', and wore 'invariably English, invariably formal clothes, in defiance of the climate and that noonday sun to which only mad dogs and Englishmen are impervious'. Despite his success, Hitchcock always stayed fundamentally middle class in his tastes and aspirations, except (perhaps) in the areas of food and wine (where he cherished the opportunity of becoming a *bon viveur* in the old Edwardian style) and art (where he added Braque and Dubuffet to the Klee and Sickert already in his collection).

I think Hitchcock was happier in Los Angeles than he was in London, largely because he was able to play the waggish and eccentric Englishman without the self-consciousness that would have overcome him in England, as if the Southland gave him licence to turn himself into something of a caricature without the shame he might have felt in London. In fact he made his image into a trade-mark, much as Chaplin had done before him—a comparison, I think, that was always in Hitchcock's mind. In his

1965 article on 'Film Production' for the *Encyclopaedia Britannica* he singled out a select group of directors as having a personal style—Lubitsch, Chaplin, DeMille, Griffith, Ince, Lang and Murnau—all of them, like Hitch, directors from the silent era: three Americans and four Europeans who ended up in LA. When Hitchcock reminisced about the silent days in 1936, he proudly quoted an English newspaper as saying, back in 1924, that *Woman to Woman* was 'the best American picture made in England'—a film on which Hitchcock had worked, on his own account, as script-writer, set designer *and* production manager. 'In the beginning', he explained, 'I was American-trained' and, as he put it, 'therein lies my debt to America'.[6] Hitchcock repaid that debt richly when he finally arrived in America, but in English cultural coinage, by bringing to Los Angeles a vision of the world, a psychopathology and an obsession with film-making as an art that were profoundly English in their roots.

While Hitch was making *North by Northwest*, he fantasized, apparently in a tipsy moment, that one day movies could be dispensed with altogether and the audience would be wired with electrodes to produce the requisite responses as the director, in John Russell Taylor's words, would 'play on them as on a giant organ console'. This, I believe, was his ultimate dream of Hollywood. He was interested, of course, in all three of the main requisites for film-making—money, professionalism and technology—and he found all three readily available in Los Angeles, whereas in London there was always somehow a bit of a problem. America permitted him to make the very English films he could only dream about making in England, yet that dream was itself rooted in his early experiences of Hollywood and his fascination with it. Where else could he make the great leap forward which he felt the cinema required if his dreams were to be fully realized? Hitchcock needed Los Angeles but, in the depths of his dreams and nightmares, he never left London. In America Hitch insulated himself in a private world of his own—a world which emerged into the public sphere in the form of his Hollywood masterpieces—yet his Los Angeles self could never escape from its London other. The two were inextricably interlocked from the beginning to the end of his career. To steal his own phrase, it was always a case of 'Handcuffed, key lost!'

6

JLG

Jean-Luc Godard's *A Bout de Souffle* (*Breathless*) and Budd Boetticher's *The Rise and Fall of Legs Diamond* were both released in 1959. I was living in Paris at that time and I went to see both of these films during the first week they appeared on the screen. In fact, I went back to see both of them a number of times. I couldn't help noticing that Godard quoted from another Boetticher movie in the course of *Breathless*, during the scene in which the small-time gangster Michel Poiccard, played by Jean-Paul Belmondo, dives into a cinema on the Champs-Elysées in order to shake off a wearisome tail. The film which is up there on the screen turns out to be Budd Boetticher's *Westbound*, one of the Randolph Scott cycle, although the voice that we hear on the soundtrack is mysteriously speaking some lines of poetry by Guillaume Apollinaire. In a way, this aberrant moment summed up Godard's appeal for me—the perverse mixture of modernism with B-movies, as if an Apollinaire poem somehow fitted quite naturally into a low-budget 'oater', a minor Warner Brothers production, as if you could love both of them at the same time. 1959 was also the year of Samuel Fuller's extraordinary *Crimson Kimono* and, sure enough, Sam Fuller showed up in a Godard film six years later, in *Pierrot le Fou*, where *le grand Sam* appears as a party guest to define film as 'like a battleground. Yes . . . Love. Hate. Action. Violence. Death. In one word . . . Emotion.' Fuller, we have been told, is in Paris to make a movie of Baudelaire's *Fleurs du Mal*.

At the time, Godard already seemed a film-maker *sui generis*, a crucial founding figure of the Nouvelle Vague, it went without saying, but also a director with his own very personal and even idiosyncratic agenda. Right from the start, he never seemed likely to develop into a respected master of the art film, a pillar of the new French cinema, as Chabrol, Resnais, Rohmer and Truffaut were all to become. If anything, he seemed more likely to become a new Cocteau, never quite integrated into the industry, always the poet rather than the practitioner, a film-maker with a fatal soft spot for the *film maudit*. Yet, although Godard was in revolt against conventional ideas of cinema, against *le cinéma du papa*, he was also an unashamed fan of minor Hollywood pictures. *Breathless*, as Godard readily admitted, was inspired by Richard Quine's *Pushover* and could be seen as the direct sequel to Otto Preminger's *Bonjour Tristesse*. The central character of the film, a small-time criminal played by Jean-Paul Belmondo, modelled his self-image on that of Humphrey Bogart in Mark Robson's *The Harder They Fall*. These films were not even 'classics'—they were little-regarded films dating from the mid-fifties, movies which a leading historian of Hollywood, Andrew Sarris, later characterized as 'widely reviled' and 'seldom, if ever, revived'. But there was method in Godard's madness. The dedication of *Breathless* to Monogram Pictures, the loving tributes to hard-boiled movies that never even made it to cult status, were part and parcel of a coherent and considered re-evaluation of classic American cinema.

My first view of Godard concentrated on this 'Americanism', linked to the auteurist rediscovery of Hollywood undertaken by the group of critics (and future film-makers) who had gathered around *Cahiers du Cinéma*— Rohmer, Rivette and Truffaut as well as Godard himself. Seen in this light, Godard's early films, his Nouvelle Vague films, echoed important trends which had surfaced within my own English culture: the emergence of early (and indeed pre-American) Pop Art after the 1956 'This Is Tomorrow' exhibition. For example, Richard Hamilton's painting *Interior 1* portrayed, as its central figure, Pamela Knight as she appeared in *Shockproof* (directed by Douglas Sirk, from a Samuel Fuller script). It seemed to echo the cultural preoccupations of Godard's *Breathless*, filled with quotations from American gangster pictures. Lawrence Alloway, who was the critical spokesperson for the This Is Tomorrow group, was the nearest thing there was in England to a *Cahiers* critic; he was a patron of the parallel English magazine, *Movie*, which promoted Hollywood repertory cinema and imported the *politique des auteurs* from across the Channel. In the end, as the sixties progressed, this cannibalizing and reworking of American mass culture became more and more dominant in Britain. In the music world, for example, it produced the Beatles and the Rolling Stones. Indeed, English mass cultural 'modernism' was itself exported abroad and became hegemonic to a degree even within the United States itself.

Godard's films appeared as the products of a similarly modernist and cosmopolitan intelligentsia when compared with the much more 'domestic' and 'French' work of Claude Chabrol, Eric Rohmer or François Truffaut, whose 'modernity' and 'Americanism' soon began to seem skin-deep. Godard had long recognized Hitchcock and Lang and Griffith as great masters—alongside Rossellini, Renoir and Eisenstein—but he also recognized the strengths of marginal and eccentric Hollywood productions, the odd films out of the studio system. Talking about his second film, *Le Petit Soldat*, he invoked Welles's *The Lady from Shanghai*, which David Thomson has seen as 'deconstructing' *film noir*.[1] *Une Femme Est une Femme* reminded him of Lubitsch's supposed 'failure', *Design For Living*, and Richard Quine's decidedly minor *My Sister Eileen*. Godard treated Hollywood as a kind of conceptual property store from which he could serendipitously loot ideas for scenes, shots and moods. On the set, he improvised, halting the filming while he disappeared to figure out what should happen next, cueing new lines to actors while the camera was rolling, even fitting them with earphones. He never once worked with a script-writer and he never gave traditional acting directions, preferring to let performers decide for themselves. In fact, his films began to turn into documentaries about their actors. In the editing, he confessed, he just used the shots he liked best, without worrying too much about continuity or coherence. His tightest film, *Vivre sa Vie*, consisted of a series of sequence shots laid end to end, each of them a first take, so that 'there was no editing. All I had to do was put the shots end to end. What the crew saw at the rushes is more or less what the public sees.' (He was scathing about Delbert Mann—best known as the Oscar-winning director of *Marty*—asking, 'What is it ultimately that makes one run a shot on or change to another? A director like Delbert Mann probably doesn't think this way. He follows a pattern. Shot—the character speaks; reverse angle, someone answers.')

In retrospect, I can now see my 'Americanist' fascination with Godard's sixties films as onesided. There were two further, and often conflicting, impulses at work in Godard's cinema, both of which were deeply French in origin. First, there was the strong strain of what we might call 'life-style modernism', which combined a journalistic sense of the topical with a more sociologically oriented mode of investigation and an attachment to the 'critique of everyday life', to use Henri Lefebvre's phrase. It is this dimension of Godard's work that made him seem both a cultural 'barometer' and an emergent political critic. In cinematic terms, this strain owed a great deal to the films of Jean Rouch, which provided models of filmic urban anthropology, first in Africa, then, with *Chronique d'un Eté*, made with Edgar Morin, in Paris itself. In intellectual terms, it was from the *Arguments* group, to which Morin belonged, that Godard drew most, but he also drew, I am sure, from the neighbouring yet bitterly antagonistic group of situationists. Godard's films exhibit any number of situationist characteristics—not only his topography of the 'society of the spectacle', but also, for example, the ideas of *dérive*, of *détournement*, and of plagiarism as a deliberate policy. Indeed, the films made by Guy Debord, the central figure in the situationist movement, pre-date many of Godard's own later preoccupations and strategies, as Debord himself couldn't help noticing and commenting on with his habitual vitriol.

Second, there was Godard's profound and yet paradoxical attachment to the idea of art, both as a repertory of great works, an available cultural heritage, and also as an anarchic project in process, which simultaneously required the reinscription and destruction of that heritage. It is here that Cocteau's heritage also made itself felt. Like those of Cocteau, Godard's films showed a contradictory reverence for the art of the past and a delinquent refusal to obey any of its rules. This applied both to the cinema and to the other, older arts. Godard's films seem to be made in a consumerist version of Malraux's 'imaginary museum,' a society full of posters and postcards of great paintings, records of great music, shelves of paperback classics and people who can quote instant lines of poetry to each other. But rather than seeing the consumer society as antagonistic to art, as did many anti-modernists, Godard saw the pervasive availability of art as an integral part of consumerism. Art had left its sanctum to become a prominent feature of 'everyday life', alongside pinball machines and advertising posters. In this aspect of his work, Godard often seems to oscillate between a critique of consumerism and mass culture and a delighted fascination with it. In this respect too, Godard's work resembles that of Jean Cocteau. It was Cocteau who first introduced the modern imagery of cabaret, café, beach and sports arena to the world of the artistic spectacle, while distancing himself through constant allusions to the classics and to 'high art', using a strategy of citations, rewritings and ironic echoes.

Eventually, of course, Godard's trajectory swept him towards a leftist political commitment, crystallized by the events of May 1968, which threw his latent neo-classicism and aestheticism into crisis. Everyday life itself had become more and more politicized until the streets were filled with militant demonstrations and home, factory and film set all became sites of political ferment. Unlike Cocteau, however, Godard did not recoil from politicization. Indeed, his whole film-making career up to this point was bound up with an unflinching determination to be topical, to keep abreast of the headlines (and particularly the city streets life-style of vanguard urban youth). Once this politicization had passed a certain point, it triggered a transformation of the whole system. Godard's cinema entered its militant phase. At first, this seemed likely to stabilize around some idea of 'Brechtian' or 'guerrilla' cinema, but it soon became clear that Godard's radicalism was impelling him even further, towards a kind of 'Cinema year zero', although even the zero point still carried echoes of earlier work: the Lettrists and Maurice Lemaître's *Le Film Est Déjà Commencé*. Cocteau broke with the surrealists when they began to move to the far left politically, but Godard moved rapidly leftward with the situationists and beyond, eventually joining a Maoist *groupuscule*, just as André Breton had once joined the Communist Party.

Instead of the Romanticism of Poe, Dostoyevsky or Garcia Lorca, it was the voice of Marxism-Leninism and Mao Tse-tung Thought that now overloaded the soundtrack of his films with quotations, providing an interminable and pitiless metalanguage, attacking the spectator with a series of inquisitorial monologues, designed, like a Lettrist film, to provoke the audience. Yet, in many respects, elements of Godard's former strategies somehow managed to survive. Films were still structured in blocks and modules (often numbered), voices were divorced from their characters, 'real people' were mingled with fictional roles, genres were shuffled together in the same film, dialogue was replaced by direct address to the camera/audience, cinematic devices and techniques were foregrounded, image track and soundtrack were filled with quotations and wordplay. There was also a new emphasis on the semiotic character of the cinema, its own codes and 'signifying practices', which were explicitly interrogated within the films themselves. Here we can also see the influence of Roland Barthes (another former member of the *Arguments* group) and his semiology of everyday life, both his inquiries into the rhetoric of images and his insistence that verbal language was always needed to anchor their meaning.[2]

The films of this brief but intense period, which lasted from 1968 to 1972, were didactic and essayistic rather than narrative or dramatic, closer to Brecht than to Hollywood. Even when there was a fictional 'story' it was subordinated to a more or less explicit ideological 'master text'. However, following the breakup of the Dziga Vertov group, the dominance of politics and the 'master text' started to dissolve and, after Godard's removal from Paris to Grenoble and the beginning of his domestic and artistic partnership with Anne-Marie Miéville, a new tentativeness began to be felt. Godard now began to be interested in video as a populist form, as people are interested in the internet today, and to develop an ongoing semiotic inquiry, not only into the meaning of photographic images as such, but also into the specific formal differences between video and film, as distinct from television and cinema. This period saw a revival of Godard's interest in semiotic investigation, now including the televisual alongside the cinematic sign. In *Ici et Ailleurs* and *Comment ça va* he picked up many of the threads he had dropped since *Le Gai Savoir*. Although his films were still political in a sense, they lost much of their dogmatism. In particular, his view of politics had changed in the wake of feminism, and he now tried to explore the ways in which the 'personal' was intertwined with the 'political'. His films and videotapes investigated the relationship between apparently 'personal' categories like 'love' and social categories like 'labour'. In many ways, this was a rich period in Godard's career.

Then, after 1976, when Godard moved again, from Grenoble to Rolle in Switzerland, his films took yet another new turn, this time towards a preoccupation with landscape, metaphysics and cosmic speculation, with the 'sublime', even with religion. It is often assumed that this happened because he was now living and working in the countryside rather than the city. However, we could also see this shift of emphasis as part of a general shift within French intellectual culture itself. Leading Marxists and structuralists began to abandon the master narratives and semiotic systems of the sixties. As the Enlightenment and 'modernity' were increasingly called into question, a process accelerated by post-1968 disenchantment, French intellectuals turned away from 'knowledge-based' approaches to the humanities and towards the more speculative domains of aesthetics, philosophy and theology, urging a decentralised vision of 'dissemination', 'rhizomes' and 'molecular' microstructures. Godard also abandoned the centre, breaking down his narrative into a mosaic of micro-elements. At the same time, there was also a clear and significant return to another element of the Cocteau tradition, the return to the classics, the development of a personal mythology. Godard's aestheticism and classicism revived and grew again as his political commitment shrank or, at least, became more ethereal.

Throughout his career, Godard had avoided following a fixed pattern, whether in story construction or editing or choice of genre or development of a theme. Writing about Jean-Luc Godard for *Artforum* in 1968, the painter and critic Manny Farber guessed that 'at the end of this director's career, there will probably be a hundred films, each one a bizarrely different species, with its own excruciatingly singular skeleton, tendons, plumage'.[3] At the time Farber wrote this, Godard had just finished his twenty-third film, *La Chinoise*, plus two episodes for omnibus films. By the time Wheeler Winston Dixon completed his compendious and insightful book on Godard,[4] the unstoppable director was already up to his seventy-sixth (including major works on video, which first appeared as a favoured medium in the mid-seventies). Moreover, just as Farber predicted, each film seems to be *sui generis*, quite unlike any of his previous work, the same only in being so unpredictably, inconsistently different. Yet Godard's films do have a kind of underlying logic, albeit one which has mutated from time to time as he changed his place of residence, his circle of intimates and his mode of production. Looking back over his biography, we can certainly see significant changes but there is also a clear sense of continuity. In the most useful sketch of Godard's biography, Colin MacCabe divided his life into seven schematic episodes, which could be summarized and recapitulated as follows:[5]

1. Childhood. Godard was born in Switzerland in 1930. His father was a successful doctor who ran a private clinic in Nyon, his mother a member of an extremely rich banking family, the Schlumbergers, founders of the Banque de Paris et des Pays Bas. Godard remembers his childhood as an idyllic time, especially the happy days spent at his mother's family estate on the banks of Lake Geneva. According to MacCabe, 'the impression one gets is of a rather dreamy child, charming and spoiled, the apple of his mother's eye, but from early on in considerable conflict with his father'.

2. Cinephilia. At the end of the war, Godard was sent to Paris to study for his baccalaureat and, subsequently, a degree in anthropology at the Sorbonne. He soon became a frequenter of the Cinémathèque, the Institute of Filmology and the many small cine-clubs which had sprung up in Paris, partly as a way of catching up with films unseen as a result of the German occupation. Godard began to write about film, first (under the name Hans Lucas [= Jean-Luc] for the tiny *Gazette du Cinéma* and then for France's soon-to-become premier film journal, *Cahiers du Cinéma*, where his colleagues, as we have seen, included Truffaut, Rivette and Rohmer, fellow-founders of the Nouvelle Vague. During this time Godard also travelled to America and Brazil and (like Truffaut) committed a number of petty thefts—from friends, family, employers—and was lucky to escape relatively unscathed after a much more serious incident, following his return to Switzerland in 1952, led to the police becoming involved. His father, however, had him committed to a psychiatric hospital.

3. The New Wave. After his release from hospital, family connections

made it possible for him to earn the money to make his first film, an industrial short. Godard subsequently returned to Paris, where he quickly made three more short subjects, continued his writing as a critic, found work in the Fox publicity department, and made a number of contacts in the French film industry. His breakthrough came in the *annus mirabilis* of 1959 when *Breathless* rocketed him to instant success. The foundations had already been well laid by his friends from the *Cahiers* 'gang'— especially Truffaut, the ringleader of what he himself called 'la politique des copains', who had made his own mark the previous year and was now able to give his old partner in crime a helping hand. Godard soon outraged the critics, provoked his audience and flew in the face of the industry protocols. All the same, nobody who saw his sixties films is going to forget them in a hurry.

4. See you at Mao. The first signs of a shift in Godard's career came as early as 1963 with *Le Mépris* (*Contempt*), in which, ironically enough, Fritz Lang quotes to him Brecht's lines on being a screen-writer in Hollywood— 'Every day, to earn my daily bread / I go to the market where lies are bought / Hopefully / I take my place among the peddlers'—and he continued moving leftwards with *Deux ou Trois Choses Que Je Sais d'Elle* (*Two or Three Things I Know About Her*), eventually reaching Maoism with *La Chinoise*—with Vertov now replacing Eisenstein in his esteem. As always, Godard had mixed up his work with his private life and everything began to implode when his stormy relationship with Anna Karina, star of seven fantastic films and also his wife, finally fell to pieces. *La Chinoise* was about a group of would-be revolutionary students, with the lead played by Anne Wiazemsky, whom Godard was soon to marry, and who appeared in five of his subsequent films. In *Le Gai Savoir*, his first film for television, he responded directly to the events of May 1968, with a film that was both his most experimental and his most politically committed work. The next year Godard and Jean-Pierre Gorin founded a Maoist film-making collective, the Dziga Vertov group, named after the founder of the Kino-Eye movement in the 1920s. Starting with ideas about 'Brechtian' or 'guerrilla' cinema, Godard's radicalism had propelled him to what he called 'Cinema year zero' (an echo of Rossellini's *Germany, Year Zero*). In 1970, he was driven away in a police van for selling the banned *Cause du Peuple* on the streets.

5. Grenoble. Three years later (in 1973), following Godard and Gorin's ill-starred attempt to make a Marxist-Leninist musical with Jane Fonda and Yves Montand, the Dziga Vertov adventure was finally wound up and Godard set off down yet another path, once again together with a new partner, Anne-Marie Miéville. Miéville was a stills photographer who had nursed Godard back to health after a motorcycle accident in 1971, just before he began shooting *Tout Va Bien*. Once the film was out of the way, she insisted that he should leave Paris behind him permanently, for his own well-being. Godard's move to Grenoble was both a stage in his personal recovery and also a way to restabilize his career by embarking on a series of video projects for French television, now in partnership with Miéville. In *Ici et Ailleurs* and *Comment ça va*, Godard picked up the semiotic trail first blazed in *Le Gai Savoir*. (Barthes, the founder of semiology, had refused to appear as himself in a Godard film, unlike other celebrities.) With Miéville, Godard now reformulated his entire political position; his self-criticism, partly carried out on screen, led him to a new concern with family and personal relationships, reflecting the emergence of a women's movement. Towards the end of this period he became involved in a utopian plan to create a do-it-yourself television channel for the Mozambique Ministry of Information, a kind of cross between Kino-Eye and *Video Nation* which eventually came to nothing.

6. Back to Switzerland. In 1976, Godard and Miéville, herself Swiss, left France for good and he returned to his childhood haunts on the banks of Lake Geneva. There they continued working together with video but, apparently in response to Miéville's urging, Godard also embarked on a series of feature films made with bankable stars and serious production values. In 1982 the great cinematographer Raoul Coutard, who had shot all fifteen of his films bar one, in the 1960s, from *Breathless* through to *Weekend*, rejoined Godard to work with him on *Passion* and *Prénom Carmen*, two films which were widely taken as signalling a partial reconciliation between the new Swiss-based Godard and the Parisian Godard of old. Predictably enough, the possibility that Godard might relaunch his commercial career came to a catastrophic end in 1987 when he signed up to make a version of *King Lear* with Menahem Golan and Yoram Globus, then heads of Cannon Films, a pair of

producers perhaps even sleazier than Jerry in *Contempt*. The script was written by Norman Mailer and he and his daughter were supposed to star as Lear and Cordelia. Predictably enough, after half a day's shooting, they walked off the set and Godard, unpanicked, began all over again with Burgess Meredith and Molly Ringwald. Woody Allen did a brief walk-on as Mr Alien and Godard himself appeared as Professor Pluggy, while Mailer's grandiose vision of the film as a version of *The Godfather* was systematically thrown to the winds.

7. Stabilization. In the most recent phase of his career, Godard, together with Miéville, has continued to put together packages that enable him to work as a director for television, very much on his own terms. Most of his TV income was reinvested in technical equipment so that he could do post-production in what is effectively his own personal facility house. He has still averaged a ruminative new feature every three or four years, while devoting the bulk of his energy to the massive eight-part video epic *Histoire(s) du Cinéma*, a protracted meditation on one hundred years of cinema as seen by one of its own most knowledgeable and unsettling figures—a fermenting collage of favourite moments, springboards for typically Godardian disquisitions and unexpected linkages and juxtapositions. *Histoire(s) du Cinéma* was finished several years ago, and is destined to be reissued as a DVD box-set. As for the future, who could hope to tell?

Thus far, although Godard's career has been one of incessant change and movement, it has somehow ended up with an almost crystalline structure. He left Switzerland for Paris, Paris for Grenoble and Grenoble to return again to Switzerland. His family gave way to the Cinémathèque and the *Cahiers* gang, the *Cahiers* gang to Karina and Coutard, Karina and Coutard to Wiazemsky and Gorin, Wiazemsky and Gorin to Anne-Marie Miéville, a fellow-Swiss with a family, who took him back to his childhood haunts on the shore of Lake Geneva. Film clubs gave way to film journals, journalism gave way to film-making, feature films gave way to TV, TV gave way to video, until he ended up editing and mixing in an artisanal workshop with a pronounced journalistic and film club feel to it, where he constructed his own video version of the ideal Cinémathèque, a televisual Rue de Messine.

Through all these phases ran Godard's own personality and preoccupations, eccentric and wayward but always rigorous and inventive. His films always displayed a fascination with both current events and the great classics of the past, they showed a taste for high art as well as for pulp fiction and pornography, they carried the traces of improvisation but also contained elaborate formal compositions. He revered old Hollywood movies from the days when studios were studios and everyone ate in the same canteen, but expressed an ever-deeper revulsion for the new Hollywood mode of production. In the seventies he developed the concept of the video script, a kind of do-it-yourself prototype for a film, shot hand-held on video, which he likened to a painter's sketchbook. He scattered quotations from other people's films throughout his own, but he was always audaciously original. He zeroed in on the crucial issues of his time (the collapse of communism, the reunification of Germany, the siege of Sarajevo) while shamelessly following red herrings and squandering his attention on side-issues.

Until recently, most of the serious writing in English about Godard still came from the 1960s—from Richard Roud, Manny Farber, Susan Sontag, Robin Wood, Raymond Durgnat and others, including myself. This reflected Godard's much greater cultural centrality during that period and his apparently secure place within the festival/art film system. When he veered off-course with the Dziga Vertov group, he not only baffled and dismayed many former admirers but he also moved into a *sui generis* mode of production which left him in a kind of cinematic no man's land. He never fitted into the experimental film world, the territory occupied by the 'underground', by structural film and the international Film Co-op movement, which shared Godard's marginalization but had their own very different history, culture and values. On the other hand, he never found safe refuge in the film festival world, the prestige sector of the industry which nurtured a stream of ambitious young directors, many of whom had been directly influenced by Godard—Bertolucci, Wenders, Akerman—but who never abandoned their audiences as irrevocably as he did. Wenders and Akerman found their niche and stuck to it, Bertolucci pulled back after 1968 and *Partner*, ending up the prisoner of his cameraman, Storaro. In France, naturally enough, Godard still retained a loyal critical following, especially in the pages of a revamped

Cahiers du Cinéma, but in the anglophone world the burden has fallen on a handful of loyal supporters, such as Jonathan Rosenbaum and Colin MacCabe, supplemented by a new generation of admirers, such as Michael Temple and Michael Witt.

In the last few years, happily, there seems to have been a burgeoning revival of interest, perhaps because Godard has now achieved the dubious status of historic monument or Grand Old Man, perhaps because of the new alliance which has taken shape between experimental film and video installations in the larger art world, perhaps even because of the cult status given him by the once-famous Quentin Tarantino, of all people. Two recent books stand out. Wheeler Winston Dixon's presents a macroscopic view of Godard's entire career to date, covering every film or video he has ever made. It is divided into five chapters, which correspond more or less to the five film-making periods of MacCabe's biographical schema, except that he divides the New Wave into two at *Le Mépris*, an elegy for the old studio system of classical film-making (as incarnated in Fritz Lang). Wheeler Dixon sees this film as the turning-point at which Godard recognized that Hollywood was now undergoing an irreversible decline, symbolized by the character of Prokosch, the producer (played by Jack Palance), who is portrayed as 'simultaneously ruthless, vain, childish, arrogant, stupid, greedy, self-deluding'. After *Le Mépris*, *Le Gai Savoir* and the work of the Dziga Vertov group seemed inevitable in their rejection of commercial cinema. Dixon rightly interprets *King Lear* as a kind of second *Le Mépris*, observing that it 'might arguably be considered Godard's final farewell to feature film production', leading him into a second period of disenchantment. Dixon also lavishes praise on *Sauve Qui Peut (La Vie)* and *Passion*, Godard and Miéville's two first Swiss features. He describes *Passion* as 'a catalogue of the difficulties and inherent transcendence afforded by the waking dream of the cinematographic process', a kind of tell-tale confession of ambivalence .

Kaja Silverman and Harun Farocki, in contrast, adopt a microscopic approach in their book *Speaking About Godard*, writing about eight select films in an exercise of what they describe as 'close reading', concentrating on specific sequences and shots within each work.[6] Their book is itself bravely experimental in form, written in alternating paragraphs of dialogue as if there was an ongoing conversation between the two authors while they watch the films. As with Godard's own work, there is a tension between improvisation and control which is both provocative and uncannily appropriate. Farocki is himself an outstanding director of what we might call 'essay films', mostly for German television, whose professional experience illuminates his understanding of Godard's choices as director and editor, while Silverman is a leading theorist and feminist scholar whose long-suppressed cinephilia finally comes out into the open as she describes with detailed and loving attention the appeal of particular shots and camera movements, just for themselves rather than as evidence for something else. They pick out eight films from Godard's massive output as key works, with five from the 1960s (*Vivre Sa Vie*, *Le Mépris*, *Alphaville*, *Weekend*, *Le Gai Savoir*) and one each from the 1970s, 1980s and 1990s (*Numéro Deux*, *Passion*, *Nouvelle Vague*). Thus their interest is weighted towards films from the second half of the 1960s, skipping right over *Breathless*, for instance. They are particularly insightful in their discussion of *Le Gai Savoir*, a notoriously difficult film, finally summing it up, in Godard's own words, as '444,000 images speaking about themselves'. While they skip over the Dziga Vertov films, they cover all three phases of the Miéville years, ending with a tightly argued paean of praise to the film *Nouvelle Vague*, the story of an industrialist and her lover who are saved from death by a miracle, saved by love, signalled by a quotation from Dante's *Inferno*: 'So while my soul yet fled did I contrive/ To turn and gaze on that dread pass once more/Which no man yet came ever out alive.'

Fredric Jameson once observed that Godard began in the sixties as a 'post-modernist *avant la lettre*' but ended up, two decades later, as 'the ultimate survivor of the modern as such', always swimming against the current of the age.[7] The futurist visionary and rebel turned eventually into the disenchanted historian in search of transcendence. This view of Godard as a premature postmodernist is based on the combination of two of Godard's qualities—his life-long penchant for quotation and recycling and his view that film-making should be a form of journalism or, perhaps, instant ethnography, seeking to grasp what is happening in contemporary society at the time of production and presenting it in a kind of visual mosaic. In fact, the contemporary French film-maker whom Godard cited most often during his years as a critic for *Cahiers du Cinéma* was Jean

Rouch, whose extraordinary films *Moi, un Noir* and *Jaguar*, set in Africa, and *Chronicle of a Summer*, made in Paris itself and co-directed with the sociologist Edgar Morin, clearly had an enormous impact on him. *Moi, un Noir*, Godard wrote in 1958, 'is a paving-stone in the marsh of French cinema, as [Rossellini's] *Rome, Open City* was in world cinema'. Rouch and Morin's film, released in 1961, contained extempore interviews on the street with passers-by, a discussion of the Algerian war with students sitting round a dinner table (including the young Régis Debray), a wrenching first-person soul-baring direct to camera by an employee at *Cahiers du Cinéma* and, in one of the great sequences of cinema, a survivor's account of her experience in a concentration camp, spoken into the Nagra tape-recorder that she carries as she walks through the old Les Halles market, filmed by a hand-held Eclair camera in classic *cinéma vérité* style.

Jameson talks, quite rightly, about Godard's 'aesthetic of quotation' but I think it is important to stress there was nothing ironic or emptily eclectic about his mode of sampling and recycling high art. It was much deeper than pastiche. It stemmed from a recognition that contemporary French society both exhibited signs of a self-destructive future and simultaneously had preserved within itself the traces of other and quite contrasting kinds of value, which still threatened to break through the crust of alienation and fetishism in a volcanic burst of romantic freedom. Godard's characters cling desperately to the hopes represented by these fragments. His New Wave films are far from celebratory. They almost all have tragic endings—Michel Poiccard is shot by the cops, Nana Klein-frankenheim (yes!) is shot by the pimps (always the bad guys for Godard—the producers), Paul Javal leaves the set of Fritz Lang's *Odyssey* with his life in ruins, Ferdinand blows himself to pieces with sticks of brightly coloured gelignite. Only Lemmy Caution and Natacha Von Braun are able to reach their goal, escape to freedom from the dystopian city of Alphaville, although we never actually see them reach the border. As Silverman points out, it is a psychological rather than a geographical barrier. They succeed because Natacha proves able to say, 'I love you'. As Farocki puts it,

Natacha does not find these crucial words at once. She claims that she does not know what to say, and, twice, like Orpheus with Eurydice, she even begins to turn around to see what she and Lemmy are leaving behind. But finally the woman with the name from the past makes that simple declaration which, no matter how many times it is repeated, brings light to those who hear it, and humanity to those who utter it. Although Lemmy and Natacha still have many miles to drive, they have already reached their destination.[8]

Silverman draws the conclusion that the surrealist commitment to *amour fou* lies at the heart of the film. *Alphaville* is a reworking of Eluard's *Capitale de la Douleur* or Breton's *Nadja* with a happy end.

In Godard's films everybody seems lost in a tangle of confusions and deceptions and pointless escapades, and yet the key which unlocks the door to freedom is usually very simple. In the end, all you ever need is to keep faith with the essential humanist values—values like beauty, love and truth. It is these values to which Godard's quotations always seem to point. On the one hand, they reflect the aforementioned society crammed with posters and postcards of great paintings, recordings of great music, shelves of paperback classics, clips from great movies and people swapping lines of great poetry—the society in which Art has left its sanctum to become a generalised feature of 'everyday life'. On the other hand, they are like the quotations assembled in a private commonplace book, Godard's own enchiridion of favourite images and sounds and citations. Godard once observed that 'people who speak should find beautiful things to say—recite Shakespeare, for instance—or else it's not worth the trouble to speak. You're better off keeping quiet.'

It is this insistence on the value of beauty that directs Godard towards the enduring art of the past. The quotations which survive, however commodified, are still emblematic figures of beauty, love and truth, carrying against the odds the durable values which alone can bring us hope. In *Nouvelle Vague*, as Kaja Silverman notes, 'virtually every line is a quotation, from sources as diverse as Dante, Proust, Chandler, Schiller, de Rougemont [on courtly love], Marx, Hemingway, Lacan, and Rimbaud'.[9] But also, as Wheeler Dixon notes, the beauty of the landscape in *Nouvelle Vague* seems somehow more important than the actions of the characters, for whom, as he puts it, 'beauty is only worthwhile if it can be possessed, or transferred to another for a price'.[10]

Over time, Godard came to distrust spectacle more and more, yet he did so without ever abandoning his fundamental cinephilia, his abiding passion for film. His disenchantment sprang from the cinema's inability to respond to its times, to act as a kind of seismographic early warning system, registering the first tell-tale tremors of social and cultural upheaval, as he tried to do in his own work. As Michael Witt has recently observed, Godard finally became convinced that the cinema was indeed a doomed art, that it had lost the will to live, when he concluded that it had abandoned its former cinematic grandeur to pander to an audience whose subjectivity had been constructed by their experience of television and video.[11] For Godard, with his usual quirky insight, cinema involved projection, a beam of light projected in the dark as in the myth of Plato's cave. 'Cinema will disappear', Godard has predicted, 'when it is no longer projected', when the beam of light has gone.[12] Entering the cinema, entering the darkness to find the light, allows us to exit from ourselves, to live for a while in another space and another time, one which casts a prophetic light on the real society and history existing outside. Television, on the other hand, lives in the ephemeral. Its space is within the home, it is a 'family affair', domesticated and insulated. Godard was always at the forefront of technical change and experiment, from bounce lighting and the Aaton camera (with whose inventor he worked in close collaboration) to technologies of video editing and digital enhancement, but his own recent work for television should be seen as a form of resistance against a symbolic but real occupation, a way of infiltrating enemy-held territory in order to maintain the memory of cinema, to keep a desire for true cinema somehow flickeringly alive for the next millennium.

Godard's return to aestheticism, and thus to a form of ultra-modernism, was the result of his refusal to submit to the norms of our post-oil-shock society, with its global system of telecommunications, its debasement of public life and its ceaseless drive towards the consumption of commodities, driven, of course, first by television and then by the World Wide Web. Moreover, he has always held fast to an exalted idea of the role to be played by art—one which came to him from such early intellectual mentors as Elie Faure and André Malraux. From the beginning, Godard had shown a profound and yet paradoxical attachment to the traditions of European art, both as a heritage of great works and, at the same time, as an anarchic project which inevitably threatens every kind of tradition and norm. (All artists, even Céline, were on the left, natural rebels, he once said.) This applies both to the older arts and to the once young, now ailing, art of cinema. As suggested earlier, Godard's films combine a contradictory reverence for the art of the past with a refusal to conform to any of its rules. His films have always been filled with references to the cinematic archive—*Le Mépris* is an extended act of homage to a classical cinema, a Homeric cinema, which was already superseded. Although Godard's own films broke with all the conventions of the classical cinema he admired, they formed a conscious coda to it.

Godard spent several years working on his massive video project, *Histoire(s) du Cinéma*. But, as Michael Temple has reminded us, in a conference paper on 'The Nutty Professor: Jean-Luc Godard, Historian of the Cinema?',[13] he thereby found himself faced yet again with the problem of narrative. In narrating the history of the cinema itself, he found himself telling a story whose end, whose death, was already inscribed within it. The persona that he chose to adopt was that of the pedagogue, a role for which he had already shown a leaning. Indeed, in the late 1970s, Serge Daney took him to task in the pages of *Cahiers du Cinéma* itself for his drill-master style of pedagogy, for setting citation against citation while avoiding responsibility for either, for his decontextualization of sources and his terroristic use of theory. Godard responded by adopting the persona of the crackpot seer who is both an utter idiot and a *poète maudit*, casting himself as the Nutty Professor, a quick-change artist whose tragic truths are presented as if they were buffooneries. But the story he now had to tell was a cruel and melancholy one—how the cinema, despite its moments of glory, ultimately betrayed us and was doomed to die. Silent film was ruined by the coming of sound. After the collapse of the old studio system, the cinema capitulated to television, accepting its insidious degradation of the visual. Most damning of all, Hollywood had fatally shirked its historic responsibility to record the seismic shocks of history when it failed to respond to the threat or the reality of the Holocaust. (Lubitsch's madcap anti-Nazi comedy, *To Be or Not to Be*, released in 1942, was perhaps the one oblique exception to Godard's indictment. Spielberg's belated *Schindler's List* was scorned as 'rebuilding Auschwitz'.) Cinema had looked the other way. Its death was overdue. Godard could tell this particular story with conviction because he knew it was true and because, although he may have been viewed as a charlatan, a provocateur and a Pied Piper, he knew that he had never been, like so many of his accusers, a collaborator. He had always been fearless and intransigent in his resistance.

Resistance can take many forms. For Godard, I believe, it has been inseparable from his mania for refunctioning the great masterpieces he admired, reincorporating them into his own work, wanting, as he put it, talking about *Breathless*, to 'take a conventional story and remake, but differently, everything the cinema had done'.[14] Not only did he cite Preminger and invoke Bogart from the *film noir* canon, but he quoted or alluded to Lang's *Tiger of Eschnapur*, Mann's *Man of the West*, Eisenstein's *October* and Rouch's *Moi, un Noir*, the film from which he drew the most—a documentary about a set of characters, in Côte d'Ivoire, who lovingly recycle, in their own style, the words and gestures of their movie heroes. In effect, the originality of *Breathless* depended on its status as creative sampling, as a remix of fragments adapted from other films or from the works of poetry or music or art which Godard revered, a remake, but different, personalized. *Breathless* was both a loving appropriation of narrative film and its desecration in the name of youth and improvised revolt, so that all the conventional rules of editing, lighting, screen-writing and direction were trashed, all the time-honoured conventions ignored. It was only a beginning. Godard's career combines an unflagging resistance to the demands of the industry with a recurrent commitment to cinema as art, classic and yet personal.

7

JEAN ROUCH

I

In his history of Henri Langlois and the Cinémathèque Française, *A Passion for Films*, Richard Roud tells the story of the Cercle du Cinéma, a private and somewhat itinerant film club founded in 1934 by Georges Franju and Henri Langlois, which began in a hired screening room on the Champs-Elysées, beneath the Cinéma Marignan, and led eventually to the foundation of the Cinémathèque Française as an institutional vehicle for screening as well as preserving films—although Langlois had always felt the two processes were indissoluble.[1] Films, he would say, are like Persian carpets: they have to be walked on. Jean Rouch, I learned both from Roud's account and from his own, was one of the first habitués of those Friday night screenings—about which he first learned from a prospectus he had picked up in Les Quatre Chemins, a Left Bank art gallery, where he had gone to see an exhibition of Dali's drawings for Lautréamont's *Maldoror*, a classic text for the surrealists. Rouch was already an avid film-goer. The first film he ever saw, as he has often recounted, was Flaherty's *Nanook of the North*, and subsequently he became an ardent habitué of cinemas such as The Lord Byron (*The Gay Divorcée*, with Fred Astaire and Ginger Rogers), Studio 28 in Montmartre (the Marx Brothers and W. C. Fields) and the Pagode (*The Scoundrel*, written and directed by Ben Hecht and Charles MacArthur). At the Cercle du

Cinéma, Rouch saw, one Friday evening in April 1937, Buñuel's *Un Chien Andalou*, Renoir's *Nana*, and Stroheim's *Queen Kelly*, followed on the next Friday by an anti-communist film from Nazi Germany, *Spartakus Bund*, and an anti-Nazi film from communist Russia, Pudovkin's *Deserter*. The next Friday, he saw Chaplin's *Shoulder Arms*, René Clair's *The Italian Straw Hat* and Protazanov's *The Mystery of St Georgion*, or perhaps that was the night, Rouch seems to remember, when *Shoulder Arms* never showed up, so instead Langlois had screened Vertov's *Enthusiasm* as its substitute. At any rate, Rouch certainly saw *Enthusiasm* and, eventually, *Shoulder Arms* too. It was also at the Cercle du Cinéma that he watched André Breton's favourite film, *Peter Ibbetson*, a film, appropriately enough, in which reality is mingled indistinguishably with dream.

Among the regular audience at the Cercle du Cinéma, Rouch also remembered seeing André Breton himself. I mention this because Rouch's early experience at the Cercle du Cinéma not only introduced him to the work of Dziga Vertov and, in more general terms, reflected his own passionate cinephilia, his consuming enthusiasm for cinema, but it was also closely connected to his interest in Surrealism. In fact, Henri Langlois had himself been a youthful disciple of Breton. José Corti's surrealist bookshop was located on the Rue Blanche, the street down which the young Henri walked on his way to school each day. It was there that he discovered Lautréamont and Rimbaud. 'I still remember', he later wrote, 'the enthusiasm I felt when I first read the Surrealist Manifesto', although subsequently he was disappointed by Breton's 'all too unrevolutionary' novel, *Nadja*! 'On the other hand,' Langlois reminisced, 'when I saw *Un Chien Andalou*, I was delirious.'[2] Langlois's early interest in Surrealism was shared by Jean Rouch, just as his love of cinema was shared by Jean Rouch. The two passions were inseparable. I believe that the tradition to which Rouch truly belongs was not so much that of Vertov, or even Flaherty, important though these two great predecessors clearly were, but—rather—the tradition of Buñuel and Dali. Important in more general terms was the way in which, for Rouch especially, Surrealism and cinema had become mixed together through the solvent of ethnography. Some of my readers will be familiar with C. W. Thompson's collection of essays, *L'Autre et le Sacré: Surréalisme, Cinéma, Ethnologie*.[3] For Thompson, the privileged year was 1931 when another of Breton's followers,

Michel Leiris, set off on his famous ethnographic expedition across Africa from Dakar to Djibouti, a journey on which he had hoped to be accompanied by none other than Luis Buñuel as the expedition's film-maker. Leiris was always quite explicit about the significance of Surrealism for ethnography—and vice versa. Seven years later, in 1938, when the Musée de l'Homme was officially opened in Paris and ethnography was thus both honoured and institutionalized, it was the surrealist poet Robert Desnos who was asked to write the words for the cantata specially composed (by Milhaud) to celebrate the occasion. Surrealists, ethnographers and film-makers shared many common interests, especially in the peoples and cultures of Africa, interests which led Jean Rouch into his own career as a cinephile inspired by ethnography, an ethnographer inspired by Surrealism.

Rouch actively entered the field of ethnography only after the war, during which he had worked as a civil engineer in Niger, an experience which encouraged him to become an anthropologist once the fighting was over. In 1946, he decided to return to Africa in order to carry out field-work with the Dogon peoples of Niger. He was encouraged by his teachers, Marcel Griaule and Marcel Mauss, to take a camera with him. In fact, Griaule had himself already made two short documentaries on the Dogon during the 1930s. So Rouch bought himself a 16mm Bell and Howell camera in the Paris flea-market, his mind, I presume, full of his experience at the Cercle du Cinéma and—no doubt—his early memories of *Nanook*. In fact, Rouch frequently remarked on Flaherty's untroubled mixture of documentary with fiction, as well as his insistence on screening the rushes of his films to the participants who had appeared in them, both practices which Rouch himself adopted. The films Rouch now made concerned magic, possession and children's games—all topics with a strong surrealist resonance, alongside their obvious ethnographic interest. We are reminded of Breton's own obsessive interest in the supernatural, in mediumistic trance states, in spontaneous play, in 'objective chance'. At the same time, cinema required technology—the Bell and Howell. Ethnography thus brought Surrealism together with technology, which in turn led to a revolution—I don't think the word is too strong—a revolution in film-making. Of course, ethnography had already been concerned with technology for many decades, longer than it had with Surrealism. In 1877, Thomas Alva Edison had made a note, reading as follows: 'Just tried experiment with diaphragm having an embossed point and held against a paraffin paper moving rapidly. The speaking [spkg] vibrations are indented nicely and there is no doubt that I shall be able to store up and reproduce automatically at any future time the human voice perfectly.' In the mid-eighteenth century Herder had envisioned a time when folk-songs would be collected in their original language, and with the accompanying music, noting enthusiastically 'how much it would enliven the chapter that the student of man reads most eagerly in every travelogue, "the nature and customs of the people! Their science and letters, their games and dances, their music and mythology!"' Just over a hundred years later, Edison made Herder's vision possible, but in an unexpected new way, using a machine which, for the first time, was able to record sounds.

2

By 1888 the Edison New Phonograph was on the market and, in 1890, Jesse Walter Fewkes took a phonograph with him on his visit to the Zuni people of the American south-west. As Erika Brady notes, in her excellent book, *A Spiral Way: How the Phonograph Changed Ethnography*, published in 1999, Fewkes's phonograph was greeted first, by the Zuni, with a degree of fear and then, by the Hopi, with

> an irreverent send-up of Fewkes and his fieldwork procedure in the course of ritual clowning in celebration of the Basket Dance. A stovepipe representing the horn was placed on a table covered with a blanket, underneath which a clown was concealed. Another clown yelled into the pipe, and the hidden man responded with nonsense, while a third clown dressed as an 'American' stood by and frantically scribbled on a piece of paper.[4]

A very Rouchian scene, I think! As Brady points out, the phonograph could easily be assimilated with the 'magic speaking object' (Stith Thompson motif D.1610), the 'speaking image' (D.1610.21) or the 'magic automata' (D.1620). Brady also notes that there was a rival claimant for Fewkes's position as the first to use the new technology—the much more flamboyant Frank Hamilton Cushing. Cushing, in comparison with Fewkes, was both more disorganized and more immersed in Zuni life, traits which often attracted criticism from fellow-workers in the field. Brady describes, for instance, how Cushing identified himself with the Zuni by having himself photographed in Zuni regalia. In sessions with Zuni story-tellers, Cushing used what he called a 'reciprocal method', by which he meant that he told tales and myths of European origin to the Zuni in exchange for their recounting their tales to him—and his phonograph. Brady comments that 'as a prototype—and a bit more—of the participant observer, Cushing can be seen as the predecessor of those seductive later epistemologies in which the demarcation between the roles of investigator and subject began to blur, finally evaporating altogether in recent works in which the investigator *becomes* the subject'. It is as if some familiar criticisms of Rouch's practice originated in those early days when camera and phonograph were first employed as alternatives to memory, note-pad and sketchbook.

Erika Brady goes on to describe the debates provoked by this new sound technology, as follows:

> Making conspicuous use of the machine and reporting on its use attracted attention to the inevitable artificiality of the encounter. Early investigators drew their professional audience's gaze away from this artificiality by drawing a veil of invisibility over the presence of the ethnographer altogether. Later fieldworkers evaded the issue by framing their role as what Morris Freilich termed 'marginal natives'. In neither case did the phonograph fit the picture. In the inevitable field-work dilemma—the tug between personal attraction to the culture at hand and the rewards anticipated from the academic culture to which the field-worker would return—the phonograph figured rather too evidently on the side of 'profitability' rather than 'sociability'.[5]

In other words, the machine was used to create an acceptable image of scientific objectivity, obtaining information through 'a mere flip of a lever' rather than a 'dramatic human interaction accomplished through skill and rapport' and, since this techno-objectivity was professionally validated, it came to be seen as preferable to actual human interaction with the subjects of research. Rouch, however, managed to undo this preference completely. He found ways to use the new technology provided by the Arriflex camera, not to distance his 'subjects', but to involve them, through the technology, in dramatic human interaction, accompanied by personal 'rapport'. He did this in two principal ways—he talked to his informants about what he wanted to do and he got them to provide the soundtrack themselves. In some ways, of course, Rouch's task was easier than that of his predecessors. He could draw upon Flaherty's early experience with the Inuit. Flaherty had worked with a technology that enabled him to make prints and project them where they had been shot, with participants as the audience. Rouch not only followed this example but also asked participants to provide the soundtrack themselves, after seeing the rushes or, as in the case of *Moi, un Noir* and *Jaguar*, while watching a fine cut of the film, improvising their words as they watched. In fact, the tape-recorder thus became the means by which participants themselves, through their own words, could take control over the way in which the images would eventually be interpreted. Rouch also noted that the Italian neo-realists shot their films without synch sound and then dubbed everything in the studio. Post-synching became an essential element of Rouch's practice.

3

In fact, even Marceline's famous monologue in *Chronique d'un Eté*, spoken into the Nagra as she was filmed walking through Les Halles, was actually post-synchronised—the location, incidentally, was chosen because it reminded her of a railway station and thus brought back powerful memories of parting and loss. Rouch's use of the tape-recorder to involve the subjects of a film in its production allowed him to discard altogether the rhetoric of scientific objectivity and use the new sound technology to foster interactivity and, indeed, improvisation. Rather than recording a pre-set (and typically ritualistic) event, Rouch began to see film-making as a process of collaborative improvisation, made possible by advances in both camera and sound technology—as the Bell and Howell was followed by Coutant's Eclair, Kudelsky's Nagra, Beauviala's Aaton—

advances which created both lighter cameras, easier to manipulate and carry, and also lighter, less cumbersome recording equipment. Rouch's strategy of improvisation was made possible, I would argue, by the curious encounter between Surrealism, with its emphasis on automatism, reverie and objective chance, and technology, its apparent enemy, but actually its friend and partner. We might almost say: like Lautréamont's famous encounter of umbrella and sewing machine upon an operating table, improvisation was made possible by the encounter of Surrealism and technology upon a cinema screen. It was Rouch's commitment to improvisation which secured him his place in the history of cinema, as distinct from the history of ethnography, although in his case, of course, the two are difficult to distinguish. It was a screening of *Jaguar*—at Henri Langlois's Cinémathèque, now located in the Rue d'Ulm—that opened the eyes of the *Cahiers du Cinéma* group to Rouch's discoveries. There they all were: Rivette, Truffaut, Rohmer, Godard   suddenly understanding, as Rouch once reminisced, who he really was, that strange fellow they recognized, of course, although 'they didn't really know what he was doing there'. Then, alongside *Jaguar* there was *Moi, un Noir*, with its film-about-film subtext, a film in which the participants, friends Rouch had made in Treichville, improvised their own action, appropriating for themselves the names of Edward G. Robinson, Lemmy Caution, Dorothy Lamour . . . names recycled in a kind of 'bricolage'.

In this context, it is interesting to look at the ways in which Jean-Luc Godard responded to Rouch's films. It is particularly intriguing, of course, because Godard was himself trained as an ethnographer. In 1958 he saw *Treichville* (as *Moi, un Noir* was then called) and described it as 'the greatest French film since the Liberation' and also, significantly, 'as Neo-Realism pure and simple'. Later the same year, he wrote of it again, this time as the film which opened up 'the possibilities of a new cinema'. The following year, 1959, the year of his own breakthrough film, *A Bout de Souffle*, he returned once more to *Moi, un Noir*, citing it as evidence for his contention that 'all great fiction films tend towards documentary, just as all great documentaries tend towards fiction'. Rouch's film, he insisted, proved that art could be consonant with chance. The film reminded him of *Rome, Open City*—Neo-Realism, but mixed in with the surrealist concept of 'objective chance'! Later that year, reporting on the Cannes

Festival, Godard grouped Rouch, together with Truffaut, Resnais, Chabrol, Franju and Melville, as one of those directors whose films now demonstrated that 'the face of French cinema has changed'. In 1960 Raoul Coutard, fresh from *Breathless*, worked as a cinematographer on *Chronique d'Un Eté*, and in 1962, in an interview for *Cahiers du Cinéma*, Godard invoked Rouch as the master of unplanned, unprepared cinema, in contrast to the classic cinema of Eisenstein and Hitchcock: 'The others, people like Rouch, don't know exactly what they are doing, and search for it. The film is the search. They know they are going to arrive somewhere—and they have the means to do it—but where exactly?'[6] In 1964, Godard listed Rouch's *Pyramide Humaine* second in 'The Six Best French Films since the Liberation', after Max Ophuls's *Le Plaisir*, but ahead of Cocteau, Renoir, Bresson, Chabrol. In 1965, he wrote about the similarity and difference between Rouch's sketch for *Paris Vu Par*, shot in one take, and his own sketch, shot by Albert Maysles, acting 'as a newsreel cameraman'. Michel Marie has also pointed out the influence of *Treichville* on Godard's subsequent use of city slang in *Breathless*, and the way he modelled Michel Poiccard's reaction to a traffic accident in Paris on Edward G. Robinson's reaction to a motor-cyclist knocked down in Treichville—'Oh! Another accident! There are such a lot of accidents in Treichville!' And then there was Belmondo's imitation of Bogart, echoing Petit Touré's imitation of Eddie Constantine as Lemmy Caution—itself a portent of *Alphaville*!

4. In conclusion . . .

The counter-cinema of the 1970s took a great deal from Godard— including, of course, his liking for elaborate movements and camera set-ups, adopting them as a kind of 'Brechtian' strategy in order to make the cinematic apparatus visible. But, in reality, this rejection of transparency in Godard's cinema was often a conscious recycling of what he had learned from Jean Rouch. In those long hand-held takes which Rouch favoured, the camera was like the dance partner in an elaborate *pas de deux*, spontaneous and yet meticulously choreographed, focusing our attention on both form and content.

How to summarize the work of such an extraordinary film-maker, a film-maker with so many dimensions? Talking about Rouch, it seems somehow right to be subjective, so I shall end upon a shamelessly personal note, throwing objectivity aside, and try to say something about the many ways in which Rouch has made an impact upon me as a film-maker.

1. To begin with: the technology. Most of the films I made—all those with Laura Mulvey—were shot on 16mm, typically with an Eclair and a Nagra—the Aaton came later. It was Jean Rouch who first showed us all what could be done, artistically, with these two instruments—instruments in the musical as well as the technological sense. Rouch erased the false line drawn between documentary and drama, between camera as recording instrument and camera as catalyst for performance. Through him, it became a way of exploring film's double nature.

2. And then, of course, improvisation. It is significant, I think, that Rouch's dramatic shift towards improvisation coincided with the spatial shift from village to city, from rural to urban, to a culture clearly 'contaminated' by modernity. It is a debt we owe not only to Rouch, of course, but also to Oumarou Ganda, Touré Mohammed, Damouré Zika, Lam, Landry, Nadine and all the others who were in *La Pyramide Humaine* (a title taken, I assume, from Paul Eluard's surrealist book of 1924). In *Crystal Gazing*, the portrait of a now lost Notting Hill that I made with Laura Mulvey, characters played themselves, unrehearsed, as performers, improvising a comedy monologue (Keith Allen) or a saxophone solo (Lora Logic).

PART II

Films and Movements

8

FREUD AS ADVENTURER*

In 1936 Freud wrote an open letter to the then-famous French writer, Romain Rolland, on the occasion of his seventieth birthday. It was published the following year under the title *A Disturbance of Memory on the Acropolis*. In this letter, Freud described an incident which occurred on an unplanned trip to Athens, which he had made in 1904, accompanied, as he often was on his travels, by his younger brother, Alexander. Naturally Freud went to visit the Acropolis, where he experienced a feeling that he described as follows: 'By the evidence of my senses I am now standing on the Acropolis, but I cannot believe it.'[1] This *Entfremdungsgefühl*, or feeling of estrangement, this unsettling doubt as to the reality of his experience, Freud saw as a defensive measure, an act of repudiation.[2] The basis for this repudiation lay in Freud's own childhood doubts that he would ever see Athens.

> It seemed to me beyond the realms of possibility that I should travel so far—that I should 'go such a long way'. This was linked up with the limitations and poverty of our condition of life. My longing to travel was no doubt also an expression of my wish to escape from that pressure, like the force that drives so many adolescent children to run away from home. I had long seen clearly that a great part of the pleasure of travel

* First published in *Endless Night: Cinema and Psychoanalysis, Parallel Histories*, edited by Janet Bergstrom, 1999. Reprinted by kind permission of the University of California Press.

lies in the fulfilment of these early wishes, that it is rooted, that is, in dissatisfaction with home and family. When first one catches sight of the sea, crosses the ocean and experiences as realities cities and lands which for so long had been distant, unattainable things of desire— one feels oneself like a hero who has performed deeds of improbable greatness.[3]

The longing to travel, to escape from the limitations of family life, to run away from home, was very deep-seated in Sigmund Freud. In the heroic period of the discovery of psychoanalysis, Freud's letters to Fliess make it abundantly clear how important it was for him, despite shortage of money, despite pressures of work and family, despite anxieties about railroad accidents and heart failure, to get away from home, to travel— to climb mountains, to descend into caves, to go on sea voyages, to visit distant cities in foreign lands. Not only that: Freud saw his intellectual work in the same kind of terms, work which we now see as laying the foundations of psychoanalysis. He was embarked, metaphorically, on a voyage of intellectual discovery, an exploration of the unknown.

On 28 April 1896, after giving his paper, 'On the Aetiology of Hysteria', to the Vienna Society for Psychiatry and Neurology, Freud wrote to Fliess complaining about the 'icy reception' given him by 'the donkeys', and Krafft-Ebing's peremptory dismissal of his thesis as a 'fairy-tale':[4] 'This, after one has demonstrated to them the solution of a more-than-thousand-year problem, a *caput Nili* [source of the Nile].'[5] On 3 January 1897, he wrote to Fliess: 'Dear Wilhelm, We shall not be shipwrecked. Instead of the channel we are seeking, we may find oceans, the more detailed exploration of which will be left to those who come after us, but if we do not prematurely capsize, if our constitutions can stand it, we shall arrive. *Nous y arriverons.*'[6] On 26 August 1898, he wrote: 'I shall be able to make good use of Nansen's dreams; they are completely transparent. I know from my own experience that his psychic state is typical of someone who dares to do something new and relies on his confidence and who, by taking a wrong route, probably discovers something original, but far less than he had anticipated.'[7] On 28 May 1899: 'I gave myself a present, Schliemann's *Ilios*, and greatly enjoyed the account of his childhood. The man was happy when he found Priam's treasure, because happiness comes only with the fulfilment of a childhood wish. This reminds me that I shall not go to Italy this year. Until next time!'[8] Throughout this period he compared the completion of *The Interpretation of Dreams* with the longed-for attainment of Rome. (And of Karlsbad, the spa-resort, to which, in a Jewish joke loved by Freud, a poor Jew is travelling without a ticket. Taken off the train at each station and beaten, he persists in his journey, confident he will get there, 'if my constitution can stand it'.)[9]

Most dramatically of all, on 1 February 1900, the dream book now published, ignored and derided, Freud wrote to Fliess, telling him that

I am actually not at all a man of science, not an observer, not a thinker. I am by temperament nothing but a *conquistador*—an adventurer, if you want it translated—with all the curiosity, daring and tenacity character-istic of a man of this sort. Such people are customarily esteemed only if they have been successful, have really discovered something, otherwise they are dumped by the wayside.[10]

And then on 7 May of the same year, he confided that 'It would be a fitting punishment for me that none of the unexplored regions of psychic life in which I have been the first to set foot will ever bear my name or obey my laws'. And, he continues, 'Yes, I really am forty-four now, an old, somewhat shabby Jew.'[11]

Freud, the adventurer—plainly this was the Freud that John Huston admired, identified with and saw as the subject of a film. Huston had cut his industry teeth as a screen-writer on bio-pics for Warners in the late thirties: the lives of Benito Juarez, the Mexican revolutionary; Dr Ehrlich, the discoverer of a cure for syphilis; Alvin York, the First World War hero recycled for the fight against fascism. Huston saw himself (or himselves) as an adventurer too. His autobiographical romance, *An Open Book*, began its narrative with the life of his maternal grandfather, John Gore, after whom Huston was named.[12] On page 7, he describes how his grandmother Adelia came to marry: 'Security played no part in Adelia's choice. She married the adventurer, John Gore. Their daughter, Rhea Gore, was my mother.'[13] Gore was a footloose pioneer in the opening-up of the West, who made and lost fortunes and died penniless in a rundown hotel in Waco, Texas, an empty half-pint whiskey bottle on the floor beside his bed. Huston's mother (Rhea), a professional reporter, married an itinerant actor, Walter Huston, threw him out, married again, left her new husband, and, 'bored with the narrow, formal society of the St Paul suburbs', eventually embarked on a life of travel.[14] Huston imbibed the ethos of adventure from his earliest years and lived it to the full, as he understood it, wandering from home to home, making and losing millions, gambling, womanizing, fighting, hunting, stealing and mesmerizing. (Literally! He learnt how to hypnotize from a psychiatrist when he made his film about war trauma, *Let There Be Light*.)

In his early twenties, Huston (who, like Freud and Sartre, became an atheist) was much impressed by William Bolitho's book *Twelve Against the Gods*,[15] a hagiographic account of the lives of twelve adventurers, with an introduction that, Huston confessed, 'had an enormous effect on my life'.[16] It is a trashy book, but the introduction provides a kind of racy justification for the wish to run away from home. A few samples:

> The adventurer is an outlaw. Adventure must start with running away from home. The moment one of these truants breaks loose, he has to fight the whole weight of things as they are; the laws, and that indefinite smothering aura that surrounds the laws, that we call morals; the family, that is the microcosm and whiplash of society; and the dead weight of all the possessors, across whose interwoven rights the road to freedom lies . . . The adventurer is a truant from obligations . . . His first enemy we know, the mechanical interlocking weight of law, social and moral. The second is the unknown itself. If he fails, he is a mere criminal.[17]

Bolitho notes that

> every age produces its peculiar type, conquerors in antiquity, discoverers in the Middle Ages, prospectors in the nineteenth century . . . concurrently the field has cramped with the mapping of the world. The geographical unknown, the easiest of access and the most naively alluring has gone. There is a telephone line to Lhassa, flags on each pole.

He asks, 'Is adventure, with these handicaps, a thing of the past?' The astute reader might well pause on the example of one of the twelve, Mahomet, and the observation that the religious adventurer must make, not an earthly journey, but 'the grand Dante circuit of Heaven and Hell'.

This was the image that governed Huston's view of Freud and, as we know ('Flectere si nequeo superos Acheronta movebo'), was in Freud's own mind from 1896 onwards.[18] The idea of a film about Sigmund Freud came to Huston and Wolfgang Reinhardt while they were writing *Dr Ehrlich's Magic Bullet* for Warners: an obvious transition from the cure for venereal disease of the body to the cure for that of the mind. 'Freud', however—an independent production, under Huston's own control—was to be different from those old genre films, with their loveable Zola and their banal Pasteur. This auteur bio-pic would be full of 'sheet lightning and sulfur';[19] it would breathe brimstone: 'Freud's descent into the unconscious should be as terrifying as Dante's descent into hell. With this in mind, Wolfgang and I went to Paris to see Jean-Paul Sartre.'[20] Huston was a long-time admirer of Sartre's work. His friend and collaborator Peter Viertel recounts how, on the occasion of his first meeting with another literary hero, Ernest Hemingway, Huston provocatively praised Sartre and vigorously defended him against Hemingway's onslaught, refusing to concede to the old monster on the worth of Sartre's *The Age of Reason*.[21] But, of course, it was *No Exit* that Huston had in mind when he went to Paris in 1958 and discussed Freud: Sartre's own vision of hell as bad faith and objectification by others, which Huston had himself produced, to great acclaim, on the New York stage.

Sartre too was surprisingly preoccupied by the theme of adventure. He traced the origin of this formative character trait in his autobiographical romance, *Words*, started just before the Freud script, but completed immediately afterwards. There he recounts how, barely able to read, he would browse in his grandfather's library: 'I launched out into incredible adventures. I had to climb up on chairs, on tables, at the risk of causing avalanches that would have buried me. The works on the top shelf remained out of reach for a long time.'[22] There he embarked on 'voyages' through the world of writing, a world of infinite variety, there he 'would be La Pérouse, Magellan, Vasco da Gama', there he 'would discover strange natives' and 'distant, impenetrable Kaffirs would spring out at the turn of a page'.[23] Endlessly reading, and taken also to the cinema, the child Sartre played out the roles of knight-errant, swashbuckler, vagabond, outlaw. Finally, aged about eight, these imaginary Poulous crystallized around the figure of Pardaillan, the adventure hero created by the popular novelist Michel Zévaco: a swashbuckler on the side of the people, fighting against tyrants, who 'made and unmade Empires, and, in the fourteenth century, predicted the French Revolution'.[24] Soon Sartre began to write, imitating and exaggerating Zévaco. 'I wanted to change the adventure novel radically. I threw verisimilitude overboard. I multiplied enemies and dangers tenfold.'[25] His explorer hero performed incredible feats, an extreme adventurer—Sartre noted—who later reappeared in his mature work as Goetz von Berlichingen, the monster-martyr of *The Devil and the Good Lord* (a play Huston had earlier wanted to film, even discussing the project with Sartre, while making his *Moulin Rouge* in Paris).[26]

Gradually Sartre transferred his investment from the adventure hero to the adventure writer: 'Great writers are akin to knights-errant in that both elicit passionate signs of gratitude . . . Despite their physical defects, their primness, their seeming femininity, writers risked their lives as free lances in mysterious combats.'[27] He chose to become 'a true paladin whose exploits would be real books'.[28] But the transference proved a difficult one: Pardaillan would never quite go away. He became one aspect of the writer, the knight who 'had never taken orders from the king', who pulled himself up out of nothingness by his own bootstraps, a self-made rather than predestined writer-knight. Gradually, Sartre claims, the writer overcame the knight; he became an 'ex-Pardaillan'. Illusory victory: on the last page of the book, he admits 'Pardaillan still inhabits me'.[29]

Indeed, we continue to meet Pardaillan throughout Sartre's career, with Sartre, in Sartre, as Sartre. In 1929, the summer he met Simone de Beauvoir, he bought second-hand copies of *Pardaillan* and *Fantomas* to give her, so that she could understand him; in the lean years of the thirties, his travel plans collapsed, his writings unpublished, he complained that Pardaillan was slipping away from him; and in the book that brought him his first success, *Nausea*, the central character, Roquantin, is a failed adventurer turned writer. In a passage cut from the published book, he noted, 'The idea of travelling, or rather of adventure, became an obsession.' And again: 'Every single one of my theories was an act of conquest and possession. I thought that one day, with the help of them all, I'd conquer the world.'[30] Like Freud, like Huston, Sartre dreamed of adventure and glory. Right at the end of his life, in the interviews Simone de Beauvoir published under the title *Adieux*, Sartre returned, unexpectedly, to the image of Pardaillan. De Beauvoir asked him about his always being 'uncomfortable' in his own body and he replied: 'Yes, but this is more complex, and it will lead us to Pardaillan.' She pressed him further: 'You spoke of Pardaillan. What did you mean?' Sartre replied that he had long ago developed 'an imaginary body'—that of Pardaillan, the swashbuckler, which gave him the feeling of being 'a powerful warrior'.[31]

With this imaginary body, he acted more violently, as though the world were 'heavier' than it really was, before being brought back to the ground by weariness and fatigue. He described how, before he could even read, he saw himself climbing up into blazing houses to rescue young girls by carrying them out on his back. He remembered going to the gymnasium and boxing (as Huston did too) and even fighting a match when he was in prison camp, disappointed that the result was a draw: 'Pardaillan didn't have drawn matches'.[32] He talked about his denial of age, his wish to be young, and, finally, most revealingly of all, his work-related addiction to amphetamines, to speed: 'I perceived myself through the motion of my pen, my forming images and ideas. I was the same active being as Pardaillan, neglecting . . .' 'The real body', De Beauvoir cut in, 'which was in the act of destroying itself and against which you always had an almost aggressive attitude.'[33]

Thus the knot was tied, linking Freud, Huston and Sartre, three musketeers, bound together by the red thread of adventure, an adventure which led all three to glory: to the Royal Society in London (Freud's name joined to those of Newton and Darwin), to the Oscar ceremony in Los Angeles (Best Screenplay, Best Director), to the Nobel Prize, a nomination refused, a journey to Stockholm gloriously unmade. It is time now to return to Athens, to the Acropolis, where, his goal accomplished, Freud felt alienated from the evidence of his achievement, from his personal moment of glory. After discussing his adolescent fantasy of running away from home, of leaving the familiar far behind, Freud went on to discuss the feeling of transgression that had ruined his enjoyment, his transgression against the paternal imago.

It must be that a sense of guilt was attached to the satisfaction in having gone so far: there was something about it that was wrong, that was from the earliest times forbidden. It was something to do with a child's criticism of his father, with the undervaluation that took the place of the overvaluation of earlier childhood. It seems as though the essence of success were to have got further than one's father, and as though to excel one's father were still something forbidden.[34]

It was the feeling of 'piety' that had 'interfered' with the 'enjoyment'.

Sartre made Freud's relationship with his father the central issue of the Freud scenario. His synopsis started with a voice off: 'Everything began with my father's death', and ended with a Wellesian 'bookend', another voice off: 'I was forty-one, it was my turn to play the role of father.'[35] Freud had finally come to the realization that he loathed and hated his father, because he desired his mother, but also because he 'reproached him with being too old, with not having been able to help him, with having left him destitute. And these reproaches hid his jealousy and his secret wish to see him die.' Freud had discovered the Œdipal drama within himself. Throughout the period of the film, Sartre noted, Freud, 'dissatisfied with his own father, has transferred his filial affection' to a succession of paternal figures: Meynert, Breuer, Fliess. At last, having completed his self-analysis, having gone 'down to the hidden depths', he is 'finally free, absolutely free'. 'He's beginning to live.' The last image of the film, as described in the synopsis, was to be that of a young doctor coming up to Freud, asking to share his compartment in the train with him, to ask him questions, to try and understand the implications of Freud's work. In a word, to play the role of son to Freud's father, an offer Freud accepts, ironically, unenthusiastically, but nonetheless willingly.[36]

Sartre's version of Freud's discovery of psychoanalysis roughly followed the standard Freudian version of the romance, which Janet Walker has described: through his self-analysis, Freud came to abandon the full-scale 'seduction theory' of hysteria, emphasizing instead the role of fantasy and infantile sexuality.[37] It was the death of his father in 1896 which freed Freud to complete his self-analysis, and thus to acknowledge the aggressivity which, Freud now believed, had led him to wish the worst of his father and even suspect him of incest. The seduction theory had posited widespread paternal sexual abuse of children in the real world, not excepting Freud's own father from guilt. In contrast, the Oedipal theory, which now moved to centre stage, accused the sons instead, but only of parricidal fantasies, a much lighter charge, and one which maintained a degree of 'piety' towards the father. His father now dead, his self-analysis complete, Freud was thus able to assume the paternal role himself (and, in Sartre's synopsis, to be treated with the proper 'piety').

It is undoubtedly odd that Sartre should end up apparently so close to orthodox Freudianism, when, as is well known, he was generally extremely critical of Freudian psychoanalysis and dubious about many of its central tenets, including the unconscious, the Oedipus complex, the role of fantasy, and so on. (Although as Janet Walker pointed out, the Magda episodes, which Huston was 'prevailed upon' to cut, did show some reservation.) To see how this alignment of Sartre and Freud came about, I think we have to look more closely at the central issue which is at stake in any attempt to tell the story of Freud's years of discovery: the role played by the father in the life of his son. Sartre himself, paradoxically perhaps, was extremely hostile to fatherhood, certainly as an institutional reality. While he was sitting around in John Huston's country house in Ireland, supposedly invited to lick the Freud scenario into shape, he received the reviews of his latest play, *The Condemned of Altona*. This was a play which clearly demonstrated the baleful influence exerted by a father, in this case a leading industrialist, the dynastic head of a Hamburg shipbuilding firm, over his son, who became an SS officer, a mass murderer. In Sartre's words, he was 'doomed to impotence by his father's power' and driven to seek a twisted form of power for himself through the SS. It is perhaps Sartre's most extreme attack on fatherhood, transferring responsibility for the son's massacres from the Nazi son, 'gripped by the past', to the capitalist father who despised the Nazis but, of necessity, for the good of the firm, colluded with them.[38] This reflected, of course, Sartre's growing anti-capitalist militancy during the Algerian war.

Then, immediately after Freud, Sartre completed *Words*, in which he celebrated his own lack of father. Sartre's own father, Jean-Baptiste Sartre, something of an adventurer himself, had died when Sartre was only one year old, of an infection contracted in Indo-China. In *Words*, he writes:

> The death of Jean-Baptiste was the big event of my life: it sent my mother back to her chains and gave me freedom. There is no good father, that's the rule. Don't lay the blame on men but on the bond of paternity, which is rotten. To beget children, nothing better; to have them, what iniquity! Had my father lived he would have lain on me at full length and would have crushed me. As luck would have it, he died young.

The same paragraph ends with the following words: 'I readily subscribe to the verdict of an eminent psychoanalyst: I have no Superego.'[39] In other words, no guilt. (Is this so very different from Huston's remark about the unconscious, which Sartre derided: 'In mine, there's nothing at all'?)[40]

In the Freud scenario, Sartre dealt with Jakob Freud's death through the analysis of a dream. On 2 November 1896, Freud wrote to Fliess thanking him for his letter of condolence and then recounting a dream which he had the night after his father's funeral. 'I was in a place where I read a sign: "You are requested to close the eyes." I immediately recognized the location as the barbershop I visit every day.'[41] Freud later gave another account of this same dream in the *Interpretation*, in which he suggested a possible variant for the wording of the sign ('You are requested to close an eye') and also noted that the 'printed notice, placard or poster' was 'rather like the notices forbidding one to smoke in railway waiting-rooms'.[42]

In the earlier letter to Fliess, significantly, Freud mentioned that he 'was kept waiting' in the barber's shop, which thus indeed became a kind of waiting room. As a result, Freud was then late arriving at the 'house of mourning' which offended the assembled family, already irritated by Freud's insistence on a 'quiet and modest' ceremony. Freud interpreted the words, 'You are requested to close the eyes', both as an expression of his actual duty towards the dead (to close his father's eyes) and as an appeal by Freud to his family to overlook his own inadequate sense of filial duty. Or, as he put it, 'the dream thus stems from the inclination to self-reproach that regularly sets in among the survivors'. (This, of course, is similar to the self-reproach that Freud felt on the Acropolis.)

Freud expanded a little on this in the *Interpretation*, reading 'close an eye' as 'wink at' or 'overlook', as he hoped that unsympathetic family members would overlook his own 'puritanical simplicity' (which he justified now as reflecting his father's 'own views on such ceremonies').

Plainly the dream may have reflected Freud's 'self-reproach' as a survivor, but the underlying wish was to be exculpated, as in the now notorious dream of 'Irma's injection'. Exculpated of what? Survival? Being late for the funeral? Delving into his father's past? Perhaps all of these, but also, of course, Freud's undeniable resentment and hostility towards his father, thrown into an embarrassing light by his father's actual death. Freud does not mention this. Indeed, in the public *Interpretation*, rather than the private letter to Fliess, he does not even mention being late for the funeral, and even changes the date of the dream to the day before it took place! Moreover, his most hostile comment on his father was still to come, only three months later, in February, when he wrote to Fliess, apropos of child abuse: 'Unfortunately, my own father was one of those perverts and is responsible for the hysteria of my brother [Freud's companion on the Acropolis] and those of several younger sisters.'[43] In October, he mentioned the Oedipus story for the first time, but only in relation to his desire for his mother and consequent 'jealousy' of his father, with no suggestion yet of parricidal impulses.

However, there was another important aspect of the dream which Freud also ignored: the association with No Smoking signs in railway waiting rooms. Three years earlier, in October 1893, Freud had written to Fliess, worried about his heavy smoking, and commenting that, 'as far as smoking is concerned, I shall scrupulously follow a prescription of yours; I did this once before when you gave your opinion in regard to it (railway station—period of waiting). But I did miss it greatly.'[44] Freud, of course, remained addicted to smoking all his life. This addiction figured prominently in Sartre's script, perhaps because of the obvious analogy with Sartre's own problems with amphetamines and other drugs. Freud also worried about the possible connection that smoking might have with his heart problems, which he feared would kill him prematurely, fuelling his 'dread of dying'. (Indeed, later scholars have wondered whether his heart problems shouldn't be classed as hysterical symptoms, without a real organic basis.) Fliess repeatedly tried to stop Freud from smoking, issuing prohibition after prohibition, which Freud somehow contrived to ignore or circumvent.

Freud also discussed his railway phobia a great deal with Fliess: a phobia which did not actually stop him travelling, but caused him considerable anxiety before boarding the train. Ernest Jones notes that 'he retained in later life relics of the latter anxiety (*Reisefieber*, travel fever) in being so anxious not to miss a train that he would arrive at a station a long while—even an hour beforehand.'[45] Thus smoking and station waiting rooms together played a crucial part in Freud's own neuroses. They were tied in to his relationship with Fliess, both because he travelled by train to see Fliess and because Fliess tried to prevent Freud from smoking while waiting for the train.

In his own analysis, of course, Freud was led to consider the light that childhood scenes could throw on these problems. In 1897 he concluded that addiction in general (alcohol, morphine, tobacco) was a substitute for the 'primary addiction' of compulsive masturbation.[46] He also argued that the sexual fantasies and longings associated with hysteria might originate from the repression of masturbation.[47] At this point, Freud had not yet made the connections between sexual excitement, autoerotic activity and train travel, which he later described so vividly in *Three Essays on the Theory of Sexuality*. Train travel appeared there as the epitome of pleasurable movement in general (rocking, swinging, shaking and so on) and Freud also noted that when the sexual pleasure of travel was repressed, it could lead to feelings of nausea, and sufferers 'will be terribly exhausted by a railway journey, or will be subject to attacks of anxiety on the journey, and will protect themselves against a repetition of the painful experience by a dread of railway travel'.[48]

Freud was quite explicit about the nature of the secondary sexual repression he had undergone in connection with railway journeys. When he was two years old, Freud's father uprooted his family from Freiberg, in Moravia (now the Czech Republic), and took them first to Leipzig, then to Vienna. This was Freud's first railway journey. Two incidents occurred which he later recounted. Passing through the station at Breslau, he remembered, 'the gas jets, which were the first I had seen, reminded me of the souls burning in hell. I know something of the context here. The anxiety about travel which I have had to overcome is also bound up with it.' On the train from Leipzig to Vienna, some time later, Freud's 'libido towards *matrem* was aroused'. During the journey, he wrote to Fliess, 'we spent a night together, and I must have had the opportunity of seeing her *nudam*.'[49] In the same letter, he also tells Fliess how he had discovered the 'primary originator' of his own sexual life. It was not his father, as he had feared, but his nurse, 'an ugly, elderly but clever woman who told me a great deal about God and hell, and gave me a high opinion of my own capacities'.[50]

It is almost too good to be true. 'You are requested to close the eyes': surely, if we are to follow Freud's own chain of associations, we should note that the blending of barber's shop into railway waiting room will lead us, via repressed memories and fantasies associated with train travel, not only to Freud's travel phobia but also to his tobacco addiction. The travel phobia takes us back to the early childhood scenes: scenes of sexual pleasure and fantasy ('libido towards *matrem*', repressed scopophilia: 'You are requested to close the eyes!') and to the fiery punishments of hell, imbibed from the Czech Catholic nurse and seductress: 'Death and sexuality', the same pairing that disturbed Freud's memory of Signorelli's great fresco at Orvieto, with its naked female bodies and its eternal flames of hell. And it was from Orvieto that Freud anxiously retreated to Lake Trasimene, Hannibal's furthest point south, only to remind him of his own frustrated longing for Rome (and for revenge on Rome).[51] Addiction, on the other hand, would have led Freud back to the prohibition on masturbation, itself related to train travel, to his seduction perhaps, and ultimately to his father. And all these passing thoughts (these free associations) were themselves, Freud noted, like the transient views unreeling through the train window, accompanied by a deep longing. Later, in *A Case of Homosexuality in a Woman*, Freud described analysis itself as a form of train travel: 'One may bring up as an analogy the two stages of a journey. The first comprises all the necessary preparations, today so complicated and hard to effect, before, ticket in hand, one can at last go on the platform and secure a seat in the train. One then has the right, and the possibility, of travelling to a distant country.'[52] Waiting, then adventure. And, of course, we should also bear in mind the historical and phenomenological linkages between train travel and the cinema, each providing a sequence of views in movement.

Finally, both smoking and trains were connected with adventure: smoking, like speed, gave Freud the sense of exhilaration he needed for his discoveries; trains, later supplemented by steamships, were his principal means of travel.

In Sartre's script, Fliess's prohibition on smoking in waiting rooms is clearly what marked him out as a father-figure, despite being younger than Freud. Freud describes him as a tyrant, and is disappointed when Fliess permits him to smoke again: 'In any case my real tyrant is you [not Breuer]. Do you know that you disappointed me when you allowed me to smoke. It gave me pleasure to deny myself in order to obey you.'[53] In essence, Sartre's view, it seems to me, was that Freud needed Fliess so that he could be both, so to speak, 'feminized' and 'infantilized', which, in turn, would enable him to understand first his own and then Cécilie's hysteria. Immediately afterwards, Freud, after demonstrating his train phobia, boards the train and dreams of his three substitute fathers (Meynert, Breuer, Fliess) whom he joins in a smoking compartment to play cards. Suddenly they are replaced by Freud's own father, Jakob, who offers his help, and Freud realizes he must understand his relationship to his own father if he is to free himself from the surrogates. Jakob then becomes the ticket-inspector, punches their tickets, and the dream ends. In this fictional dream, the surrogate fathers have been revealed as 'dead men', dummies (in the card-playing sense), and, on awakening, Freud muses on his need, as 'the living one', to free himself from them.[54]

Sartre's view was that autonomy and freedom could only be achieved when the paternal bond was fully broken, not displaced onto others. In Sartre's own autobiographical example, the death of his father, Jean-Baptiste, freed him from an otherwise inevitable crushing weight of prohibitions, expectations and mandates. In the script, Freud, after Jakob Freud's death, is now able to exculpate his father from the accusations of sexual abuse Freud himself had made. The guilty father becomes innocent, no longer a burden, and this in turn leads to Cécilie's exculpation of her father. As required by the romance, the feeling of guilt is thus displaced from the father on to the children.[55]

Soon afterwards, Cécilie's cure is completed after Freud explains the Oedipus story to her and she exclaims: 'It's the children who are guilty.' But Freud replies: 'Nobody's guilty' (i.e. 'Don't lay the blame on men but on the bond of paternity') and tells how his own father's failures in life were brought about not by his own shortcomings but by rampant anti-semitism, not by an interior character flaw but by an exterior social force. Freud's earlier reproaches were thus based on a misunderstanding, a misrecognition of his father. Similarly, Cécilie now comes to understand that her 'monstrousness' too was simply imagined. The guilt she bore for driving her mother to suicide was a misunderstanding—'It was an accident!'—based on a misrecognition of her mother, who explains: 'I swear to you. I never thought of killing myself. We're used to hardship in my family, and we live with our misfortunes.'[56] Again, I think there is a subtext here. In Sartre's script, Freud's father once again becomes the shabby Galician Jew, and Cécilie's mother is once again the working-class prostitute. Psychoanalysis was necessary to reach the point of cure, but the final moment of cure depended on the subjects (both Freud and Cécilie) realizing that they have misrecognized their oppressive parents; instead they must now see their parents as themselves victims within a social (and political) perspective. Then, by implication, the aggression, instead of being mistakenly and guiltily directed against the imaginary parents, can presumably be freely turned on the real villains of the piece: the anti-semites and the exploiters.

Sartre's project was one of enfolding a critique of psychoanalysis within Marxism, and a critique of Marxism within what we might call existential phenomenology, to create the foundations of a practical ethics. In the script, this final enfolding is demonstrated by the way in which the psychoanalytic work is presented as the joint project of Freud and Cécilie, Freud's 'teacher'. They work through their neuroses together to arrive at a cure together. The unconscious, in this view of things, is not an entity, a continent to be discovered, but a history of secrets, masks and deceptions, encapsulated by the command, 'You are requested to close the eyes'; it is the result of repeated choices not to see, not to acknowledge, not to remember. These choices may be motivated by a self-protective impulse, but, in Sartre's opinion, it is precisely this attempt to safeguard the self from reality that causes neurosis. The self-as-identity must be repeatedly undone, nihilated, in order for the subject to arrive at the point where he or she is free.[57]

Analysis, in this sense, is similar to the progressive–regressive method which Sartre explained in his 1957 *Search for a Method*, a cyclical movement back into history and then forward again to the present, repeatedly narrowing and expanding the field of inquiry from individual detail to social generality, always rethinking oneself as one rethinks the other. In preparing his script, Sartre worked from four main sources: Freud's own letters to Fliess, *The Studies on Hysteria*, *The Interpretation of Dreams* and Volume I of the Jones biography. It is amazing to me how faithful to the Freudian record, as established by these books, Sartre was able to be, while at the same time proposing and experimenting with his own method of inquiry, one which was radically different from Freud's in its methodology. The key to this achievement, of course, was Sartre's assignment (by Huston) to the period of Freud's early self-analysis, a period before Freudianism congealed into a system and psychoanalysis into an institution. Precisely, we might say, the period when Freud was still an adventurer, not yet (quite) a law-giver.

A final word about 'filial piety', the root cause of Freud's strange and quixotic feeling on the Acropolis. At the end of Sartre's synopsis, Freud, now cured, able to assume the paternal role, is faced by a son who comes to him in a spirit of 'filial piety'. In the script, as opposed to the synopsis, the son never appears. Instead, Freud goes to lay a wreath on his father's grave. There, by chance, he encounters one of his 'dead fathers', Breuer, who asks him, 'Will you be able to love again?' Freud replies, 'Yes. My children . . . and adopted sons—men who'll believe in my words—if any such can be found. I'm the father now.'[58] It is a very Sartrean moment. In real life, Sartre had only adopted children: surrogate sons, young men who believed his words (or wanted to)—André Gorz, Olivier Todd (who rebelled), Benny Lévy—and finally, a daughter, Arlette El Kaim, whom he adopted legally and who thus became his sole legitimate heir. In this sense, he chose to burden a daughter with the paternal weight, leaving the sons, lighter, to leap forward. In his book *Search for a Father*, Robert Harvey points out the ethical implications of Sartre's concept of the surrogate son, able to start from nowhere, but guided by a father-figure who could help him, without possessing or mandating him.[59] This, of course, was what Jakob Freud was quite unable to do. Hence, in Sartre's view, Freud's conditional need for the three surrogate fathers. To run away from home, as far as the Acropolis, Freud needed to forge a more burdensome paternal bond to be broken. Sartre himself never faced this problem, or so he claimed. The bond was broken for him.

John Huston's problem was quite different. He notes, on the third page of his autobiography,

> My only recurrent dream is one in which I'm ashamed of being broke and having to go to my father for money—something that happened only a time or two, and then he pressed the money on me. There was an instance when I was flat-assed broke and didn't go to him, and, when he found out afterwards, he was deeply hurt. Why then should I have that dream in which I feel weak, dissolute and shiftless? It doesn't match up with anything, symbolically or otherwise.[60]

Suffice it to say, on the subject of the paternal bond, that the Hustons are the only family to have had three consecutive generations of Oscar winners: grandfather, father, daughter. Strangely enough, Huston too had a surrogate son, Pablo Albarran, a teenage Mexican extra on the set of *Treasure of the Sierra Madre* whom Huston took a liking to, made his personal assistant and then brought home to California. Lauren Bacall remembered, 'He was like a little pet. He was very cute and John decided he was this perfect little mascot.'[61] Back in California, Huston's then-wife, Evelyn Keyes, found herself looking after Pablo: 'This was one of the careless things John did. You don't bring a kid home when you're married without asking your wife.'[62] Soon Pablo was sent off to boarding school and to college, eventually returning to Mexico and becoming a photographer, the first of many failed careers.

Somehow Huston never got around to adopting Pablo officially and never seemed to have felt much responsibility for him. 'That's your problem, isn't it?' he would say. He hired Pablo for illegal jobs in Mexico occasionally and then blamed him if things went wrong. Huston didn't reply to his letters and didn't visit when he went to Mexico. Finally, on location for *Reflections in a Golden Eye*, Huston did something: he hired Pablo as a messenger. 'I thought I was treated like a slave,' Pablo remarked. When Pablo's marriage broke up, Huston took his wife's side: 'That was the end.' Pablo finished up as a caretaker. He never tried to contact Huston again. 'I think he would have felt better if I had,' Pablo said. 'But he taught me never to crawl. And that's the best lesson anybody could teach you.'[63] Perhaps this story of surrogate fatherhood, the paternal bond and filial piety does something to explain John Huston's own single repeated dream.

Finally, there is Freud's own family. His daughter Anna became a model of filial piety, outlasting the surrogate sons, Jung, Jones, etc., never going too far, preserving Freud's memory and safeguarding his legacy. Loyal to her father, she opposed the making of the film of Freud and influenced it in an unusual way. Both Huston and Sartre, in a meeting of minds, thought that Marilyn Monroe was perfect to play Cécilie, but her analyst told her that Anna Freud was against the film and she refused the part. Marilyn Monroe had seen Anna Freud herself briefly for psychoanalytic help, in 1956, and her New York analyst was Marianne Kris, the daughter of Freud's family doctor. It was through Marianne Kris that Monroe left a substantial sum to Anna Freud's Hampstead Clinic. So there was nothing surprising in her rejection of a role in a film of which Anna Freud disapproved. Marilyn Monroe was simply the instrument of filial piety.

As Freud finally hinted in his letter to Romain Rolland, there was an insoluble contradiction between the two mandates his father had left him: first, to go far, to become an adventurer, to run away from home, from God and religion, to leave Galicia far behind and travel, not just to Freiburg, or even the Viennese ghetto of Leopoldstadt, but all the way to the Acropolis; and then the second mandate: to observe filial piety, the core of the very tradition that Freud was expected to leave behind. In this sense, Sartre, who had no filial piety of his own, was the ideal person to portray Freud the adventurer and, at the same time, show piety to his father, the ineffective, old, uneducated, somewhat shabby Galician Jew who said nothing when his hat was knocked off into the gutter.

9

BLADE RUNNER

In his book *City of Quartz*, which first came out in 1990, Mike Davis categorized *Blade Runner* as noir revival, setting it in the context of an ongoing struggle between utopians and dystopians for control over the representation of Los Angeles.[1] The chapter in which he briefly comments on the film is titled, 'Sunshine or Noir', and recounts the contrasting histories of boosterism and its pessimistic alter ego, the 'nightmare anti-myth of noir', which between them shaped Los Angeles's divided vision of itself.

Two years later, in 1992, the year of the 'Director's Cut', Mike Davis was more precise. He now took issue with what was already the dominant academics' view of the film—a postmodern classic—and categorized it as simply 'another edition of the core modernist vision' of the city as either Ville Radieuse or Monster Manhattan. Essentially, he now argued, *Blade Runner* provides us with what is 'recognizably the same vista of urban gigantism that Fritz Lang celebrated in *Metropolis*'. He dismisses the 'teeming Ginza' aspects of *Blade Runner*, the 'Noir', the 'high-tech plumbing retrofitted to street-level urban decay', as 'overlay', texturing on top of the basic *Metropolis* core. Los Angeles, he points out, is not the same as Gotham City or Metropolis. It is not a Wellsian city, but an endless unspectacular vista of 'great unbroken plains of ageing bungalows, dingbats and ranch-style houses'.

Of course, he is right about this. Philip K. Dick's novel *Do Androids*

Dream Of Electric Sheep?, from which *Blade Runner* was adapted, is set in San Francisco. The first screen-writer, Hampton Fancher, very soon changed the location to Los Angeles and there it stayed. However, the director, Ridley Scott, once appointed, moulded the film to his own vision, steering it through several rewrites from a second screen-writer, David Peoples. He was never deeply committed to the Los Angeles setting. His main inspiration was, indeed, New York, as Mike Davis surmised. He also thought about setting the film in either Los Angeles or Atlanta. But, in the end, he decided to stick with Los Angeles, largely because the decision to film in the Bradbury Building identified the location in an unmistakable way. Once this decision was taken, he then went on to shoot the opening sequence, portraying an unmistakable Los Angeles, as seen from Terminal Island, looking north towards downtown across a smoke-belching industrial landscape, a caricature version of the refineries and cat-crackers of Torrance and El Segundo.

It would be a mistake, however, to see *Blade Runner* as simply exchanging New York for Los Angeles. In reality, it provides an image of a generic world city, rather than any one particular conurbation. It is a conceptual montage of many different urban phenomena, drawn from a variety of sources. The main exterior set for the film, christened 'Ridley-ville' by those working on it, was built on the classic old New York street on the Warner Brothers lot, where scenes from *The Big Sleep* and *The Maltese Falcon* had been shot nearly forty years before. To this were added elements from contemporary New York, from London, Tokyo, Hong Kong and Milan. The overall look of the set was inspired by futurist illustration—Moebius's work for *Heavy Metal* and Syd Mead's for *The Sentinel*. Ridley Scott also refers to Hogarth's 'Gin Lane' prints of eighteenth-century London as an important source. Essentially Scott, Mead and the others were constructing a composite world city, which incorporated a number of different features of contemporary cities extra-polated into the future, to 2019.

The topography of world cities is well known by now. There is a postmodern downtown (a 'citadel' as Mike Davies dubs it) where corporate headquarters and financial nerve-centres are clustered together, instantly linked to outposts around the world by satellite, fibre optics and data compression. This is the command-and-control centre for key

sectors of the global economy. Around the hub, there is a dense
environment of refurbished industrial spaces (for loft living), restaurants
(for ethnic eating), cultural centres and art museums (for the upmarket
flaneur), designer boutiques (for prestige shopping) and luxury hotels
(with easy access to the international airport). These are all there in *Blade
Runner*, except for the art museums and the opera houses. Nearby there
are the humming hives of a range of specialized just-in-time service
industries—suppliers, sub-contractors, bankers, lawyers, accountants, PR
people, advertisers, publishers, architects, and their retinues of researchers, software experts, drug dealers, visual designers and niche marketing
consultants. Hurrying and scurrying, in the shadows, on the sidewalk, at
the lunch-counters, in the public transit system, are the low-paid
immigrant workers and, just a cut above them in status and salary, the
part-time and freelance cultural workers—the immigrants and ethnic
minorities who work in the restaurant kitchens; the installation artists
and off-Broadway actors who work as the restaurant waiters.

Los Angeles has many crucial elements of this model, but it does not
quite fit all the necessary specifications. To begin with, Los Angeles is
weak on banks and corporate headquarters. It doesn't have a serious stock
exchange. There are too many mini-centres. The art museums and luxury
stores are scattered all over the city. The Getty, LA's nearest equivalent
to the Tyrell Corporation, with its view out to Catalina Island, is located
somewhere on the 405. Lacma is on the old Miracle Mile, half-way down
the Wilshire corridor. The Norton Simon is in Pasadena. The Gehry
Music Center is endlessly delayed. You can tell there is something
missing just by glancing at the silhouette of downtown, if you can see it
through the smog. This is not New York or London or Tokyo. Los
Angeles has not undergone the same massive change that has transformed
other cities. In many ways, it maintains elements of the mythic city of
Chandler, Nathanael West and Aldous Huxley, presences still to be felt
in *Blade Runner*.

Los Angeles is a second-tier world city, like Miami or Singapore or
São Paulo. But, in one respect, it is a paramount global centre. It is the
undisputed capital of the world's entertainment industry, dominating
both New York and Chicago, far out-reaching London, Bombay and
Hong Kong. LA provides the metaphors which model our imaginative

perception of the world and it does so in ways which reflect its own carefully cultivated civic narcissism. Ridley Scott's *Blade Runner* was not an instant commercial success. The modest amount of money it eventually made came from secondary or tertiary markets—Japan, video-stores, TV rights, the Director's Cut. But it has been an immense cultural success in updating the noir image of Los Angeles into the next millennium. Its impact can be discerned both in a series of subsequent films and in the cultural shockwaves it sent through the futurist imaginary.

The idea of the world city as command-and-control centre for global capitalism, one of an archipelago or Hanseatic League of such cities circling the globe, housing transnational corporate headquarters, their business services, transnational institutions and telecommunications and information processing centres, goes back to John Friedmann's essay of 1986, 'The World City Hypothesis', postdating Ridley Scott by four years.[2] Manuel Castells's *The Informational City* followed in 1989; Saskia Sassen's *The Global City: London, New York, Tokyo* in 1991.[3] The economic model postulated by these books brought together elements from Wallenstein's concept of the global system with elements, it has to be admitted, of McLuhan's earlier idea of the global village.[4] Sharon Zukin, from *Loft Living* onwards, played an important part, as did theories of postmodernism developed in other fields and introduced to urban studies by Ed Soja and Fredric Jameson.[5] It was in the shadow of postmodernism that Giuliana Bruno wrote her seminal study of *Blade Runner*, 'Ramble City', published in the art journal *October* in 1987.[6]

In this context, I would like to discuss three aspects of *Blade Runner* which I believe should be seen as crucial to our understanding of the world city, in a number of interconnected ways. First, the Tyrell Corporation; second, the replicant; and third, City-Speak. The Tyrell pyramid is the central and dominating building in *Blade Runner*, supposedly one mile high, like Frank Lloyd Wright's notorious and never-realized skyscraper project. It is the headquarters, not simply of a transnational corporation, but of one which operates off-world, in space. The corporation, rather than the political elite, is the centre of power in the city, and, through its manufacturing interests, is presumably responsible for the massive pollution which poisons the city's air and causes the climatic transformation which brings endless downpours of acid rain to fall upon the city. It is also responsible for the manufacture of replicants as slave labour and for the sharp social polarization between elite and underclass. Hampton Fancher, the original screen-writer, is explicit about this: 'Blade Runner was always meant to be cautionary. For instance, BR was shot during the dawn of Reaganism. And I was flabbergasted by Ronald Reagan and everything he stood for. So the cruel politics portrayed in the film were my rebuttal of Reaganism, in a sense.'[7]

The Tyrell Corporation is already, I think, somewhat anachronistic as a symbol of 'globalization', because it represents manufacturing rather than financial capital. Nonetheless, maufacturing remains the foundation of the new capitalist order, despite the hegemonic role played by banks and the other FIRE sectors (Finance, Insurance, Real Estate). Manufacturing did not become truly 'global' until the 1970s when, as Alain Lipietz pointed out, in his 1982 essay 'Towards Global Fordism', manufacturing in the periphery accelerated much faster than in the core—more than three times faster in Bangladesh, Kenya, Yemen, Indonesia, Lesotho, Thailand, Nigeria, Ecuador, Tunisia, South Korea, Malaysia, Algeria, Hong Kong and Singapore.[8] Essentially a new international division of labour was created during this period. At the same time, multinational corporations continued to remain dominant, the top thousand companies controlling over three-quarters of world manufacturing output. This expansion, moreover, was financed by borrowing on the international money market, rather than by domestic accumulation.

Its corporate headquarters, the Tyrell pyramid, with its Sant'Elia elevators copied from the Bonaventure Hotel, also invokes pre-Columbian architecture, a style which shaped Los Angeles during the 1920s through the designs of Robert Stacy-Judd, Francisco Mujica and, of course, Frank Lloyd Wright, whose Ennis House, drawing on Mayan temples, is explicitly used in the film. The pyramid, moreover, is also the site of death and entombment. Right up to the point of shooting, the script of Blade Runner contained a scene in which the 'Tyrell' killed by Batty is revealed to be a fake. The real Tyrell is preserved in a cryonic chamber in the heart of the pyramid, waiting for a cure to be found for his incurable disease. Thus global capitalism is represented as a culture of death, artificially preserved beyond its time. Plainly, there is no building closely resembling the Tyrell pyramid in LA today, but that is hardly the point. Like *Who Framed Roger Rabbit?*, a film much more closely based on the history of the city, *Blade Runner* works as allegory, in both story and visual dimensions. The Tyrell pyramid represents the global power of the corporation as well as its location in Los Angeles and the death drive which sustains it. It also contributes to the image of city as spectacle, optical rather than tactile, to use Walter Benjamin's terms—a city to be looked at rather than lived in.

The replicants manufactured by the Tyrell Corporation are intended for use off-world, in the Colonization Defence Program, for political homicide, for handling nuclear materials, and so on. They are part of the infrastructure of an industrial complex which involves both ruthless economic exploitation, colonial expansion into undeveloped territories and tight paramilitary control. There are also references in the film to the exploitation of Antarctica and the oceans, logical areas of expansion for a predatory capitalist system. The replicants themselves are not simply industrial products but products with built-in obsolescence, like the automobiles Vance Packard wrote about in the 1950s. As Hampton Fancher put it, 'So the idea from the beginning was that Tyrell had purposefully built in this breakdown so people would have to buy a new replicant every few years. He did that to keep his commerce running.'[9]

The replicants, however, are customized in ways which Detroit never managed to achieve. In *Blade Runner*, we are dealing with a post-Fordist rather than a classically Fordist economy, to use the concepts developed by Lipietz and Aglietta, an economy in which assembly lines have become, so to speak, 'intelligent' and can tailor their products unit by unit within a spectrum. Moreover, as we know from the 'Eye Works' scene in the film, production of important elements, such as eyes, is subcontracted out to small specialized workshops, run on a craft rather than an industrial basis. 'Ridleyville' is presumably full of such 'out-source' workshops, alongside the animoid suppliers, noodle bars and night-spots. Similarly, Sebastian, the toy-maker, is a freelance genetic engineer, who has both a research and design relationship with Tyrell and a small craft business of his own as a luxury toy-maker.

Most of the academic discussion of replicants in *Blade Runner* takes off from a postmodern discourse of originals, copies and simulations or from a neo-Lacanian interest in the psychology of sophisticated robots. In both cases, it is a discourse of identity and difference, whether this is looked at philosophically or psychologically, whether in terms of ontological decidability or Oedipalized subjectivity. The origins of these *topoi* are to be found in Philip K. Dick's original book, where the issues, however, are explicitly political—capitalism destroys the realm of nature and sets out to replace it with a world of manufactured goods, animoids as images and commodities rather than as living creatures—a vision distinctly similar to Guy Debord's concept of the 'Society of the Spectacle' and one which therefore reflects directly on Los Angeles, as capital city of the Spectacle.[10] Or, as Manuel De Landa might have described it, in his book *A Thousand Years of Non-Linear History*,[11] we could see the replicants as signs either of the 'mineralization' of the proletariat itself, if we see them in terms of micro-chip implant technology, or of a long-term biological mutation as genetic engineering changes the realm of nature into that of culture, biology into technology.

At first sight, the principal characters of *Blade Runner* seem to be classical figures of modernity—the replicant rebel is the outlaw dandy, a kind of Nietzschean aesthete who is also the leader of a slave rebellion, while Deckard is the working stiff, the plebeian who just gets on with the job. Both of them despise the master of Metropolis, the ruler of the Tyrell Corporation, but they take very different paths. But there are also significant differences between Ridley Scott's film and Fritz Lang's. In the character of Tyrell, the Master is submerged into the figure of Rotwang, the evil magician and automaton maker, creating a much more negative vision of the Master, no longer capable of redemption. In Lang's *Metropolis*, the slaves are presented as a mass rather than as individuals, transformed from mindless drudges into a mindless mob, whereas the replicants in *Blade Runner* are intelligent individuals, an outlaw elite. Deckard, who is the counterpart to the Master's son, is far from a wide-eyed innocent—instead he is the typically world-weary protagonist of noir. Nor is there any final reconciliation between Deckard and the replicants, although there is mutual esteem, springing from Deckard's suspicion (and ours) that he is really one of them, a renegade replicant rather than a blade runner.

In *Blade Runner*, the drama is no longer between the proletarian mass-man and the gilded youth. There is no proletariat—or, if there is, it is off-world. In the city, there is only what we have come to call an underclass, mingled with a plethora of small-time peddlers and service providers, on the one hand, and a lone, single figure at the apex, a situation typical of contemporary postmodernity rather than the classic modernity of Weimar Germany. Perhaps, at this point, it is worth saying a few words about the question of 'postmodernism'. In a recent study, Perry Anderson proposes that postmodernity in the arts is really split between two trends, one which 'adjusts or appeals to the spectacular', the other which 'seeks to elude or refuse it'.[12] The replicants, it seems to me, are both figures of the spectacular, especially in their deaths, but also renegades who seek to revenge themselves upon it. The same paradox marks the film as a whole—it is both an explicitly spectacular production, with its astonishing sets and stunning effects, and, at the same time, an implicit critique of the spectacle as a culture of death. It is clearly a product of the image industry and yet intellectually detached from it. It appeals to our fascination with postmodernity while distancing itself from it. Again, this ambiguity probably reflects the underlying legacy of Philip K. Dick, the master of the dystopian 'trip', who consistently swings in his own work between euphoria and paranoia. In Dick's fiction, too, there is a consistent interpenetration of the public and the private, the world as outside force and the world as inner vision. It is as if the two poles of postmodernity—the global and the local, or the public rhetoric of advertising and the private world of fantasy, have become hopelessly entangled.

In the film (or, more accurately, in the Director's Cut) it is Gaff, Deckard's rival, played by Edward James Olmos, who appears to have access to the blade runner's dreams, as suggested by his poisoned gift of a dream image—an origami unicorn—at the very end of the film, thus raising the question of privacy. This is an issue with which we we are all now much more familiar than we were when *Blade Runner* first came out, due to the way in which we seem to sense that our personal computer files are somehow part of our own identity, external to our body, of course, yet still as private as our bodily memory itself. Edward James Olmos was also, it seems, responsible for the use of 'Cityspeak' as a polyglot street jargon, incorporating words from many different languages—Spanish, French, Chinese, German, Hungarian and Japanese. Olmos recounts how he 'went to the Berlitz School of Languages in Los Angeles, translated all these different bits and pieces of Gaff's original dialogue into fragments of foreign tongues and learned how to properly pronounce them. I also added some translated dialogue I'd made up myself. All that was a bitch and a half, but it really added to Gaff's character.'[13]

It did more than that. It pinpointed the importance of language, as opposed to visual design, in defining the nature of the world city, as well as the nature of identity in the city. There are four categories of language spoken in *Blade Runner*—there is English, the 'standard' language, used as a lingua franca; there are a number of vernacular languages, such as Chinese or Spanish; there is the code-switching sub-creole of Cityspeak; and finally there is the hyper-language of computers. The Esper, the talking computer network, which we see in use in Deckard's apartment and in a display of 'Incept tapes', was conceived as a system run by the police. 'Originally it was going to be everywhere—inside cars, out on the sidewalk, everywhere. But they got whittled down during rewrites until the Esper made only two appearances.' Similarly cars were to travel on an intelligent highway, a road with a mind of its own, exchanging information with vehicles through a sensor and controlling their path, flow and speed.

These languages each have their own socio-cultural context. English is 'unmarked', but besides being an interlingua, it is both the language of the elite and the language used in public or official situations by the police and by corporations. It is also, of course, the language implanted in replicants. Vernacular languages are used within ethnic groups who are represented as members of an underclass of petty entrepreneurs, casual labourers and 'street people'. Cityspeak is an ad hoc contact language, not far removed from a pidgin. Esper is a specialized network which is available only to a privileged elite who have private access to advanced communications technology. This linguistic landscape is one which reflects a sharply hierarchical system with a multitude of immigrant communities at the bottom. At the same time, the presence of a private communications network, while explicitly supporting the power of the local ruling elite, also implies that it has the global (or trans-global) reach characteristic of a world city. It is both a whirlpool, sucking immigrants in from the periphery, and a hub, controlling the periphery. By 1990 Los Angeles was already the North American urban region with the highest proportion of foreign-born residents (27 per cent, as opposed to New York's 20 per cent and Chicago's 11). At the same time, it had become increasingly bi-polar, as wealth was redistributed from rich to poor. The distribution of wealth thus parallels the distribution of linguistic skills between a technocratic lingua franca and a vernacular proto-creole, the germs of which we already see in the World Wide Web and the hubbub of the urban street.

In fact, the 'future metropolis' of *Blade Runner*, located in the year 2019, is surprisingly plausible as an extrapolation from trends which were dimly perceived in 1982 but have since become quite clear and the subject of considerable academic study. Underlying this type of city are a series of what we might call 'stratified mobility zones' (SMZs)—mobility of capital, mobility of elites and mobility of labour. Back in the 1950s, Marshall McLuhan's mentor, Harold Innis, noted that speed of communications favoured centralized power. Speed of global communications favours centralized global power and this creates the conditions for the growth of world cities with specific social, demographic, cultural, spatial, architectural and linguistic characteristics. In this respect, *Blade Runner* was indeed premonitory on many different levels.

Credit for this must go to its writers (official and unofficial), to Ridley Scott for his fanatical interest in the creation of a richly detailed environment, full of metaphoric meaning, and also to Syd Mead, who had previously worked in both the automobile and electronics industries as a 'futurist', giving visual form to his visions of feasible hardware set in a complete future environment. The city *Blade Runner* portrays is not precisely Los Angeles. In a way, it is both the city which Los Angeles wishes to be, perceived in boosterish, optimistic terms from the vantage-point of an elite, and the city it yet fears it will become, looked at in noir, pessimistic terms from the point of view of its critics and its immigrant and underclass population, numerically much greater but politically, of course, much weaker. Mike Davis is right in seeing it as an extension of the Fordist city of New York-Metropolis, but it is a New York which has been privatized, retrofitted and 'noir-ified'. The privatization and retrofitting are both typical of the transition from Fordism to post-Fordism. The 'noir-ification' represents a new postmodern phase in a long-standing tradition of radical cultural critique, nurtured in Los Angeles itself.

This is not the same as a radical political critique—Fancher, obviously, is a left-liberal interested in ecology, but it was Ridley Scott, whom Fancher characterizes as politically conservative, who describes the power of the Tyrell Corporation as 'patriarchal'. Radical cultural critique is, however, a long tradition in Los Angeles, going back, as Mike Davis has chronicled, to Nathanael West (a favourite of Philip K. Dick), to Aldous Huxley (the great pioneer of prophetic science fiction), to Raymond Chandler and Dashiel Hammett (models for the creators of Deckard). In this sense, *Blade Runner* is certainly an LA movie set in a great local tradition, a critique drawing on West and Chandler. At the same time, it has a global relevance and a global reach, of the kind Hollywood has long enjoyed, but not yet Los Angeles. It reflects both the vision of LA as a future world city and the unsustainable dystopia which that would involve.

10

SPIES AND SPIVS:
AN ANGLO-AUSTRIAN
ENTANGLEMENT

1948. Ruins, the detritus caused by the massive Allied bombing of
March 1945 (747 American bombers, 1,667 tons of explosives) and then,
almost without respite, the Red Army assault on the city the following
month—artillery duels, raging fires, 37,000 soldiers dead (Russians and
Germans) while the Viennese hid underground in their cellars. It was the
ruins which struck Graham Greene when he visited Vienna in February
1948 to research the script for *The Third Man*. 'I never knew Vienna
between the wars, and I am too young to remember the old Vienna with
its Strauss music and its bogus easy charm; to me it is simply a city of
undignified ruins which turned that February into great glaciers of snow
and ice.' It is the images of desolation which we remember best from *The
Third Man*, the classic film for which Greene wrote the shooting script—
the ruins, the big wheel and the sewers. By July 1948, clearance and
repair of the ruins were well under way—the effects of the the Marshall
Plan were already beginning to be felt. By the autumn, when filming
began, Vienna was clearly beginning to change: reconstruction was on
the agenda and it was not to be long before the damaged monuments
were restored and the city returned to a kind of normality. It was not
until after Stalin's death, however, that a peace treaty was finally agreed,
the occupying powers withdrew and Austria became, once again, an
independent, although constitutionally non-aligned, country.
    What was it that took Graham Greene and Carol Reed, the director

of the film, and Orson Welles, its most striking personality, to Vienna, not the easiest city in which to work? The original idea, the idea that eventually became *The Third Man*, came from the film's producer, Alexander Korda. Korda was himself Hungarian in origin. He had begun his film career there as head of Corvin Films immediately after the First World War, after the great collapse of the Hapsburg Empire, producing films first under the liberal Karolyi government, then under the communist Béla Kún regime. Arrested by the police of the incoming anti-semitic, anti-communist Horthy government, he was held and tortured in the beautiful and picturesque Hotel Gellert, a fate from which he was rescued by Brigadier Maurice, a British army officer who, according to Korda's nephew Michael, could be 'variously described as the representative of MI-5 in Budapest, the British government's secret link to Admiral Horthy and as an adventurer, profiteer and speculator'.[1] Maurice intervened personally with Horthy, and Alex Korda left for Vienna to pursue his career as a producer, travelling first class in a *wagon-lit* under British protection, accompanied by his film star wife, Maria Corda. How Korda must have smiled on encountering the figure of Harry Lime, the classic cinematic adventurer, profiteer and speculator, and also, in the context of post-war Vienna, very likely a spy—a legendary figure who had been conjured up for him at his own instigation.

In his accomplished family memoir *Charmed Lives*[2] Michael Korda, recounts how he was invited to his first grand Alex Korda dinner party—it must have been 1948, because Carol Reed was there and the conversation turned, at one point, to the problem of getting Orson Welles to appear in a film which Reed would be directing for Korda, the future *Third Man*. As Michael Korda remembered it, the film they were talking about was one which would be 'a spy story'. It was a project which his uncle had been toying with already 'for nearly three years', a time-span which would take us back into 1945, to the very end of the Second World War and the establishment of a joint Allied authority in the city of Vienna, which was divided up into five zones administered by the four powers, Russia, Britain, America and France, with an international zone in the centre of the city where all four co-operated—or not, as the case might be. From other sources it seems that Korda's first thoughts were of Paul Tabori's book *Epitaph for Europe* as a possible film project and that he then zeroed in on the idea of setting the film in Vienna.[3] According to Tabori, he was invited to meet Korda as the war neared its conclusion, after Korda had read *Epitaph for Europe*, a book (written, of course, by a fellow-Hungarian) which describes the first year of a completely ruined city in Eastern Europe following the end of the war. 'I want to buy your book,' Korda told him. 'You kept me awake all night. It will make a great film.' Tabori told Korda he hoped it might turn out like King Vidor's great saga of the Depression, *Our Daily Bread*, a film which, as it happened, was one of Korda's own favourites. Time passed, and quite soon after the war had finally reached its end Korda sent Tabori on a research tour of the Balkans. On his return Korda informed him that he had now severed all connections with his former partner, MGM, which had retained the rights to Tabori's book. Korda balked at buying his former property back at MGM's high price and the project fell through. Later that year, however, Tabori was called back to Korda's office for an immediate meeting. The Vienna project was still on his mind.

At the headquarters of London Films, at 146 Piccadilly, Tabori found Korda waiting for him, together with Karl Hartl, the Austrian director and producer who had been Korda's production manager and closest associate on his Austrian films way back in the 1920s. Now, however, they had a very different kind of project—no longer a costume romance or a biblical epic, like his early Viennese films, but instead a comedy set in contemporary Vienna whose 'basic idea', Korda told Tabori, 'is "invisible frontiers". I want you to do a treatment as quickly as possible.' Drawing on his own memories of Vienna, where he had been early in 1946, Tabori set to work, delivered his manuscript, discussed it at length with Korda and then waited for something to happen. This draft was presumably the 'spy story' which Korda eventually dropped when he decided to turn the Vienna project over to Graham Greene, after the runaway success of *The Fallen Idol*, the film which Greene and Reed had made for Korda in 1947, set in an embassy. In the end, the 'spy story', in Greene's hands, turned into quite another kind of story, one I would call a 'spiv' story—'spiv' being the English term for a certain kind of flashy black marketeer.

The spiv cycle of British films first came into view towards the end of the war. In essence, the cycle reflected a mutation in the traditional British crime film, a shift which took place in response to the changing pattern of crime itself that developed in wartime as a result of state regulation of the economy. Controls and rationing—and rising prices— led inevitably to the emergence of a black market. 'Spiv' itself seems to have been a fashion term as much as a job description. In the words of Raynes Minns: 'The archetypal spiv wore yellow shoes, a wide-lapelled suit and wide tie, and sported a shifty little trilby pulled rakishly over the forehead. He symbolized a flashy flaunting of authority—especially towards the end of the war when people were long tired of self denial and the many wartime restrictions.'[4] Other sources suggest that the spiv costume was consciously derived from Hollywood gangster pictures. Be that as it may, the crucial difference between the spiv and the classic gangster was the degree of sympathy the spiv attracted for the transfer of black market goods from army camps, docks, railway yards, lorry parks, industrial depots and so on, to a grateful mass of consumers, weary of wartime and post-war shortages. Black marketeers may have been outside the law but they performed an obvious public service. They could even become heroes.

At the same time, of course, official ideology portrayed the spiv as an enemy of the war effort who was prospering while others paid the price. This ambivalence between sympathy and distaste runs right through the spiv cycle of films, in which the spivs are clearly marked as villains, ruthless and violent, while at the same time they are frequently fascinat- ing precisely because of the strange way in which living and working in and even for the community combined with dissolute rakishness and demonic transports of evil. Partly for this reason too, the line between 'spiv' and 'spy' was a surprisingly thin and permeable one. For Graham Greene, *The Third Man* was an entertainment rather than a serious film. Nonetheless it had serious aspects, some of which at least overlapped with the serious business of spying—being a black marketeer, like being a spy, involved living in a world marked by illegality, subterfuge and betrayal, being at all times a man on the run. I don't know whether Greene ever saw Alberto Cavalcanti's great film, *They Made Me a Fugitive*, made in 1946, about a criminal on the run, wanted for murder, who infiltrates a gang of spivs and black marketeers to clear his name, but I feel sure that he did, if only because he had previously worked with Cavalcanti as screen-writer for *Went the Day Well*, a film which had been made only a short time earlier (in 1942) about a group of undercover German infiltrators who are finally unmasked due to a series of tell-tale slips.

Everything to do with *The Third Man* seems to take us back into the world of espionage. Greene himself worked as a professional spy during the war, in a team headed by the future traitor Kim Philby. His own family had a background in espionage and it provided a repeated theme for his stories. His uncle worked on secret business at the Admiralty and helped to establish the Naval Intelligence Department. His elder brother spied for the fascist side in Spain and then worked for the Japanese, although he also kept the British and the Americans informed about what he was doing. His younger sister worked for MI6, the British Secret Intelligence Service, and recruited Graham himself into the ranks of the service during the war. One of his cousins was jailed as a collaborator with the Nazis around the same time, clearly under suspicion of helping German intelligence. Greene's father ran a boys' boarding school in which every pupil was kept under constant surveillance through a well-organized network of teachers, staff and fellow-pupils and was also subjected to routine interrogations, mainly to make sure that all sexual activities had been totally repressed. It is hardly surprising that Graham too should have joined the ranks. Indeed, as Michael Shelden has noted, 'it is impossible to make sense of Greene's life until one acknowledges the extent of his devotion to spying'.[5] Greene joined the SIS in 1941, working in the section responsible for counter-espionage. Posted first to Africa, he soon returned to London to work under Philby, the legendary master-spy, double agent and defector, at Section V, as the counter-espionage division was known. Although he resigned in May 1944, it is clear that he did not sever all his ties with the 'old firm', but continued working informally right up to the 1980s, as Shelden has shown. Probably, in fact, he had been working freelance even before he joined the staff payroll in time of war. His Soviet code-name, incidentally, was LORAN.

Sheldon writes that 'often Greene's main contact was not even an officer of the service but another independent operator like himself. In the early post-war years this contact was primarily his future film producer, Alexander Korda.'[6] Korda was particularly close to Winston Churchill, whom he even hired as a screen-writer in order to support him during his years in the political wilderness, along with his son Randolph and his confidant, Brendan Bracken, who was alleged, maliciously, to be Churchill's illegitimate child. Bracken was also one of the guests at the Claridge's dinner party attended by Michael Korda where *The Third Man* was discussed. During the war Korda left England for America and was derided as a coward by the English, but, on his return, in mid-war, Churchill, now Prime Minister, immediately awarded him a knighthood, clearly for intelligence services rendered in the United States. In America he had worked clandestinely with BSC (British Security Co-ordination) and became close to Wild Bill Donovan, head of the OSS, which later evolved into the CIA. In fact, isolationist members of the US Senate specifically (and validly) attacked Korda Productions as a centre for British espionage. Another guest at Claridge's, I might add, was the deeply ambiguous Baroness Budberg, Maxim Gorky's mistress, who had briefed Greene on the first of many foreign trips, in 1934, to Estonia, a country Greene later picked as the site of another spy drama, another film treatment.

The making of *The Third Man*, moreover, also proves to have been inextricably bound up with the world of espionage. It has frequently been asserted, for instance, following Greene's own account of events, that Colonel Charles Beauclerk, who was serving as an intelligence officer in Vienna, gave him the information about the penicillin racket and the sewer police which he subsequently used in his script. Beauclerk may indeed have been helpful to Greene, particularly since Greene himself was so well-connected to the intelligence racket, if I may use the word. However, Greene had another source. As Norman Sherry notes in his standard biography of Greene,

he was met at the airport by Elizabeth Montagu, daughter of Lord Montagu [Beauclerk, incidentally, was the future Duke of St Alban's], who worked for Korda and had the job of looking after Greene and making sure that he saw all that he needed to. She introduced Greene to a friend of hers, the London *Times* correspondent, now known as Peter Smollett (although his original name was Hans Peter Smolka), who was extremely knowledgeable about conditions and confusions involved in the four-power occupation.[7]

According to Sherry, Smolka 'was better informed than the young intelligence officer [Beauclerk] about the dirty rackets then operating in Vienna'. During Greene's reconnaissance trip he spent several nights with Smolka and 'once visited the Russian sector [Harry Lime's sector] so that Greene could call on an old, retired servant who had worked for his mother'. According to Elizabeth Montagu, Sherry notes, Smolka also showed Greene some unpublished stories of his, one of which contained information about the watering-down of penicillin, which features prominently in *The Third Man*.

Further research, however, reveals that Smolka had some rather special qualities which must have intrigued Greene as a connoisseur of espionage. Smolka had been a close friend and partner of Greene's good friend Kim Philby. Philby had become converted to communism during his time in Vienna, in early 1934 (before, of course, the meteoric rise through British intelligence which Greene had so keenly observed). This was the moment when fighting broke out in Vienna as the armed socialist militia, the Schutzbund, was provoked into an ill-prepared attempt to overthrow the Austro-fascist regime of Chancellor Dollfuss. After heavy fighting the regime used artillery against the working-class housing projects from which the socialists drew their political support. The fighting was quickly over, with hundreds of dead and wounded on both sides, maybe over a thousand in the Schutzbund. The mayor of Vienna, a socialist, was arrested and replaced by a conservative. Many others fled the country or, if they remained, were tried, imprisoned and, in many cases, executed. During this time Kim Philby was living in Vienna. He had gone there as a young leftist, not yet a party member, in order to work with the Austrian Committee for Relief from German Fascism, which turned out to be a communist organization. There he was directed to stay with Litzi Friedmann, a communist activist, who later became his wife. Philby delivered packages from Vienna to Prague or Budapest, using a sprig of mimosa as a visual password. It was in Vienna that Philby made his decision to commit himself to the communist cause and acquired his first taste of clandestine political activity.

It was also where he met Hans Peter Smolka, through Litzi. Like Philby and his new wife, Smolka and his wife left Austria after the débâcle of the uprising, but the two couples soon met again in London. Philby and Smolka (now Smollett) started a small press agency which they named the London Continental News Ltd, to supply Central European news to journalists working in London. The project failed but Philby stayed in close touch with Smolka (Soviet code-name ABO) and, according to Shelden, 'there are some students of Soviet espionage who believe that both men were working as spies for Moscow'[8]—although Smolka, it seems, was providing information first to Philby, then to Burgess, without these links being cleared by Moscow Centre. Evidence in recently published KGB files shows that Smolka was in their service at least by 1939, when he had started work as a journalist for the London *Times*. After the war broke out, he became head of the Soviet Relations Division at the British Ministry of Information, a government department run, incidentally, by Korda's good friend Brendan Bracken. During this period Philby, according to his own account, approached Smolka and 'said to him, "Listen, Hans, if in your present job you come across some information that in your opinion could help me in my work *for England*— and I winked at him—come over to me and offer me two cigarettes, I'll take one, you'll keep the other, and that will be a signal that you want to tell me something important." '[9] Smolka agreed. The deal was done.

Philby always disclaimed any knowledge about what happened to Smolka after the war—as we know, he left Vienna for Prague, where he ran into serious problems at the time of the Slansky trials, eventually returning to Vienna and ending up, it is said, as an economic adviser to the socialist Prime Minister, Bruno Kreisky. Shelden provides another interesting sidelight on Greene's relationship with Smolka. He puts it as follows: 'It does seem a great coincidence that Elizabeth Montagu would lead Greene straight to Smolka [on his reconnaissance trip to Vienna for *The Third Man*]. He was the one man in Vienna who could discuss Philby's past in detail, and who could do it in English. The plot becomes even more complicated when one knows more about Elizabeth Montagu. The daughter of the second Baron Montagu of Beaulieu, the Hon. Elizabeth Montagu is listed in the film credits of *The Third Man* as 'Austrian Advisor'. Earlier, during the war, she had worked for the

Political Warfare Executive in Switzerland, and had eventually been given a job as one of two personal assistants working for Allen Dulles in his OSS office at Berne [Dulles, that is, the future head of the CIA]. After the war, Korda hired her, for reasons we can well guess, but as a dialogue coach. In 1948, Shelden reveals, Korda dispatched her to reopen some of his old offices in Europe, offices that had served as covers for secret service agents during the war. Elizabeth Montagu has denied that she was involved in any intelligence work during her time with Korda but she certainly served as the intermediary between two players in the intelligence world, Greene and Smolka. The other key link between them, of course, was Kim Philby.

One last comment on Smolka. In his book on Korda, Tabori suggests that it was actually Smolka (referred to in his public capacity as 'the *Times* correspondent in Austria') who originally suggested the idea for *The Third Man* to Korda, by providing him with 'a graphic description of the once-proud Hapsburg capital, now divided between the four occupying powers, on the very edge of the Iron Curtain and (as in 1920, when Alex arrived there first) a happy hunting ground of profiteers, spies and black marketeers'.[10] This would certainly explain why Greene was steered so promptly to Peter Smollett/Smolka on his arrival in the city and why, out of gratitude perhaps, although with more than a touch of irony, he gave the name of 'Smolka' to Major Calloway's driver. Smolka, according to Philby, could not himself be considered a communist, although he was a sympathizer, but he took a personal decision not to betray either Philby or Burgess or his friend Maclean or the art historian Anthony Blunt, all of whom worked for British intelligence and simul-taneously spied for the Soviet Union. When the Russian writer Genrikh Borovik gained access to the Philby files in the KGB archive, following the collapse of the former Soviet Union, he also spoke to Philby at length about a project, suggested to him by none other than Graham Greene, of producing a book which would juxtapose Philby's own recorded account of his career as a double agent with the archival material which was to be found in the KGB files. Philby, in Borovik's view, was pained by KGB suspicions, at Moscow Centre, that he was really a treble agent, working for British intelligence while pretending to be a double agent feeding secret material from London to Moscow. Smolka, in Philby's view, as interpreted by Borovik, was that rare figure in the world of intelligence, a man from the world of espionage, with all to lose, who could nonetheless be trusted and who respected personal ties, even when difficulties emerged.

Holly Martins, it turns out, in *The Third Man*, could not be trusted despite his close personal loyalties. He betrayed his oldest and dearest friend, Harry Lime. Lime, it should be noted, was living and operating out of the Russian zone. In fact, black marketeers frequently based themselves in the Russian zone, as Inge Lehne has pointed out, because, having acquired uniforms, they would become immune against arrest there, as persons wearing uniforms could not be seized, even if they were caught committing a crime.[11] 'To a certain extent', moreover, Lehne explains, 'the Allied clients in each of the occupational zones protected their blackmarketeers in order to guarantee an uninterrupted supply of merchandise.' In an economy where there were endless shortages and money was virtually worthless, the black marketeers provided a necessary service (on the black market, cigarettes were the currency, with flint lighters worth six cigarettes). Penicillin, the new 'silver bullet', was also traded, as in the film. In his memoir of post-war Vienna, *Hunger's Rogues*, the self-confessed Vienna black marketeer Jacques Sandulescu describes a 'penicillin baron' eating heartily in a restaurant.[12] Penicillin was also used for purposes of espionage, surprising though this may sound. According to Jim Milano, moving spirit of the American Military Intelligence Service in post-war Vienna, one of his operatives, a Major Chambers, discovered a Bulgarian doctor who had opened a clinic for venereal disease in Wiener Neustadt, south of Vienna in the Soviet zone. Chambers, rather like Josef Harbin in *The Third Man*, had access to penicillin from the American Military Hospital in Vienna and supplied quantities to the clinic, which was thus able to attract patients from the Russian military. In return, the Bulgarian doctor was able to obtain information from his grateful patients, meeting weekly with Chambers to establish a wish-list and even persuading a steady stream of Red Army officers to defect. This operation was actually in effect while *The Third Man* was in production in Vienna, finally closing down in 1949, when the Bulgarian doctor was secretly shipped out by the so-called 'rat line' to South America.

Thus spies and spivs, the worlds of espionage and the black market, not only coexisted in post-war Vienna but even converged. It is worth remembering that soon after the cat has rubbed up against Harry Lime in a dark doorway and Holly has intuited that somebody is there hiding, the first words he addresses to Harry are 'What kind of spy do you think you are—satchelfoot? What are you tailing me for?' In this context, *The Third Man* could be seen alternatively either as a political thriller or as a spiv film. On the one hand, its roots were in Hitchcock's *The Lady Vanishes* and Reed's own *Night Train to Munich*, while on the other hand it echoed Cavalcanti's *They Made Me a Fugitive* and Reed's own *Odd Man Out*, with its setting in Belfast, another violent and divided city. In films like these, 'riff-raff realism' (as it is often called) verged on *film noir*, minus the key figure of the *femme fatale*, seductive but treacherous, a type which never seems to have captured the British imagination. Reed's Belfast and Vienna are both variants of wartime London, cities where he found an exotic and extreme version of his own backyard, where the social fabric was devastated by bombing, where crime prospered in conditions of penury and the old civil society seemed suddenly precarious. The British spiv films are full of bombsites and rubble, peopled by rakes and black marketeers. But they are also full of what we might call the 'vernacular fantastic': pinball arcades, ghost trains ('Dante's Inferno' in the film version of Graham Greene's *Brighton Rock*), race tracks, dance halls, wrestling rings, tattooing parlours—and, in the case of *The Third Man*, the merry-go-round and the big wheel in the Prater amusement park.

The style of the early spiv films pointed the way towards the 'urban nightmare' expressionism of *Odd Man Out* and *The Third Man*, both shot by Robert Krasker (as was David Lean's *Brief Encounter*)—an Austro-German cameraman in exile, whose roots were in Weimar Expressionism and the 1920s 'street film' genre. In fact, the first important post-war spiv picture, Alberto Cavalcanti's *They Made Me a Fugitive*, made in Hammersmith for Warner Brothers and released in 1946, had pushed nightmare Expressionism even further than *The Third Man*. Narcissus, known as Narcy, a sadistic racketeer whose headquarters are located in an East End funeral parlour, deals in black market goods (cigarettes, Scotch whisky, New Zealand lamb) which are transported in coffins accompanied by mourners in full regalia. 'Narcy', of course, suggests 'nasty', 'nark' and 'narcotics'—and Narcy does also have a line in what he calls 'sherbet'. The spiv character is split into two—Narcy is vicious and depraved, while Morgan, his nemesis, is an innocent man on the run, betrayed by Narcy who has informed falsely on him to the police. In *The Third Man* the same dramatic strategy is given a reverse twist—it is the monster who is on the run and it is his loyal friend who informs on him, betrays him and finally shoots him dead. We sympathize with the black marketeer, the charming rogue, while Martins is left alone and unwanted, abandoned by the woman he loves, unable to stomach his betrayal of the man that she loved. The treachery at issue here, it goes without saying, is not of one's country, but of one's friend. In fact, Reed's Austria was not really anybody's country. It was a montage of zones spliced together without any unity, a jigsaw puzzle in which the pieces didn't fit. At best, it was a battered and decayed museum piece, a baroque stage reset for an all-too-modern melodrama.

By 1948 the British film industry was beginning to falter after losing a disastrous trade war with the United States. *The Third Man* imported two American stars, Welles and Cotten, just as Edmond Gréville's late spiv film *Noose* (also made in 1948) featured Joseph Calleia as a racketeer and Carole Landis as a fashion reporter obsessed with Christian Dior's New Look, symbol of an end to austerity. The next year saw the last of the cycle, complete with its own bombed-out cityscape, Jules Dassin's *Night and the City*, with Richard Widmark as Fabian, a club tout who has a tragic fantasy of controlling London's wrestling arenas, trying desperately to survive as he is hunted across bleak rubble-strewn bomb-sites by the gangsters he has crossed. In all three of these films, our hearts go out, ambivalently, to the doomed and defeated American villains. We remember Lime's fingers desperately quivering through the grating which blocks his flight to freedom, just as we remember Narcy plunging to his death off the roof of the Valhalla, with its flashing electric sign, down into the grimy alley below, and the wanted man on the run in Hamer's *It Always Rains on Sunday*, throwing himself on the track as a locomotive rumbles towards him through the dark, deserted marshalling yard. Our sympathy goes even to Narcy, the most evil of all, if only for his stubborn refusal to show a single spark of goodness, even as his rotten life ebbs away in the rain. Similarly, we are charmed by Harry Lime, whereas Martins unsettles us. He is being 'run' by Calloway, a British intelligence officer, he has acquired some tricks of tradecraft, such as how to rid himself of a shadow by slipping into a cinema, he betrays his oldest friend and comrade to the other side for a price, as Anna protests when she realizes that her own freedom has been secretly bartered for Harry's. I can't help wondering whether Greene, who certainly knew how to keep a secret, consciously created Holly Martins in antithesis to Hans Smolka, the man who never betrayed his friend's trust, however many deaths lay on that friend's conscience.

Finally, a last word about Vienna. The twentieth century saw Vienna collapse from being a centre to being a frontier—at first, after the First World War, a frontier with the Balkans (the Wild West for Holly Martins), and then, after the Second World War, a frontier with the Soviet bloc. *The Third Man* was conceived and made in a transitional period—the Balkans are still there, as they were in Graham Greene's earlier novel, *Stamboul Train*, with its fateful departure from the station in Vienna for the instability and chaos of Yugoslavia, where the train is stopped and passengers are removed, but the Soviet bloc—'Eastern Europe' as it came to be known—was not yet quite in place. Vienna was no longer at the centre in a positive sense but only in a negative sense, at the half-way point, as the Iron Curtain began to come down. The frontier was still, as Korda suggested, an 'invisible' frontier but it was becoming more visible every day, as the rubble of war was cleared away and the geopolitical lines began to harden. Greene—and, in different ways, Korda and Reed—were all fascinated by the metaphoric power of the sewers, the network of tunnels underground which provided a way of escaping over the frontier, crossing secretly, unobserved, invisibly from one zone to another. The death of Harry Lime, like a rat in a trap, signalled a goodbye to all that. It was almost like the future shooting down of would-be refugees from East Germany—the grating through which his fingers stretch is like the wall which finally came to symbolize the impermeability of the Iron Curtain.

Reed made one key decision early—there would be no Strauss, no waltzes in his film. That Vienna, the Vienna which could imagine itself at the centre of Europe, was gone for good. Reed's Vienna is a crooked

city, a city shot with tilted angles, a city in which the cobbled streets are
wet and glistening, as if from melted snow, a city in which a few beams
of light cut through deep darkness, in which the shadows are all
exaggerated. For Reed, who saw himself as a director who respected the
script, Vienna was essentially Greene's Vienna. For Greene, as I have
suggested, it was a no man's land, a city on the edge, in which the old
values were in ruins, a city with no future. By the old values I mean, not
the values of Mozart or Strauss, but the values of the old political left,
which Greene could now find neither in America nor in Russia. It was
Greene, we should remember, who published a review in 1937 of an
Austrian film, *Tales from the Vienna Woods*, in which he wrote:

> An Austrian film and you know what that means: it means Magda
> Schneider's deep-sunk eyes and porcine coquetry; courtyards where every-
> one in turn picks up a song as they mend cars, clean windows, wash
> clothes, a festival in a beer-garden with old Viennese costumes, balloons,
> slides, laughter, and driving home together in a fiacre; Magda Schneider's
> trim buttocks and battered girlishness; a musical tour of Vienna—no
> sign, of course, of the Karl Marx Hof, only palaces and big Baroque
> dictatorial buildings.[13]

A few months earlier he had reviewed *Pépé le Moko*, the central film of
French 'Poetic Realism', a film he very much admired which tells the
story of a wanted man's failure to escape from the trap of being forced to
live in a 'shabby, alien quarter', followed inexorably to its 'grim conclusion', a film in which 'the theme of no freedom anywhere is not lost
in a happy ending'.[14] Or as Kim Philby put it, reflecting on his own life,
'Long ago, back in Vienna, when I was already working for Moscow, I
began to prepare myself for the thought that the threat of failure is
always present in intelligence work, and so, therefore, is the death
sentence.'[15] It never came to Philby, as it came to Lime. But then Lime
was an American. Had Philby been American, he told Borovik, there
would have been

> a more 'radical solution'. An 'accident', you know, a car crash, murder by
> an 'unknown terrorist', 'accidental poisoning', anything like that, includ-
> ing 'suicide', or a slow death that takes six months but requires only a
> grain of a special drug in a glass of whisky. By the way, that would have

been the simplest way to avoid a widespread scandal. No person, no problem.[16]

No person, no problem. Lime too had wanted a quick death. He gave Holly a nod, almost a wink, a signal just before the finger tightened on the trigger. No freedom, no happy ending. Falling leaves. Theme music. End credits.

11

RULES OF THE GAME

Jean Renoir's career spanned nearly fifty years. He made his first films, *Cathérine* and *La Fille d'Eau*, in 1924, and his very last, *Le Petit Théâtre de Jean Renoir*, in 1969, when he was in his mid-seventies. He was one of the extraordinary pioneer generation which dominated the history of film from silent days right up to the end of the fifties and beyond: Cavalcanti, Chaplin, Disney, Dreyer, Ford, Hawks, Hitchcock, Lang, Mizoguchi, Ozu, Sternberg . . . Yet Renoir's own reputation as one of the great directors did not really take off until the 1950s. Before that he had always been overshadowed by his somewhat younger French colleagues, René Clair and Marcel Carné, the masters of French 1930s 'Poetic Realism'. It was the very last films he made in France, at the end of the 1930s, only just before the outbreak of war (*La Grande Illusion*, *La Bête Humaine* and *La Règle du Jeu/Rules of the Game*), which assured his reputation. Almost immediately after that he took stock of the political situation, left for America, stayed there for fourteen years, and did not make another film in France until 1954, as he turned sixty.

The crucial turning-point for his reputation came, in fact, long after the war, with the reissue, in 1958 and 1959 respectively, of newly restored archival prints of both *La Grande Illusion* and *La Règle du Jeu*, both of which had been lost and had vanished completely from public view. In 1956 two French researchers, Jean Gaborit and Jacques Maréchal, found 224 boxes containing negative and positive footage, and sound mixes, in the bombed-out ruins of the film studios at Boulogne-Billancourt. With Renoir's own help, they were able to restore the edited footage to its original length and re-release it at the 1959 Venice Film Festival. *Rules of the Game* was now recognized as one of the great masterpieces of the cinema. Every ten years the British film magazine *Sight and Sound* publishes a poll of film critics from around the world, each critic submitting a 'Ten Best Films' list. These are then totalled up to produce an overall ranking. Since 1962, *Citizen Kane* and *Rules of the Game* have topped the list in every single poll, holding absolutely steady, while there has been considerable change beneath them: *Battleship Potemkin* alone has maintained its regular place, a little further down, around five or six.

La Règle du Jeu is generally seen as summing up Renoir's talents and preoccupations—his sympathetic understanding of an extraordinarily wide range of human characters and types, their passions, confusions and foibles; his mixture of craftsmanship with spontaneity, order with anarchy; his subordination of intricate and complex narrative to character and milieu; his fascination with sudden switches of mood; his love of both the countryside and the city; his taste for both tragedy and comedy, his underlying humanism and sense of history. Yet when the film first came out in July 1939, it was a critical and commercial disaster. Literally howled at by sections of the audience, it was savagely cut down from 113 to 87 minutes or, according to Renoir himself, from 100 to 85 minutes, an act of disavowal and vandalism which only made matters worse. For Renoir, the episode was one of humiliating self-abasement. Many years later, commenting on the reduction of his own on-screen appearance to practically nothing, he felt he had acted 'as though I were ashamed, after this rebuff, of showing myself on the screen'.

As a result of the catastrophe, *Rules of the Game* became a *film maudit*—a doomed film—and it was in those terms that we find it being rehabilitated after the war. Above all, the magazine *Cahiers du Cinéma*, especially through the writings of its most aggressive and influential critic, François Truffaut, saw it in these terms—as a doomed film which had been wrongfully dismissed and whose claims needed to be reasserted as forcefully as possible. Truffaut was a protégé of the great French critic André Bazin and it was Bazin who proved to be Renoir's staunchest critical supporter. He saw Renoir retroactively as the protagonist of a great cause, the renewal of cinematic realism, and *Rules of the Game*, in particular, as a kind of prefiguration of Italian Neo-Realism, a high point in a counter-tradition of film-making which reacted against both Russian montage and American continuity cutting in favour of a style marked by long takes and deep focus, a way of film-making which encouraged events to develop in their own space and time, apparently unforced. For Bazin, *Rules of the Game* was the immediate precursor of *Citizen Kane*, the two films which inaugurated the new post-war cinema of Rossellini and the Italian neo-realists. Neo-Realism, in turn, opened the door for the French New Wave, whose directors themselves looked back to Renoir's film as their model for French cinema: the spontaneity, the disconcerting mixture of comedy and tragedy, sentimentalism and social comment.

Bazin thus helped change cinema history when he made the direct connection between Renoir's film and Orson Welles's *Citizen Kane*, which he also saw as a great realist masterpiece, on both stylistic and dramatic grounds. *Citizen Kane*, which came out in 1941, two years after *Rules of the Game*, was, of course, another classic example of the *film maudit*, a critical and commercial disaster more or less disowned by its studio ('To succeed is to fail', wrote Truffaut. 'All great films are "failed".') We might also add that both films were to be interpreted as critiques of a political establishment and a social class which was oblivious to the political peril of Nazism. Both Renoir and Welles emerged from the culture of the Popular Front, the alliance of communists, socialists and radicals formed to combat fascism during the 1930s. Politically they had much in common, although Renoir was even more explicit in his commitment, actually working directly with the French communist trade union confederation, the CGT, to produce what was virtually a committed propaganda film. Certainly, both *Citizen Kane* and *Rules of the Game* suffered partly as a result of their directors' known politics, each of them militantly anti-fascist and openly supportive of the Popular Front in his respective country.

It is hardly surprising that *Rules of the Game* should have been seen from the start as a deeply political film. It was made in the immediate aftermath of defeat in Spain and appeasement at Munich. In December 1938, Renoir and a group of friends announced the formation of a new production company, NEF, which would be managed co-operatively by the film-makers themselves, somewhat on the model of United Artists in 1920s Hollywood. The first film to be made by the new company was to be Renoir's *Les Caprices de Marianne*, which later turned into *Rules of the Game*. The next month Barcelona fell to the victorious fascist forces in Spain and Renoir settled on the cast for the new project. With Karl Koch, a refugee from Germany, he began work on a final version of the script. Shooting began in the country, with exteriors in the Sologne, on 15 February. In March Madrid fell and the Franco regime took power in Spain. At the end of September, the prime ministers of Britain and France—Neville Chamberlain and Edouard Daladier—went together to Munich to sign the agreement with Hitler and Mussolini that ratified the German occupation of the Sudetenland, formerly part of Czechoslovakia. The Munich agreement was widely welcomed in France. In November an attempt to launch a strike against Munich at the Renault factory outside Paris was defeated and a subsequent attempt by the anti-fascist left to launch a General Strike quickly collapsed. Shortly afterwards Hitler occupied the rest of Czechoslovakia. Renoir returned to Paris to shoot interiors and to work on the editing. In July, the film opened in Paris. The next month, Hitler and Stalin signed a non-aggression pact. France began to mobilize. At the beginning of September, Hitler invaded Poland and war began.

Renoir said later that, in making *Rules of the Game*, he had wanted to make a film in which French society was seen as 'dancing on a volcano'—a volcano which indeed erupted almost as soon as the film was completed. '*La Règle du Jeu*', he observed, 'is a war film, and yet there is no reference to the war. Beneath its seemingly innocuous appearance the story attacks the very structure of society. Yet all I thought about at the beginning was nothing avant-garde but a good little orthodox film.' When Renoir first embarked on his project he had seen it as 'a gay film', a light-hearted film, conceived in reaction both against his previous production, the gloomy and tragic *La Bête Humaine*, and against the depressing political situation. He wanted a change of mood, a return, perhaps, to the atmosphere of the *commedia dell'arte*, which he later celebrated in *Le Carrosse d'Or*, a film with many parallels to *Rules of the Game*, a film to be set, in Renoir's words, in 'the Italy from before Verdi and romanticism'. He deliberately chose a story with a light eighteenth-century atmosphere, as if drawn from the world of Beaumarchais, Marivaux and de Musset.

The film begins with an invocation of Beaumarchais, the author of *The Marriage of Figaro*, accompanied by a few bars of dance music by Mozart, the composer most associated with the French writer. From Marivaux, another late-eighteenth-century playwright, came the dramatic device of a symmetrical grouping of upper-class and lower-class characters, aristocratic masters and dependent servants, a dramatic form whose distant descendant can be traced in the British television series *Upstairs, Downstairs*. Marivaux had his own roots in the Italian *commedia dell'arte* and wrote for an Italian company. The original title of *Rules of the Game*, *Les Caprices de Marianne*, refers directly to de Musset's play of the same name, written in the early nineteenth rather than the eighteenth century, in 1833, but still retaining the same pre-revolutionary spirit and atmosphere. Marivaux and de Musset, incidentally, were the inspiration for Jean-Luc Godard's most recent film, a meditation on Bosnia which draws a direct parallel between the 1990s and the 1930s in terms of their appeasement of evil. Godard drew his idea from an article by Philippe Sollers written in criticism of Susan Sontag for producing *Waiting for Godot* in Sarajevo, rather than Marivaux or de Musset.[1]

This eighteenth-century, pre-revolutionary background to *Rules of the Game* inevitably reminds us that the French *ancien régime*, despite a series of upheavals, had nonetheless succeeded in prolonging its ascendancy right through to the end of the 1930s. In particular, Munich, the failure of the General Strike and the collapse of the Popular Front inevitably lent disheartening support to the idea that the *ancien régime* was still effectively in place, as France adopted what seemed at *least* passive support for counter-revolution in Germany, in its fascist form. At the same time, Renoir took the radical step of updating the world of Marivaux and de Musset, transposing it into the twentieth century and thereby throwing it into sharp contrast with contemporary modernity.

I think it is fair to say that Renoir himself was often fairly ambivalent in his attitude to modernity. After the war, on his return to Europe from America, this retreat from modernity became very marked. *The River* was set in India during the period of the British Empire; *Le Carrosse d'Or* (*The*

Golden Coach) was set in Peru during the time of the Spanish Empire, *French Can Can* and *Paris Does Strange Things* were set in France, but in the nineteenth century. Both films are full of regret for a long-gone milieu. It seems, in particular, that Renoir looked back nostalgically to the period of French Impressionism—Manet's *Lunch on the Grass*, Toulouse-Lautrec's Montmartre and, of course, his own father's landscapes and interiors. (Renoir openly regretted that his father had never painted in the Sologne, where the rural exteriors for *Rules of the Game* were shot. It was a landscape which he thought appropriate for his father's style of lush pastoralism.)

In *Rules of the Game*, however, modernity was foregrounded in two major ways: through the intrusive presence of radio and aviation, aspects of modern life each of which had a direct relationship with film. Radio, of course, was the major form of modern mass communication in the thirties, the medium of a public sphere which, as is made clear in the film, intruded into every private space. It was radio which was associated, in particular, with the consolidation of power by Hitler, and in America Roosevelt also was renowned for his fireside radio chats. Radio, as we see illustrated in the case of André Jurieu, the hero of Renoir's film, also created a new kind of mass celebrity. Jurieu's love for the Marquise is known to all the characters in the film by his outburst on the radio when he arrives at Le Bourget after his solo transatlantic flight. In *Rules of the Game* the characters are initially connected together through the radio, before they are gathered together physically in Robert de la Chesnaye's country house. The film begins with the clamour of radio and ends with the croaking of frogs.

Radio is also present, I think, in the way the soundtrack of the film is itself constructed. The use of radio at the beginning of the film is simply the first instance of a series of inventive ways in which Renoir uses sound-sources in the film, 'diegetic' rather than 'non-diegetic', to use the technical terms. For example, de la Chesnaye's musical automata, at first sight simply decorative, come to play an important role with the display of his great mechanical musical instrument, the Limonaire, which plays music from *Die Fledermaus*. The mechanical organ becomes a metaphor for high society itself, a passionless world of automata, and its breakdown is paralleled by the breakdown of order in the society (although, at the same time, perhaps, it can also be seen as a nostalgic return to a rococo fascination with automata and mechanical toys, devices which gave the culture of the machine an air of ludic frivolity). In another key, the player piano which plays its phantom *Danse Macabre* prefigures the fatal ending of the film, the conclusion of the masquerade party by the death of Jurieu. The sound of hunting horns, boots and gunshots also echoes through the film. Finally, there is the extraordinary sequence in which Octave conducts a non-existent orchestra. *Rules of the Game* is one of the great films of sound cinema simply because of its command of sound itself.

This is another crucial feature which it shares with *Citizen Kane*. Welles, of course, came from a radio background and deliberately introduced innovative techniques of radio recording and mixing to the cinema. (And, in *Citizen Kane*, the *March of Time* newsreel at the beginning plays much the same role as the radio broadcast in *Rules of the Game*, both establishing the leading characters and the main lines of the story as well as placing private events in relation to the public sphere. Kane, too, echoes Chamberlain with his claim, 'There will be no war.') The year before *Rules of the Game* was made, in 1938, Rudolf Arnheim wrote his great essay on sound film, 'A New Laocoön: Artistic Composites and the Talking Film', where he argued that a completely new approach to film sound was needed, seeing its function not as realistic but as formative, and its role in film as one in which sound rather than dialogue should be dominant.[2] Film sound must develop its own aesthetic, rather than dominating the image through spoken dialogue. Arnheim was seeking a sound cinema which, in effect, would be silent film plus radio. Renoir and Welles produced the cinema which he wanted within the next few years, but in both cases their breakthrough was to be disregarded, only surfacing again much later, in the work of the 1960s New Wave, especially Jean-Luc Godard.

Within the film itself, radio serves two principal functions thematically. First, it contrasts the private world of the aristocracy with the public world of radio—and by implication, the realities of modern life. It intrudes and disturbs. Second, it acts as the vehicle of sincerity and honesty, as Jurieu blurts out his love for Christine. Here it contrasts with the closing speech of the film in which de la Chesnay papers over the reality of the tragedy that has occurred with a carefully, even exquisitely, phrased speech delivered to the very same audience of assembled guests, but designed to cover up the truth of what has actually happened. Public speech is the vehicle for truth, private speech is the vehicle for lies. It is truth which is the intruder, which disrupts the old order, and artifice (falsehood) which restores its equilibrium.

In 1933 the great modernist painter Fernand Léger observed that 'Cinema and aviation go arm in arm through life.' 'The cinema', he announced, 'is the machine age.' For Léger, aviation and the cinema were the two great contemporaneous mechanical inventions which had revolutionized the realm of human perception—allowing us to move through space with unprecedented velocity, to look at the world with a completely new perspective, and to change point-of-view in an instant while remaining seated in the same row of plush chairs. In *Rules of the Game*, the aviator is the crucial representative of modernity, the prospect of rapid and uncertain change. He is also a celebrity, a star, in the same sense that a film star is a celebrity, because of his command of the mass media. Unlike a film star, however, he is an authentic hero, one who has achieved fame, not as a vehicle for the fantasies of others, but for his extraordinary exploits, the realization of his own fantasies, his palpable authenticity. Jurieu is the modern hero—as the aviator was the modern hero for Brecht in his radio plays or for Auden or for Faulkner. *Rules of the Game* is cognate with Brecht's *Lindberghflug*, futurist aero-poetry, the heroic airmen of Yeats, Auden and Day Lewis, and, especially, Faulkner's 1935 *Pylon*, with its ironic contrast between tragic barnstorming aviators and the sordid carnival world of Mardi Gras.

This is perhaps not so obvious now as it was when *Rules of the Game* was first released. The image of the aviator has changed, first because of the Second World War (and the association of the aviator with mass destruction of non-military targets); second because of the arrival of mass cheap air travel in the 1960s and the consequent reduction of the plane from an image akin to Phaethon's chariot to that of a Greyhound bus burtling through the sky; third because of the increased technologization of aviation so that the pilot became more like an adjunct of the technology than a controller of it. By 1939 these changes had already begun—after the bombing of Guernica, the image of the aviator had already, perhaps, become threatening. Yet Jurieu clearly falls into an older tradition—the heroic explorer, ready to risk his life for the woman he loves, seeking out danger and conquering the skies for humanity, a modern *conquistador*. Jurieu is the heroic symbol of modernity, its celebrity icon, and yet at the same time a lonely, confused man, a solitary who has lost touch with the world below, the world of modern society.

In France there was a long tradition of aviator-heroes: Blériot, Santos-Dumont, Roland Garros and, in the 1930s, two artist-aviators, André Malraux and Antoine de Saint-Exupéry. Malraux, who flew in Cambodia, the Yemen and the Spanish Civil War, wrote at least two great novels and a fundamental book on art, as well as directing a film and ending up as a cabinet minister, but it is Saint-Exupéry I want to talk about in more detail. He is remembered today mainly for his children's book, *Le Petit Prince*, written right at the end of his career, but his literary reputation was founded on the series of books he wrote about aviation, which drew upon his own experiences as a pioneer pilot. Saint-Exupéry was both an aviator hero and a writer of outstanding talent. Moreover, at the time Renoir began work on *Rules of the Game*, they were already known personally to each other. In February 1939, when Renoir had completed around a third of the final script of the film, Saint-Exupéry published his *Terre des Hommes* (*Wind, Sand and Stars*), which was an instant critical success and commercial best-seller. In fact, drafts of much of the book had already been published in a newspaper, *Paris-Soir*, late the previous year.

Subsequently, in 1940, after Renoir had met Saint-Exupéry again in Lisbon, he shared a cabin with him on their transatlantic crossing and the first film project he tried to get off the ground in the United States was, precisely, a film based on *Wind, Sand and Stars*. Saint-Exupéry actually uses the phrase 'the rules of the game' at a crucial point in *Wind, Sand and Stars*. In the section of the book called 'The Centre of the Desert', he writes of his experiences at an isolated air-courier staging field in the Sahara, his own crash-landing in the endless sands and his encounter there with the Bedouin, who saved his life. In the desert, he must 'accept the rules of the game, the game formed us in its own image. To enter it is not to visit the oasis, but to make one's religion of a fountain'—i.e. the desert imposes its own values and its own order on those who enter it, a web of relationships which the Bedouin must observe or die. I can't demonstrate that Renoir read *Wind, Sand and Stars* as soon as it came out (or even the *Paris-Soir* articles) or that Saint-Exupéry thus directly influenced *Rules of the Game*, but we do know that he felt an affinity for Saint-Exupéry as a friend and that he wanted to film his friend's book.

We should also remember that during the First World War Renoir had himself been, first, an aerial photographer (and, by some accounts, cinematographer) and then a fully fledged pilot in the French air force. Later he reminisced about his experience at the flying school: 'Hitherto I had only been an observer, which I had not enjoyed at all. I was in love with machinery, and to be ferried about in the air by another man gave me the feeling of being shown a toy which I was not allowed to play with. Toys are only interesting if you can take them to pieces.' Renoir's career as a pilot in the reconnaissance squadron ended when a faulty landing in his wooden plane damaged his leg, aggravating injuries he had already incurred from a bullet wound. During the thirties, Renoir began to feel a certain nostalgia for those wartime days, mainly as a result of swapping stories with friends, and eventually he wrote a treatment with a wartime subject, a project which eventually turned into *La Grande Illusion*, a film about captured French pilots.

La Grande Illusion was released in 1937, only two years before *Rules of the Game*. The parts of the aviators were originally written for Jean Gabin and Pierre Fresnay, with a third part for Marcel Dalio as a Jewish prisoner of war named Rosenthal. Gabin actually wore Renoir's old pilot's tunic for the film. Erich von Stroheim played the German pilot who had shot the two Frenchmen down. Gaston Modot and Julien Carette also appeared in the film. Dalio, Modot and Carette, of course, all play significant roles in *Rules of the Game*: the Marquis (who has a Rosenthal in his ancestry), the gamekeeeper and the poacher. Gabin was offered the role of André Jurieu but turned it down (to make *Le Jour se Lève*) and was replaced by Toutain. We might think of Renoir himself as the replacement for Stroheim, two directors playing a role as actors. *La Grande Illusion* is a film about comradeship across class and ethnic lines, about the community of fliers created by their sense of a common experience, even if Stroheim must shoot the escaping prisoner at the end, as duty demands.

Rules of the Game is a film about the isolation of the aviator, who is shot because of a farcical misunderstanding, in a kind of parody of his own misunderstanding of the fashionable world.

In *Rules of the Game*, the aviator is a hero only when he is in the air. Once he lands, he reveals his complete inability to understand the socially acceptable 'rules of the game'. In *Rules of the Game* the phrase is used in a sense both similar and opposed to the way in which Saint-Exupéry uses it. There are rules which the aviator is incapable of understanding and his failure indeed leads to his death. But these rules do not come from the kind of existential risk which underlies those of the Bedouin, but from an elaborately devised system of etiquette and pretence. Reading Saint-Exupéry, one is reminded of another great film director who was also an aviator, Howard Hawks. Hawks celebrated the life of pioneer aviators in films like *Ceiling Zero* and *Only Angels Have Wings*, made in 1936 and 1939 respectively. It seems a strange coincidence that *Only Angels Have Wings*, which celebrates American mail-plane fliers in Latin America, should have been released the same year as *Wind, Sand and Stars*, which celebrates French mail-plane fliers in Africa and Latin America—and also, of course, *Rules of the Game* with its related aviator hero. Hawks, too, was a director much praised for his modernity—in cinematic terms. Hawks was also Hollywood's most successful director of screwball comedy, a genre based, as Stanley Cavell has shown, on ambivalence about marriage.[3]

Seen in this perspective, *Rules of the Game* looks like a strange hybrid in which a classic Hawksian hero, no-nonsense technological man, intrudes into an alien social world, an intrusion which proves fatal, when screwball comedy flips over from farce to tragedy. *Rules of the Game* can be measured against those typical Hawks films which, in Andrew Sarris's words, 'have quasi-suicidal climaxes in which characters accept fatal missions, but the moral arithmetic balances out [i.e. they have not recklessly chosen death] because in each instance the martyr is a replacement in an obligatory situation'.[4] In other words, once Octave had refused the assignation with Christine, André Jurieu could not honourably refuse to go to his death. The comparison between Hawks and Renoir is not as far-fetched as it may sound. It was, after all, the very same critics whose re-evaluation of both directors elevated them into the canon. Moreover, Eric Rohmer, perhaps after André Bazin the most important *Cahiers* critic, mentions films by Renoir and Hawks in one sentence as early as 1948. The context is a defence of ambiguity in the cinema, and the use by both directors of a gap between sound and image. Interestingly enough, this article was published in Sartre's journal *Les Temps Modernes*, and Sartre's own debt to *Wind, Sand and Stars*, with its proto-existentialist ethic, is a matter of record. *Rules of the Game* could certainly be interpreted in this light, as a film based on inchoate existentialist concepts of bad faith, contingency and commitment.

Thematically, the embedding of modernity in the cinema can be seen, in a general sense, in terms of the supersession of a Manichaean cinema of clear moral distinctions, free will and effective action (classical Hollywood) by a more complex cinema of moral ambiguity, the entanglement of necessity with freedom, and the mismatching of actions with goals. The modernity of *Rules of the Game* stems precisely from these characteristics. Traditionally, Renoir is seen as a humanist director, optimistic and confident in human potential. There is indeed a great deal to be said for this assessment. It is clear, for example, that fraternity, a sense of human solidarity, was important to Renoir in life and art (as it was to Hawks and Saint-Exupéry), and certainly during the early years of the Popular Front he committed himself to a clear moral and political choice. In *La Règle du Jeu*, however, this limpid clarity and sympathetic confidence is clouded and challenged. A dark side begins to overwhelm the enjoyment and good humour, the happy, sunny world of his father's painting. A sense of tragic fatality begins to dominate.

Renoir was not alone in this. A look at English writing at the same time, between Munich and the outbreak of war, reveals the same sense of fatality. In 1939, for instance, Henry Green wrote his novel *Party Going*, in which a group of spoiled, rich, bright young things are stranded by fog on a train journey to the Continent.[5] They wait for the fog to clear in the station hotel, flirting and drinking, while an onlooker comments, 'What targets . . . what targets for a bomb.' Or T. S. Eliot in *The Idea of A Christian Society* (also 1939), reflecting on Munich: 'What had happened was something in which one was deeply implicated and responsible. It was not, I repeat, a criticism of the government, but a doubt of the validity of a civilization.'[6] Or Virginia Woolf's *Between the Acts* (written later, just before her suicide, but set in June 1939, the month when Renoir edited *Rules of the Game*), with its interruption of a village pageant by low-flying planes, its repeated evocation of startling violence—a snake trying to swallow a toad in parallel with talk of Daladier and the falling franc—and its delineation of a group of solid citizens completely unable to grasp the tragic dimensions of the historic moment in which they find themselves.[7]

Renoir had made the acquaintance of another film-director shortly before beginning work on *Rules of the Game*. This was the maker of the great documentary films *Nanook of the North*, *Tabu* (co-directed with Murnau) and *Man of Aran*—Robert Flaherty. The two men got on very well and became close friends. At first sight, *Rules of the Game* has little to do with Flaherty. Yet there is a sense in which *Rules of the Game* can be seen as a kind of ethnographic film, the portrait of a vanishing, doomed society, just like Flaherty's films. Looked at this way, de la Chesnaye's country house, La Colinière, is an idyllic society, like those of the Canadian Inuit, or the peoples of Tahiti or the isle of Aran. But, unlike them, it is portrayed as unnatural, artificial, far removed from honest work or passion. It is bound to end in tragedy, despite its attractive features. Moreover, it is unable to resist. It is dancing on the edge of a volcano. Its resistance to the intrusion of modernity cannot save it. Gradually an atmosphere of nostalgia, of admiration for the charm of bygone ways, gives way to bitterly pointed exposé.

At the same time, Renoir described *Rules of the Game* as 'my most improvised film'. Like Flaherty's films, it strives to capture life in the raw, with a sense of events unfolding naturally, spontaneously. The script was written and changed while the film was being made and it drew on the invention of its actors, including, of course, Renoir himself. It is an ethnographic film in the sense that, despite its intricate plot, it truly tries to capture an impression of life as it is lived. This was only possible because it was the film over which Renoir had the most personal control—at least, till it fell into the hands of producer and distributor—and on which he embarked co-operatively with a group of his most trusted collaborators and friends. As a project, as the founding film of his new co-operative venture, it represented another kind of isolated society, a utopia of fraternity and creativity. It is this tension between utopian dream and tragic reality which permitted Renoir to make his masterpiece, a tension which ran both through the film as dramatic narrative and through the historic experience of making and releasing the film. It was an unalloyed auteur film, conceived and produced outside the film industry. Seemingly doomed, it became the classic *film maudit*. However, not only did it survive its time, but, out of the ashes, it recreated the cinema itself, modern, progressive and free.

Finally, I want to return to the opening sequence of the film in order to contrast it with the closing sequence. The opening sequence, as we have seen, shows André Jurieu as the modern hero, the national idol and celebrity. Confronted with the radio interviewer, he blurts out the truth, unable to conceal his emotions, irredeemably honest, unable to engage in the charade of sophistication which 'society' demands. Across Paris, his audience listen with amusement or concern, dimly aware that a fuse has been lit which must somehow be extinguished if calm and order are to be maintained. At the end of the film there is another public speech, this time from the Marquis, standing on the steps leading up into the house, addressing the same company of listeners, now assembled as guests to hear a version of events which is completely fabricated, delivered with utterly cynical charm. Only one of the listeners, from a younger generation, has been unable, at first, to dissemble and conceal her emotions. To the others, da la Chesnaye appears the last of a dying breed, a consummate exemplar of the skills and attitudes of his class, as he veils the tragedy of Jurieu's death with a tissue of lies.

Renoir himself, the failed artist, has already left with the poacher, Marceau. The poacher is a recurrent figure in Renoir's films, a character with whom he clearly identified. Artists, after all, can be seen as poachers, getting away with things, ignoring the rules, indulging themselves, whereas producers and censors are like gamekeepers, endlessly negative, powerful figures who exert their power to constrict creativity and play. Octave, Renoir's alter ego in the film, is himself, in a sense, a poacher, but a failed one, a *raté*. He gives up his reckless attempt to 'poach' Christine from her husband, offering her instead, in an act of fatal generosity, to his friend, André Jurieu. The gamekeeper, Schumacher, duly shoots the poacher and order is restored, at the cost of a tragic misunderstanding. But the misunderstanding derives from masquerade, from things being presented as other than they are, from surface appearances mismatched with reality, from *commedia dell'arte* encountering the dark side of modernity, its grim truth.

12

THE LAST NEW WAVE

For many reasons, British cinema has never been regarded as an art cinema with the same value as other European cinemas: French, Italian, German—or indeed, in a different context, Japanese. Indeed, many critics and historians have simply taken at face value François Truffaut's notorious dictum that the idea of British cinema is a contradiction in terms. In this chapter, I want to argue against this negative judgement. In my view, British cinema is as important, aesthetically, as that of any other European country. In order to argue this, however, I shall need to rewrite the whole history of British film, schematically demoting the work of some periods, genres and directors, and—conversely—promoting that of others whose films have been unjustly neglected. Above all, I want to argue that the essential spirit of British film has not been one of 'realism', as is generally assumed, but rather one of 'romanticism' and fantasy. Moreover, I want to claim that there was indeed the break-through of a British 'New Wave', but it occurred, not in the sixties (with the films of Anderson, Reisz, Richardson, etc.), as is often hopefully suggested, but, instead, in the eighties, during the Thatcher years, with the work of Peter Greenaway, Derek Jarman, Mike Leigh and others.

Independent film-makers of the eighties reacted strongly against the effects of Thatcherism. They responded in their films to the imposition of market criteria in every sector of society, to political authoritarianism, to the 'two nations' project of Thatcherism and to the leading role of the

City, in films as various as Greenaway's *The Cook, the Thief, his Wife and her Lover* (1989), Jarman's *The Last of England* (1987), Terry Gilliam's *Brazil* (1985), Frears and Kureishi's *Sammy and Rosie Get Laid* (1988), Mike Leigh's *High Hopes* (1988), Mulvey and Wollen's *Crystal Gazing* (1980) and Reece Auguiste's *Twilight City* (1989). Paradoxically, these are all London films, precisely because of the success of Thatcher's polarization of the country between North and South—a polarization which, as shown in the films, is doubled back within the metropolis itself. Their roots can be traced back to the sixties—to the art world, the cabaret and television satire boom, experimental theatre and the post-1968 avant-garde. It was in these areas that a modernist impulse had finally made itself felt in British culture and had eventually combined with an emphasis on the visual dimension of television, theatre and film. Together, these films provide a definitive picture of the Thatcherization of London.

Negatively, Thatcherism (and its soft-spoken footnote, Majorism) aimed to destroy the post-war Keynesian settlement which both Labour and Conservative governments had respected, to dismantle the public services provided by the state and to eliminate obtrusive foci of political opposition.[1] Positively, Thatcherism combined three elements: (1) an economic 'unregulated market' neo-liberalism; (2) a politically neo-conservative authoritarianism; and (3) a social 'two nations' project, dividing the country geographically, between North and South, and socially, in terms of the labour market, between a de-unionized 'peripheral' sector and a 'core' company union sector. The 'two nations' project, of course, hit ethnic minorities especially hard and encouraged a sharp division between 'inner city' and suburb. Thatcherism was a radical modernizing movement in a very specific sense. It aimed to modernize the finance, service, communications and international sectors of the economy, but not domestic manufacturing industry or civil society. New 'core' industries, largely dependent on international capital, were consolidated in the South, while the North of the country was left as a peripheral, often decaying hinterland. The South, organized around the City of London, traditionally the hegemonic pole of the economy, was increasingly decoupled from domestic manufacturing industry. Thus Thatcherism, terrified that the City would lose even more of its world role given the continuing relative decline of the British economy, had an Atlantic rather than a European outlook in its international policy and aimed to provide the point of entry into Europe for both American and Japanese capital. Money, rather than goods, was paramount. Socially and visually, the citadels of international capital were abruptly juxtaposed with the decay of London's old industries and docklands.

The Thatcher years provoked a long-delayed efflorescence of British film, still largely unrecognized in Britain itself. It can be seen, I believe, as a 'British New Wave', coming long after the idea of a 'New Wave' had crumbled away in most other European countries. The first 'New Wave', of course, exploded on the world from France in the 'Miraculous Year' of 1959, which launched Truffaut's *Les Quatre Cents Coups*, Resnais's *Hiroshima, Mon Amour* and Chabrol's *Les Cousins*. Godard's *A Bout de Souffle* followed in 1960, also the year of *L'Avventura*, the first film of Antonioni's trilogy. This, in turn, drew attention to the work of Pasolini and, soon, Bertolucci. A few years later, Fassbinder, Syberberg and Wenders were grouped together as the core of a somewhat belated 'German New Wave'. Since then critics gathered at festivals around the world have sought out 'New Waves' wherever they could, broadening their net to include the Third World and hailing the Brazilian, African and Chinese 'New Waves'. No one thought of looking again at Britain which, having missed the bus in the sixties, could hardly expect a second chance. Besides, the British were notoriously unvisual, unartistic and uncinematic. What was it Truffaut had said? 'Aren't the words "Britain" and "Cinema" incompatible?'[2]

As I noted, it has sometimes been argued that the 'Angry Young Men' films of 1959–63 were the 'British New Wave', rather than the 'Jeune Cinéma Anglais', as the French, who certainly ought to have known, dubbed it at the time.[3] Yet surely to call these films 'New Wave' is both inappropriate and misleading. First, the idea of a 'New Wave' was intimately linked to the project of directorial 'authorship'. A good case could be made for Lindsay Anderson as a bilious but authentic 'auteur' (something he himself might well deny in a fume of irascibility), but nobody has ever made a serious claim for the auteurist credentials of Reisz, Richardson, Schlesinger *et al*. In fact, it would be much more plausible to argue for the despised producer-director duo of Relph and

Dearden as auteurs, film-makers whose 'social problem' cycle, beginning with *The Blue Lamp* in 1950 and continuing, via *Sapphire* (1959) and *Victim* (1961), to *A Place to Go* in 1963, preceded and paralleled the work of the 'Angry Young Men' group.[4] Moreover, in 'daring' to deal with race and homosexuality, for whatever headline-grabbing reasons, they showed greater courage, prescience and, indeed, political sense, than their more celebrated and supposedly more progressive and innovative younger colleagues.

Second, the idea of a 'New Wave' involved putting film first and not subordinating it to literature or theatre, as Truffaut argued in his notorious polemic against adaptation in *Arts* magazine.[5] The 'Angry Young Men' films, however, plainly put film second. Their success was directly derived from the success of the original plays and novels by Osborne, Amis, Braine and Sillitoe. *Look Back in Anger*, *Room at the Top*, *The Entertainer*, *A Taste of Honey*, *Saturday Night and Sunday Morning* and *The Loneliness of the Long Distance Runner* came out in their original forms between May 1956 and September 1959. The film versions which came out after a three-year interval, between 1959 and 1962, clearly depended for their initial impact on the pre-publicity and acclaim already generated by their literary sources. Moreover Woodfall Films, beginning with *Look Back in Anger* (1959), set a pattern by having the original writers first collaborate on the film scripts with professional script-writers and then write them entirely. Osborne, Sillitoe and Delaney all wrote their own scripts for the film adaptations of their work. The same procedure was followed with *This Sporting Life* (1963), written by the author of the novel, David Storey, and directed by Lindsay Anderson, and with John Schlesinger's *Billy Liar* (1963), written by Keith Waterhouse and Willis Hall, based on their own play of Waterhouse's novel! This film of an adaptation of an adaptation is about as far from Truffaut's ideal of auteurism as you can get.

Third, both critics and the directors themselves explicitly justified the 'Angry Young Men' films in terms of 'realism'. Their attitude reflected an old shibboleth and plaint of the British cinema establishment, both in production and reception, best summed up by Michael Balcon's programmatic preference for 'realism' over 'tinsel'.[6] This system of value, though most strongly entrenched on the left, ran all the way across the political spectrum. For the right, as for the left, the aesthetic preference for 'realism' was bound up with nationalism. 'Tinsel', of course, was identified with Hollywood escapism and, in contrast, 'realism' evoked local pride and sense of community. It meant showing ourselves honestly to ourselves, rather than indulging in other people's alien and deceptive fantasies. British critics praised films they liked in terms of their realism and damned those they did not as escapist trash. The French New Wave, however, aimed to transcend this shallow antinomy. The third term which made this possible was, of course, 'modernism'. The films of Resnais and Godard, even when adaptations, placed themselves clearly in a modernist tradition, as did Truffaut's crucial *Jules et Jim* (1962). Resnais, to take the most obvious example, collaborated with writers like Robbe-Grillet and Duras. The *Cahiers* group followed the path blazed by the 'Nouveau Roman' and recognized Jean Cocteau as their godfather. Yet in Britain supposedly progressive film-makers fetishized the second-rate literature of regionalists, realists and reactionaries.[7]

The history of modernism in Europe followed a definite geographical pattern which reflected an underlying historical reality.[8] The more a country felt the ambition to catch up economically and culturally, the more an aggressively avant-garde section of its intelligentsia embraced and radicalized a version of modernism. After the collapse of the old absolutist regimes, avant-garde artists often rejected the search for new modes of personal expression in favour of a depersonalized rationalism or functionalism. They attempted to subordinate the arts to industrial and technological needs and imperatives, and to merge the artist with the masses. Thus in backward Russia, the avant-garde moved rapidly from Symbolism to Futurism and then, after the impact of the October Revolution, to Constructivism. In Italy Futurism developed its own technocratic ideology and, in Germany, Expressionism gave way to the Bauhaus. In France, where the *ancien régime* had been toppled more than a century before, Cubism was followed by the much weaker current of Purism, around Le Corbusier, but also, more significantly, by Surrealism. The surrealists, like the constructivists or the later Bauhaus artists, lined up on the left politically, and yet reacted with hostility to the norms of modern industrial development, unlike their counterparts in Russia or

Germany. In Britain, after the very brief flurry of Vorticism, modernism never took root at all in any lasting way.

Britain, of course, was both the homeland of the Industrial Revolution, the pioneer of manufacturing capitalism, and the European country with the most remote and attenuated experience of absolutism. Modernism, in its pure form, appealed to very few in Britain, especially few in England. England's most committed modernists were very often expatriates— Eliot, Pound, H.D., Wyndham Lewis. In the visual arts, Vorticism rapidly dissolved and modern currents were smoothly amalgamated into the English landscape tradition, as in the work of Ben Nicholson or Henry Moore. A mild and heavily romanticized anglicization of Surrealism surfaced briefly and then sputtered to a halt. In the world of literature and in taste-setting journalism, there was a bloodless transfer of power to the Bloomsbury group, within the traditional intelligentsia itself, and an increasingly emollient modernism was assimilated into the ongoing high culture with hardly a break. Indeed, the most powerful and effective protagonists of modern literature—Eliot and Leavis— argued for modernism in frankly traditionalist terms. Far from wanting a break with the past, they saw modernism as the culmination of a long national literary history. This history now needed only to be reassessed retrospectively, rather than brusquely overthrown. Moreover, modernism was treated as something which had already happened and been absorbed, rather than as an ongoing project.

Modernism first impinged on British film culture during the silent period with the London Film Society and the small journal *Close Up*. But the coming of sound quickly wiped out these tender plants, as it did much stronger film avant-gardes elsewhere. The *Close Up* circle, around the writers Bryher and H.D., produced Kenneth MacPherson's *Borderline* (1930), financed by Bryher (then married to MacPherson), and starring H.D., alongside Paul and Eslanda Robeson. It remains the one outstanding British avant-garde film of the period.[9] However, *Close Up* folded shortly thereafter, and its contributors lost heart and dispersed. Meanwhile, after the collapse of the London Film Society, its moving spirit, the irrepressible Iris Barry, left for New York in 1930.[10] There she met Philip Johnson at a cocktail party and, soon afterwards, she was hired by

Alfred Barr to run the new Museum of Modern Art's film programme. Thus the modernist impulse was transferred from London to America where the Museum played a crucial role in the survival of avant-garde film through the thirties, enabling it to resurface again in the forties. In Britain, of course, this did not happen.

The London Film Society's most significant outcome was its impact on Alfred Hitchcock, a habitual and doubtless punctual attender at screenings. There Hitchcock not only mingled with the cultural elite but also absorbed modernist aesthetic ideas, which he later attempted to nurture within narrative film. Hitchcock experimented with sound in his first talking picture, *Blackmail* (1929), but soon retreated into conformity. Nonetheless, once he felt his career in the industry was secure, both in Britain and subsequently in the United States, he cunningly contrived a place for experimental ideas inserted into commercial genre films—the Salvador Dali dream sequence in *Spellbound* (1945), the ten-minute takes in *Rope* (1948, produced by another Film Society alumnus, Sidney Bernstein), the 'pure cinema' project of *Rear Window* (1954), the montage murder sequence in *Psycho* (1960) and so on. Hitchcock's collaborator, Ivor Montagu, whom he met through the Film Society, also worked with Eisenstein, many echoes of whom appear in Hitchcock's own work. But, in general terms, Hitch seems to have drawn the conclusion that modernist experiments were best contrived as a kind of illicit contraband, which he could smuggle in and secretly enjoy, while lapping up the praise and the dollars for his popular success within the mainstream of the industry.

During the thirties, the surviving vestiges of twenties modernism were channelled into the state-sponsored British documentary movement. John Grierson, a Scot, remained more open to modernism than other British producers and hired co-workers (like Alberto Cavalcanti, a Brazil-ian, and Len Lye, a New Zealander) who had impeccable experimental film credentials: Cavalcanti's *Rien que les Heures* (1926) was a landmark of the French avant-garde and Lye had made his pioneer abstract film, *Tusalava*, for the London Film Society in 1928. Nonetheless, the main drift of Grierson's project was to subordinate modernism (in its Russian form) to realism and to national propaganda. Grierson was impressed by Eisenstein's vision of an epic silent cinema based on the masses and achieving its dramatic effects through formal means rather than character identification, and he believed this aesthetic could be transposed to fit British documentary and propaganda film. Grierson's documentaries aimed to represent the society at large rather than particular individuals. They were meant to inform rather than entertain. In this context, he could draw productively from Eisenstein and Pudovkin. Similarly, other modernists could have a role to play within his team. Thus, in this unlikely setting were to be found artists like Lye, W. H. Auden (who wrote the voice-over for *Night Mail*, 1935), and Humphrey Jennings (a chief organizer of the London Surrealist exhibition of 1936).[11]

To critics at the time, Grierson's efforts seemed to combine the realism they desired with a prudent preservation of modernist elements in an acceptable, marginal role. Meanwhile, the Hungarian émigré Alexander Korda became the standard-bearer for narrative film in Britain, launching a series of costume dramas celebrating the popular high spots of British history and a cycle of extravagant imperialist epics, mainly directed by his brother, Zoltan Korda.[12] Korda's initial success with *The Private Life of Henry VIII* (1933) sprang from a canny combination of grandiose costume spectacle with vernacular music-hall comedy, but he was never able to repeat it and his backers, Prudential Insurance, abruptly withdrew their support in 1937. Korda, however, did succeed in inspiring the British cinema world with the idea that they could and should set their sights on Hollywood as a model to be emulated. He pointed the way towards Rank's brave attempt to take on Hollywood after the war and, more recently, the pathetic false dawn of David Puttnam. Meanwhile, British cinema continued to churn out a series of 'quota quickies': George Formby vehicles and vernacular pot-boilers for the domestic audience. But when the deadly grip of heritage drama and pierhead comedy finally broke down during the 1939–45 war, it was romanticism, not realism, that carried the day:[13] whether the operatic Technicolor romanticism of 'The Archers' and Gainsborough or the contorted black-and-white 'man-on-the-run' romanticism of the 'spiv' film and Carol Reed. The spiv film was a riveting British equivalent to *film noir*—and a 'spiv', I should explain, was a petty racketeer involved in the post-war black economy. He wore flash ties, suits with wide lapels and a sneer or grin.

The war years saw a revival of English romanticism in response to the need for an idealized reaffirmation of British history and shared values (as perceived within the dominant ideology) and, on the other hand, for release into fantasy and dream to relieve the stress, hardship and agony of war. During the war, film production was necessarily limited, but nonetheless the national mood was much better conveyed by the visual ambition and expansive romanticism of Olivier's *Henry V* (1944) than by the restrained grittiness of Coward and Lean's *In Which We Serve* (1942), however much the critics may have welcomed the realism they felt that it conveyed.[14] After the war was won, still sheltered from American competition, British cinema blossomed. This period saw not only Powell and Pressburger's trilogy of *Black Narcissus* (1947), *The Red Shoes* (1948) and *Gone to Earth* (1950), in which a series of intensely desirous women are thwarted and finally plunge over the edge to their death, but also Carol Reed's trilogy of *Odd Man Out* (1947), *The Fallen Idol* (1948) and *The Third Man* (1949), in which appealingly desperate heroes are caught in paranoid labyrinths of pursuit and betrayal.

This movement in the cinema ran parallel with movements in poetry, painting and dance, exemplified, for example, by the work of Dylan Thomas, Francis Bacon and Frederick Ashton. Thomas was the leader of the 'New Apocalyptic' movement in poetry, which drew on Surrealism to create a new style of visionary writing. In the 1950s Michael Powell asked Thomas to collaborate with him on a 'composed film', along with Picasso as designer and Stravinsky as composer, and, although the project never came to fruition, it is emblematic of the affinities I am talking about. Surrealism was an influence on Powell, as it was also on Jennings, who turned to neo-romanticism in the 1940s. Powell also collaborated with Robert Helpmann on the choreography of *The Red Shoes*, Powell's most internationally successful film, and with Frederick Ashton on *The Tales of Hoffmann* in 1951. During the same period, the neo-romantic painters Leslie Hurry, Robert Medley, John Minton and John Piper also designed the posters for a series of neo-romantic films: *Dead of Night*, *Saraband for Dead Lovers*, *The Loves of Joanna Godden*, etc.

It is important to stress the strength of this 'new romanticism', as the parallel movement in painting and poetry is called, because it partly explains the success of the 'Angry Young Men' films in the next decade. In 1945 the top box-office film was *The Seventh Veil*, a sublimely over-the-top drama of female desire, classical music and psychoanalysis. The same year, Cavalcanti, having left Grierson's documentary unit, made a small masterpiece of the grotesque in *Dead of Night* and followed this up, in 1947, with *They Made Me a Fugitive*, the definitive expressionist 'man-on-the-run' film. Thus even a hero of 'documentary realism' showed himself the master of 'docklands romanticism' (along with Robert Hamer and his *It Always Rains on Sunday*, 1947). British films, none of them remotely 'realist', dominated the domestic box-office for four straight years, until American political and economic power became irresistible and the British finally capitulated to Washington arm-twisting and a Hollywood boycott in 1948.[15] Both *The Third Man* and *Gone to Earth* were co-productions with Selznick and, apart from them, the most impressive films from 1949 onward were Hitchcock's transatlantic *Under Capricorn* (1949), Dassin's *Night and the City* (1950) and Huston's series of 'runaway productions' beginning with *The African Queen* (1952). The stage was now set for the critics at last to welcome a truly 'realist' counterblast to a victorious Hollywood, one which simultaneously reacted against the romanticism and aestheticism of earlier British film.

However, the realist Angry Young Men were not the only cultural counter-current of the fifties. In 1956, the year that *Look Back in Anger* was produced at the Royal Court Theatre (first performance 8 May), the exhibition *This Is Tomorrow* opened at the Whitechapel Gallery (8 August).[16] This was the culmination of the work of the Independent Group of artists, architects and critics and the emblematic beginning of British Pop Art. Both the Angry Young Men and the Independent Group, founded in 1952, reacted strongly against the diluted modernism of the traditional intelligentsia, a decaying amalgam of Bloomsbury and Cold War pieties. However, while the Angry Young Men turned back towards a provincial Little Englandism, the Independent Group openly welcomed American consumer culture in their struggle against the English countryside and the villa in Tuscany, celebrating science fiction, Hollywood movies, tail-fins and advertising. The Angry Young Men were resentfully anti-American, although they did energize their English populism with a taste for traditional jazz, uncontaminated either by Tin Pan Alley or by post-bebop modernism. 'Trad' enlivened the soundtracks of Reisz's *Momma Don't Allow* (1955) and Richardson's *Look Back in Anger*

(1959). Visitors to *This Is Tomorrow*, on the other hand, were greeted by a giant *Robbie the Robot* (from the sci-fi movie *Forbidden Planet*) and a wall montage celebrating CinemaScope.

Pop Art was a way to outflank the dominant elite culture by turning simultaneously to popular consumer culture and to the avant-garde tradition. Reyner Banham, for instance, carefully placed pop technophilia in the context of the Modern Movement, and Richard Hamilton, the pioneer pop artist, turned back to Marcel Duchamp as a revered ancestor. Pop broke through to a wider cultural audience with the 1961 appearance of a new phalanx of artists, the Young Contemporaries, encouraged by Alloway, and then Ken Russell's benchmark television show *Pop Goes the Easel*, the following year. In retrospect, we see that the non-existent British 'New Wave' of the time would have been much more closely linked to pop than to the Angry Young Men. Pop prefigured the sixties transformation of British culture.[17] When the transformation came, however, it was expatriates who showed the way, at least as far as the cinema was concerned: Richard Lester, Canadian, especially with *The Knack* (1965), Joseph Losey, American, who made *Modesty Blaise* (1966), and Antonioni, whose *Blow-Up* (1967) became the archetypal film of the decade. These directors aligned themselves much more closely with their French counterparts. Their scripts derived from absurdism rather than realism. Local directors appeared very late in the decade—Cammell and Roeg's *Performance* was shot in 1968, but its distributors cravenly delayed its release until 1970. Alongside Roeg, John Boorman and Ken Russell eventually developed into 'auteurs', but basically they were neo-romantics (low-key and high-key, respectively), clearly anti-Kitchen Sink, but only incidentally modernist.

We can better see the long-term importance of the sixties for British film in the subsequent work of Derek Jarman and Peter Greenaway.[18] Both went to art school in this period, Jarman after getting a Literature degree at London University, in deference to his family, and Greenaway in preference to going to university, in defiance of his family. Jarman and Greenaway both set out to make films within the visual arts tradition. The dominant painters in Jarman's world were gay—David Hockney and Patrick Procktor. He was also close to Ossie Clarke on the fashion scene, which interlocked tightly with the art world during the sixties. Hockney's significance, of course, sprang not only from his success as a painter, but also from his public declaration of homosexuality and its increasingly crucial presence in his art. Jarman himself, however, was not a pop painter, but a landscapist who moved towards abstraction—an abstraction fully achieved in his astounding film *Blue*, released in 1993, in which the screen remains blue throughout, reflecting both Jarman's growing blindness and his 1960s memories of Yves Klein. His own early paintings show monoliths on English 'west country' hills—descendants of Paul Nash or Henry Moore. Jarman was deeply attached to the landscape round Swanage in Dorset (which appears many times in his films), where he spent many childhood holidays and whose unique features Paul Nash also celebrated in his surrealist paintings. Jarman's own landscape tour de force at Prospect Cottage on Dungeness, a garden of Elizabethan flowers, stones and driftwood, over which looms a massive nuclear power station, recreates the surrealist world of Chirico, with the respect for the 'genius loci' always felt by Nash. There is a lasting tension in Jarman's work between a delirious neo-romantic Englishness and a pop modernism, always in touch with 'street culture'. His two influential teachers at university were Eric Mottram, who introduced him to William Burroughs's *Naked Lunch*, and Niklaus Pevsner who directed him to Gothic cathedrals, Lincoln, Canterbury or Ely. The eerie elegiac tone of his late films has its roots in this metaphysical historicism and in his deeply ambivalent nostalgia for childhood, fed by an intransigent anger and a will-to-resist rooted in gay culture.

In his films, rather than his paintings, Derek Jarman first articulated the gay world in which he lived, its tastes, routines, extravagances and crises. Film-making began for him as a personal art of home movies, strongly contrasted with his professional work as a set designer for Ken Russell. The crucial turning-point came when he turned down Russell's invitation to design *Tommy* (1975) and determined instead to make his own first feature, *Sebastiane* (1976). What strikes me now about *Sebastiane* is no longer its place as a pioneering transposition into film of age-old visual motifs aestheticizing beautiful, tormented boys in Mediterranean settings, but its 'high camp' silver Latin dialogue track. To me, this makes the film like an opera whose libretto is in a foreign language, foregrounding the role of performance and visual composition. Dialogue always seemed an awkward necessity for Jarman, and he increasingly became happiest with pre-existing literary texts—*The Tempest* (1979) or *The Angelic Conversation* (1985)—or, as with *War Requiem* (1989), musical texts. (Here he carries out Michael Powell's old ambition of the 'composed film', in which the music preceded the filming, as in episodes of *Black Narcissus* or, of course, *The Red Shoes*.)[19] Greenaway, on the other hand, is fascinated by words and overloads his soundtrack with dialogue, sometimes as though the characters were mouthpieces for an abstruse disputation taking place outside the film.

Peter Greenaway was much more directly influenced by sixties pop artists, such as R. B. Kitaj (after whom a star is named in *Drowning by Numbers*, 1988) and Tom Phillips, the creator of *A Humument*, with whom he collaborated on his television *Dante's Inferno* (1989), the pilot project for *Prospero's Books* (1991).[20] In Greenaway's case, the fascination centres on artists who explore the relationship between words and images, between literature and painting. Greenaway discovered Kitaj's paintings at the same Marlborough Gallery show in 1963 that Derek Jarman also visited. Like Greenaway, Kitaj maintains an impenetrably enigmatic relation to his sources.[21] Like Greenaway, too, he is drawn to the arcana of old engravings, incunabula, emblems or maps. Kitaj has sought to people his paintings with imaginary characters, like those in novels, who appear in a series of works. In the same way, Greenaway also has his cast of imaginary characters, presided over by Tulse Luper, who crop up in film after film, sometimes in central roles, sometimes as fanciful marginalia. At heart, Greenaway, like Kitaj, is a collagist, juxtaposing images drawn from some fantastic archive, tracing erudite coincidental narratives within his material, bringing together Balthus and Borges in a bizarre collocation of arcane eroticism and *trompe-l'oeil* high modernism. Kitaj also, of course, is a cinephile, through whose painting *Kenneth Anger and Michael Powell* (1973) we can trace a strange connection between the myth-worlds of Greenaway and Jarman.

At first sight, Derek Jarman and Peter Greenaway have little in common. Indeed, Jarman was notorious for his vitriolic attacks on Greenaway. Yet both were products of sixties art schools, both were trained as painters, both developed a strong visual style and dedicated themselves to making personal films marginal to the populist mainstream of the industry, both paid court to narrative while shamelessly revealing that their true interests lay elsewhere. Both can be seen, in a certain sense, as modernists. Both, in another sense, can also be seen as neo-romantics, steeped in a personal vision of the English landscape, endlessly revisiting and rejecting the temptations of Victorianism and antiquarianism, returning much more willingly to their memories of childhood, mediated through home movies and family snapshots for Jarman, and through pored-over children's book illustrations for Greenaway. Derek Jarman accuses Greenaway of succumbing to antiquarianism in *The Draughtsman's Contract* (1982), a vice he attributes first to Poussin and thereafter to the Victorians. In contrast, he cites his own *Caravaggio* (1986) with its contemporary references on image track and soundtrack, its obvious debt to Pasolini, its inauthentic modernity. But Greenaway does not see *The Draughtsman's Contract* as authentic. On the contrary, he reacts angrily to a comparison with Kubrick's *Barry Lyndon* (1975)—'My film is about excess: excess in the language, excess in the landscape, which is much too green—we used special green filters—there is no historical realism in the costumes, the women's hair-styles are exaggerated in their height, the costumes are extreme. I wanted to make a very artificial film.'²² In the same interview, he dismisses *Chariots of Fire* (1981, also Derek Jarman's most hated film) as reactionary and lacking any real aesthetic, even that of a *Saturday Night and Sunday Morning* (1960).

The difference between them, of course, lies in their divergent strategies for avoiding antiquarianism. Derek Jarman explicitly modernizes, introduces contemporary references and false touches, interprets Caravaggio's life and art through a filter of topical and personal preoccupations and tastes. Greenaway, on the contrary, exaggerates the archaism, pushing all the elements into an unreal and peculiarly inauthentic realm of caricature and pastiche, trying to turn a Restoration comedy into *Last Year in Marienbad* (1961). *Prospero's Books* follows in the same tradition by recreating the high Renaissance world of masque, pageant and emblem in exaggerated splendour, while at the same time placing the play within Prospero's mind and experimenting with video effects and infography. The risks run by the rival strategies are clear. Jarman opens himself to the charge of anachronistic travesty, Greenaway to that of lavish overindulgence. When I saw *The Draughtsman's Contract* at its première at the Edinburgh Film Festival, I was nauseated by the excess of Englishness, the hyperbolic heaping of English language on English acting on English landscape on English country-house murder on English preciousness and whimsy, the dilettantish celebration of eccentricity and games-playing. The modernist dimension of Greenaway's work, the side which takes us towards Hollis Frampton's *Zorn's Lemma* or towards the game-playing Oulipo writers in France, towards an intricate conceptualism or a Nabokovian dandyism, can appear over-ingenious and wilfully bizarre— another rerun of Lewis Carroll, yet with its shadow-side made ever more apparent in erotic tableaux and Jacobean cruelty.[23]

Derek Jarman was much more intimately linked to 'new romanticism'.[24] His most prominent disciples (John Maybury and Cerith Wyn Evans) were part of the 'Blitz crowd' and his own work is related not only to this 'club scene' new romanticism, but to a much deeper, more long-lasting tradition: to the medieval poets, to the Elizabethans (not only Marlowe and Shakespeare, but magicians, alchemists and herbalists), Blake and Shelley, the late Victorians, the Apocalyptics and, of course, Michael Powell and Emeric Pressburger. Modernism in Britain has prospered precisely in alliance with the underground currents of this broad national-romantic strain in the culture. As I have observed, neo-romanticism fitted intimately with the experience of the war, in poems by Edith Sitwell, Dylan Thomas or T. S. Eliot, in drawings or paintings by Moore and Piper, in films by Humphrey Jennings and Powell and Pressburger. This wartime mood still runs through Jarman's films, especially in *The Last of England* (1987), with its recurrent imagery of a blitzed and burning London, recalling also the Great Fire of 1666, the burning of the Houses of Parliament painted by Turner and the burning down of his own studio. 'Fire turned nasty.' It was no longer the comforting glow of childhood hearth and picnic bonfire. The palette of *The Last of England* too, like that of Jarman's later paintings, is all tarry black and fiery red, made to look like cathedral stained glass.

Whereas the mainstream of romanticism has always expressed and consolidated national myths, Jarman's subverted them. Underlying the imagery of the Blitz and the wasteland lies a critique of a destructive society and government—in a word, of Thatcherism. The desolate cityscape is contrasted with the imagery of the garden, as the state terrorism of *Jubilee* (1977) was contrasted with the closing masque of *The Tempest* (1979), the two films linked through the role of two Renaissance magicians, John Dee and Prospero. Jarman's political commitment drew on the sense of an alternative tradition, on the great homosexual texts—Plato's *Symposium*, Shakespeare's sonnets, the paintings of Caravaggio. At the same time, it is inseparable from his day-by-day involvement in the gay world, in the struggle against Clause 28 and the solidarity of gay men in the face of Aids as they confronted an authoritarian and homophobic regime whose leader's insistent moral appeal was to 'Victorian values' and against the 'permissive society'.[25] The key turning-point, for Jarman, came with the Royal Jubilee of 1977 and its riotously sinister shadow, punk. Jarman's *Jubilee* is a protest against the whole horrendous notion of the 'second Elizabethan age', the backdrop of national grandeur and creativity against which Britain's economic and cultural decline was played out for twenty-five years. After that, of course, Thatcherism came as a movement not of renewal but of vengefulness against everything she disapproved of that had somehow still managed to survive.

Peter Greenaway emerged from a strangely contradictory background. On the one hand, he worked for the government Central Office of Information, making films meant to express the British way of life, and, on the other hand, he made idiosyncratic 'structural films' in his own free time. His affinities are with 'international' modernism—before making *The Draughtsman's Contract*, he screened films by Fellini, Bertolucci, Rohmer, Straub and Resnais for the crew, so that they could understand his intentions. At the same time, he secretly remade his own earlier *Vertical Features Remake* (1979), in which a group of film-scholars try to reconstruct a lost film from a series of surviving views. Greenaway is also close to movements in modern art and music which employ modular and serial structures. Like many conceptual artists, he is fascinated by lists, grids, catalogues, counting games and random procedures, which appear in his work as 'coincidences' or 'accidents'. He is also fascinated by mysteries and their concomitant troop of red herrings, deceptive riddles and false trails, the stock-in-trade of the peculiarly English form of the cerebral detective story. His films are made under the twin signs of the taxonomy and the enigma. Such an aesthetic is perhaps strongest in an intrinsically non-realist art like music, but even in literature and painting it subordinates content to formal preoccupations, so that subject-matter often seems no more than a pretext. The structure comes first and the content—say, a series of fictions—is then fitted into it, a lesson Greenaway learned from John Cage. This school of modernism, unlike neo-romanticism, was historically decoupled from politics, yet, under the pressure of Thatcherism, Greenaway too turned to political invective in his *The Cook, the Thief, his Wife and her Lover.*

Greenaway's antipathy towards Thatcherism stems from an ethical and aesthetic dislike for the philistinism and vulgarity of her regime, her exaltation of the profit motive, her determination that art and scholarship should only be supported if they served an economic function, her authoritarianism, her social philosophy of frugality and order for the poor combined with greed and licence for the rich. Thus an expensive restaurant was a logical setting for his film, a place where Spica's own authoritarianism, greed and licence can be publicly indulged. Moreover, one of Greenaway's recurrent preoccupations is with the food chain, the process of ingestion of the weak by the strong and the dead by the living, in curious configurations of cruelty and death with sex and dinner. At the same time, the restaurant is symbolically a cathedral, a cinema and an art museum, the chef its officiating priest and artist. As in other Greenaway films, the woman is the controlling character, bent on revenge on the world of men, destroying the figure of the artist en route. The brutalization of an innocent child recalls that of Smut in *Drowning by Numbers* (1988), a gruelling moment when a ludic *commedia dell'arte* is suddenly transformed into a macabre Jacobean drama. Indeed, as Greenaway puts it,

> The Jacobeans were looking over their shoulder at the grand Elizabethan age; Britain still looks over its shoulder at the Great Empire. In Jacobean times, syphilis was the new sexual scourge; we now have AIDS. There's a certain comparison in that sexuality has become complicated, so there's a similar spirit of melancholy. The same sensation of fatalism exists vis-a-vis the sort of cruelty we see every day, especially cruelty in the home, the abuse of children, and so on.[26]

From their very different angles, Greenaway and Jarman unexpectedly converge on a surprisingly similar standpoint.

Both Greenaway and Jarman made key films for the British Film Institute Production Board, under Peter Sainsbury: *The Draughtsman's Contract* (1982), suggested by Sainsbury, who asked Greenaway whether he had ever thought of making a dialogue film, and later, Jarman's *Caravaggio* (1986). The Board had become completely divorced from its experimental function until Sainsbury, former editor of the avant-garde journal *AfterImage*, was appointed in the mid-seventies. Sainsbury became something like a new but decisively modernist and anti-realist Grierson. Towards the end of the sixties, under the dual impact of New York 'structural film' and the European experiments in narrative of Godard and others, a film avant-garde crystallized for the first time in Britain since *Close Up*. It was built around the BFI, the journal *Screen*, the Other Cinema, the 'Workshop Movement' and the Independent Film-Makers' Association. Neither Greenaway nor Jarman participated in the avant-garde debates and activities of the time, which they saw, perhaps, as too politically doctrinaire or too potentially time-consuming. In a way, their non-involvement probably made it easier for them to break out of the earlier pattern of their film-making, unencumbered by a baggage of past positions and pronouncements. Also, they did not confront Thatcherism head on, as 'political film-makers', but from a less explicit artistic position within which their political anti-Thatcherism emerged.

Nonetheless, films like those of Greenaway and Jarman should be seen as elements of a wider and disparate shift in British film, due in part to a decisive shift towards the visual arts as a source for cinema, and in part to the theoretical and practical consolidation of a film avant-garde in the IFA and at the BFI.[27] The emergence of a post-Godardian 'political modernism' at the BFI, although it never achieved even the limited popular success of Greenaway or Jarman, helped to create an alternative pole of attraction within British cinema and thus the space between mainstream and counter-cinema which they later occupied.[28] Greenaway and Jarman were much closer in background and outlook to other directors emerging from the BFI and the Workshops than to the upscale TV drama and ad directors who constituted the rump of the 'film industry' left behind in Britain after the more ambitious of them had been called to the Coast. The other important condition, of course, was the fabulous collapse of Puttnamism and the flight of its leader to Hollywood, where his pretensions were ignominiously liquidated. 'The British are coming'—indeed, 'The British are coming!'—was the media slogan propagated after *Chariots of Fire* (1981) won a screenplay Oscar. It is strange that the next British Oscar sweep, for *The Last Emperor*, had no discernible impact whatever in Britain, presumably because its director, Bertolucci, was an Italian. Conversely, a director like Ridley Scott, even though he has retained his personal and working ties with Britain, has never been treated as British, although his vision of the city in *Blade Runner* (1982) has much in common with its domestic counterparts.

Thatcherism, by breaking the mould of British politics and trying, with considerable success, to carry through radical right-wing cultural policies which were directed, in essence, against the legacy of the sixties, succeeded paradoxically in politicizing a generation of film-makers who had been formed during the comparatively liberal years of Wilson, the decade of sexual liberation, the last hurrah of welfare Keynesianism and the belated entry of modernism into the general culture. This 'delayed modernism', however, proved resilient enough to survive into the eighties. It decisively influenced a generation then in a position to make oppositional films first for the BFI, later for Channel 4, and eventually for independent producers within the industry or in Europe. As a result, Britain saw an efflorescence of film-making paralleled only in the forties, whose strength has been revealed by successive IFA Biennales. Britain finally produced the 'Last New Wave', a series of uncompromising films made by original—and often oppositional—visually oriented and modernist auteurs. It was worth waiting for. Let's hope it survives.

13

RIFF-RAFF REALISM

This chapter is about an intriguing aspect of British cinema during the 1940s. I should begin by acknowledging that I owe the term 'riff-raff realism' to Robert Murphy, who coined the expression in the pioneering chapter on 'The Spiv Cycle' in his 1989 book *Realism and Tinsel: Cinema and Society in Britain, 1939–49*.[1] But although I am going to zoom in on a particular cycle of films, I believe that they also have much wider implications for our whole approach to British cinema. We have now reached a point when, after several years of study and research, we can begin to think seriously about synthesizing a wide range of new information and new insights in order to create a comprehensive new vision of British cinema, seen as a whole. Way back in 1960 at a British Film Institute (BFI) seminar group, Alan Lovell presented a paper with the melancholy title 'British Cinema: The Unknown Cinema'.[2] In 1985, in a new essay which he now titled 'British Cinema: The Known Cinema?', he reflected on the advances that have been made:

> Today, British film scholars can hardly be accused of neglecting their national cinema. In the space of twenty-five years we have moved from scarcity to abundance. There are now available solid histories of the British cinema; detailed explorations of British genre film-making; analyses of important historical 'moments'; critical examinations of influential film-makers; wide-ranging anthologies; informed discussion of the econ-

omic and cultural context of current British film-making; informative accounts of Welsh and Scottish film-making.[3]

But Alan Lovell then goes on to warn against the dangers of complacency by asking, 'What are the consequences of this work? How is the British cinema now perceived?' He argues, in response to his own question, that the traditional view of realism as the dominant aesthetic drive underlying the best of British films has been increasingly countered by a stress on work which privileged excess rather than restraint, melodrama and horror rather than documentary or the kitchen sink, a form of 'diluted surrealism' rather than the realism which Michael Balcon famously called for, in response to the wartime emergency, in his programmatic speech, 'Realism and Tinsel'.[4] The best British films, Lovell goes on to argue, are marked by an interaction between restraint and excess, between realism and melodrama. The classic examples he gives are David Lean's *Brief Encounter* and Michael Powell's *The Small Back Room*, a polemical choice, given the fact that Powell has been revalued precisely as the great hero of an anti-realist aesthetic in British film. Essentially, Lovell is attempting to redirect discussion of British film back to basic questions of aesthetics, asking us to evaluate as well as to describe, to interpret and to contextualize. If I understand correctly, he doesn't want us to discard the realist impulse, as we are bewitched by *Black Narcissus* or *The Wicked Lady*, but to incorporate it into a more complex and even paradoxical aesthetic of, so to speak, 'realist melodrama' or 'romantic slice-of-life'.

My argument is that 'riff-raff realism' gives us precisely the mix which Alan Lovell was looking for, the disturbing and difficult combination of realism with excess and fantasy. Beyond that, I believe a closer look at the spiv cycle of films will raise a number of important issues about British cinema as a whole and our evaluation of its artistic standing as a small but significant sector of world cinema. First, however, I want to address the specific historical context of the spiv cycle in order to make some modest proposals about the vexed question of cinema and national identity. The spiv cycle first came into view towards the end of the Second World War. In essence, the cycle reflected a mutation in the traditional crime film which took place in response to the changing pattern of crime that emerged in wartime as a result of state regulation of the economy. Controls and rationing—and rising prices—led inevitably to the emergence of a black market. As Raynes Minns explains in her book, *Bombers and Mash*, rationing actually created demand for a black market in two contrary ways—either when the supply of rationed goods exceeded the ceiling imposed by the total of rationing allocations, thus creating a surplus, or, of course, when overall supply fell short, creating a situation of scarcity.[5] In one situation, then, there was a surplus of goods which could only be sold illegally; in the other situation, a demand for goods which could only be bought illegally. The black marketeer catered enthusiastically for both.

As Minns puts it,

> People talked of 'knowing a man' who might have spare parts for radio, alcohol, rubber tyres, petrol, or even dolls, nylons and perfumes—known to be illegally acquired . . . Attitudes were mixed to these dealings. They varied from moral outrage at even a whiff of Black Market dealings to the view that if sharp dealing was the only way to provide for family and friends at a time of stress, then it was the obvious course to take.[6]

Black marketeers, a category closely overlapping that of spiv, could be viewed either as unscrupulous parasites and law-breakers, 'vermin . . . waxing fat'—in the angry words of *War Illustrated*—while others 'faced death night and day to bring in the food necessary to our salvation', or else welcomed as libertarian benefactors performing a relatively harmless public service in times of adversity and oppressive bureaucratic control. Thus, as Minns concludes, 'the grinning spivs, the barrow boys and the "wheelers" gradually endeared themselves to the general public'.

As suggested in an earlier Chapter ('Spies and Spivs'), 'spiv' itself seems to have been as much a fashion term as a job description. To quote Minns again: 'The archetypal spiv wore yellow shoes, a wide-lapelled suit and wide tie, and sported a shifty little trilby pulled rakishly over the forehead. He symbolized a flashy flaunting of authority and petty regulations—especially towards the end of the war when people were long tired of self denial and the many wartime restrictions.' The crucial difference between the spiv and the classic Hollywood gangster was the degree of sympathy the spiv gained as an intermediary in the transfer of black market goods from army camps, docks, railway yards, lorry parks, industrial depots and so on, to a grateful mass of consumers. At the same time, official ideology presented the spiv as an enemy of the war effort (and hence the people) who was prospering while others paid the price. This ambivalence runs right through the spiv cycle of films, in which spivs are clearly marked as villains, ruthless and violent, while at the same time they are frequently fascinating precisely because of the strange mix of living and working in the community combined with demonic transports of evil.

In *Waterloo Road*, the first true film of the cycle, made at the end of the war and released in 1945, the spiv Ted Purvis, played by Stewart Granger, of all people, is clearly unsympathetic, not so much because of his racketeering activities but because, by avoiding military service through bribing a doctor, he is able to pursue the female lead after her fiancé is drafted into the army. He also, of course, uses and orchestrates violence, and the film implicitly contrasts the good and necessary violence of war directed against the Nazi aggressor with the bad violence of the spiv exercised or threatened against members of the community and even against a soldier, albeit one who has gone AWOL to try and retrieve his wife. As in other spiv films there is implicit or even explicit comparison between the spiv and the enemy, as though the racketeer was a kind of fifth columnist or virtual counterpart of the fascist foe. The spiv is portrayed as a destructive force, threatening to the working-class community of Waterloo Road at a time when the value of 'community' seems more important than ever. The film begins with a bustling Cockney street-market, moves on to show heaps of rubble where houses have been bombed and then takes us into a terrace home, complete with HP sauce on the table alongside a teapot with the morning paper propped up against it. The working-class living room is vividly contrasted with the Lucky Star pinball arcade operated by the spiv, Ted Purvis. Early in the film, we see Purvis, sporting a spotted bow tie, waiting for the errant wife under the clock at Waterloo Station; then there is a cut to the frantic husband who arrives, desperately searching for his wife. His search soon takes him to the Lucky Star arcade with its garish décor and sinister clientele. The arcade, where he gets into a fight intercut with pinball lights, provides us with an example of the vernacular fantastic, the typical trope of spiv films which zero in on ghost trains, race tracks, dance halls, wrestling rings, goods yards and other such sites of violence and tawdry glamour—*Waterloo Road* even boasts a glimpse of a tattooing parlour.

Stewart Granger, who plays Ted Purvis, the suave and unscrupulous spiv, had established himself as a star for Gainsborough by playing, in his own words, the 'romantic, heroic lover' (with James Mason as his rival, the bad Lord Rohan of *The Man in Grey* repeated in various versions). It is interesting that in *Waterloo Road* Granger was cast against type—and, in his own opinion, against his interests as a star. By undercutting Granger's star image the spiv becomes a heady mixture of romantic lover and unscrupulous villain, more in the Mason mould of the fascinating rake. In a way Launder and Gilliat's film, besides following in the community-realist tradition they had established with their earlier *Millions Like Us*, also establishes a link between the Cockney spiv and the 'monstrously nasty' Lord Rohan tradition of Gainsborough cos- tume pictures ('monstrously nasty': Mason's own words!). The hero, played by John Mills, in contrast, plays the ordinary member of the local community, desperate to get his wife back from the Masonic spiv. He is also a 'man on the run', pursued by the military police as he attempts to track down the spiv–seducer, and helped to outwit them by a sympathetically portrayed Canadian deserter (a figure who reappears decades later in John Boorman's nostalgic *Hope and Glory*). As we shall see, the spiv cycle of films overlaps surprisingly closely with the 'man- on-the-run' picture, in which the hero himself is the wanted man, the persecuted innocent. It is through the charisma of the spiv and the melodrama of the persecuted innocent motif that the spiv film starts to push the aesthetic of populist realism over the edge towards romantic excess.

In 1943, just two years before *Waterloo Road*, the great British producer Michael Balcon, head of Ealing Studios, had gone down to Brighton from London, first class on the Brighton Belle I presume, to give his address 'Realism and Tinsel' to a gathering of the Film Workers Association. In effect, he had gone down to Brighton in order to confess publicly that he had now experienced a 180-degree change of heart. In the past, he confided, he had paid no heed whatever to realism:

> What I am telling you, in fact, is a frank admission that I was not at all concerned with the sociological aspect of films [i.e. what today we would call the cultural aspect]. If I realized their potential importance it was not from the same point of view in which today I regard them as important. I visualized merely a prosperous industry giving employment to many thousands of people, providing a profitable investment, and so on.[7]

It was the war, of course, which had changed Balcon's mind and led him to abandon 'tinsel' and embrace 'realism', the authentic representation of Britain on the screen, rather than theatrical flimflam and the primacy of entertainment values. 'Entertainment' now fell to third place on Balcon's list of desirable qualities in films, after 'the projection of our own ideas' and even after 'instruction'. Balcon's choice of nationalist 'realism' before cosmopolitan 'tinsel' became a kind of article of faith for critics, film-makers and public figures who wanted to foster a national cinema in Britain. Heritage and identity must be realism, they all agreed, not tinsel.

This view that national cinema should, almost by definition, be a realist cinema is very limited, to say the least. During the second half of the 1940s, when British film-makers still believed that they might be able to compete against Hollywood, before the crushing defeat of Harold Wilson's ambitious plans to challenge the Americans, the most successful films exported were flamboyantly romantic melodramas, for example *The Seventh Veil* and *The Red Shoes*, everything Balcon meant by tinsel. These films were not particularly welcomed by the British critics, who found them visually and emotionally excessive. In fact, in Julian Petley's words, they were 'desperately disliked' by the English critics. Yet, in many ways, they tell us a great deal more about England and Englishness than any films made in the realist tradition, precisely because they expose wild fantasies, however delirious, which realism seeks to suppress. Strange films, like films by strangers, are often the most revealing. Nonetheless, the realist imperative, enunciated by Balcon and by the critics, led to a long-lasting emphasis on realism as the destiny and duty of a truly British cinema, in contradistinction to Hollywood tinsel.

This led, as we have seen, to a series of films being made which showed the seamy underside of British life as well as its positive side. Prominent in the new genres which grew out of the turn towards riff-raff realism, of course, was the 'spiv' film, which flourished between 1945 and 1950, the years of the first post-war Labour government, the reforming Attlee government, which brought the working class—or its representatives—to real power for the first time in British history. The 'spiv' film was the breakthrough British cycle, albeit a branch of the crime genre, to be clearly based in a working-class milieu. 'Spivs' were racketeers with roots in the working-class. Despite their wide-lapelled suits and flash neckties, they were an indigenous type originating, as we have seen, from the black market economy which grew up during wartime and continued growing with post-war scarcity and rationing. While it is true that the 'spiv' film has some (misleading) similarities to American *film noir*, it remains a very British type of film, in its setting, in its attitudes and in its style. (Unlike American noir, the British spiv films never revolved around the seductive but treacherous *femme fatale*.)

It was for this reason that when I started to look back at the history of the 'spiv' film, in such sharp contrast to the traditional film image of Britain, I was surprised to find that it had actually been anticipated in Hollywood, by none other than Clifford Odets, in his 1944 film, written and directed for RKO, *None but the Lonely Heart*, starring Cary Grant and June Duprez, also English-born, which portrayed the petty criminal underworld in contemporary London. In fact, to my bewilderment, *None but the Lonely Heart* actually pre-dated *Waterloo Road*, which Robert Murphy and others, including me, had all assumed was the first real spiv film. At first sight, Odets's film seems a somewhat strange concoction, with its weird gallimaufry of accents, ranging from pure Hollywood through Barry Fitzgerald's heritage brogue and Cary Grant's half-remembered Bristolian twang, to some fairly passable South London bit players. But the core of the film, of course, comes from its literary source, a novel by Richard Llewellyn, best known as the author of *How Green Was My Valley*, the story of Welsh working-class life set in a mining community, which had been made into a successful film by John Ford in 1941.

Llewellyn's novel is a model of popular street-smart vernacular writing. Odets, of course, adapts it to suit his own preoccupations, but the underlying theme of his script remains characteristically British: crime as a way out of a working-class life-style felt as a kind of imprisonment by the sensitive and idealistic central character. The same theme can be found in Carol Reed's pioneering *The Stars Look Down*, in which three classic avenues of escape from the working class are posited: crime, football and education. In *None but the Lonely Heart*, Ernie Mott, the central character, is played by Cary Grant, who won a much-coveted Oscar nomination for his performance as a Cockney drifter who has fantasies of becoming an artist but ends up involved with a small-time racketeer, a 'wide boy' in Llewellyn's phrase, who is based in a South London garage and, having acquired a nightclub and a slot-machine arcade, is branching out into shaking down pawnbrokers ('had to wallop the old bloke') and doing smash-and-grab raids on Brompton Road furriers. (Much to Grant's chagrin, the Oscar went to Bing Crosby for his role as Father O'Malley in Leo McCarey's unctuous *Going My Way*.)

Odets gives the film a topical anti-fascist inflection by implicitly linking the violence-and-racketeering theme to Nazism, a Brechtian tactic (as in *Arturo Ui*) supported by his use of Mordechai Gorelik as set-designer and Hanns Eisler as composer, both of whom had worked with Brecht and were probably his closest associates in America. Odets, for example, highlights the significance of the fact that the pawnbroker beaten up by the spiv's two enforcers is Jewish, and thus makes Ernie Mott's change of heart about the value of the criminal road into a kind of moral decision against fascism, linked to the war by a single shot in which the shadows of planes passing overhead move across his face. *None but the Lonely Heart* could almost have served as a model for Cavalcanti's *They Made Me a Fugitive*, with its expressionist design style and its strange and eerie details of the London criminal-cum-proletarian milieu—the meal of sheep's heart, the budgerigar brought in to be pawned, the awe at the first refrigerator in the street, the arcade with its Test Your Strength machines and peepshows, the startling appearance of Dan Duryea in the fish-and-chip shop ('Special Today—Fresh Hake') and Ernie Mott's perfect pitch, which leads him to comment 'E-Flat!' when the getaway car he is in crashes into a lorry, whose driver is killed and whose horn is jammed, droning away on the same note.

The fascination I felt watching *None but the Lonely Heart* for the first time sprang primarily, I think, from the strange confrontation of Odets's very American proletarian-cosmopolitan aesthetic with its very English source-material and subject-matter. Odets drew both on the 'New Masses' vision of the vernacular representation of proletarian life and on the much more intellectualized aesthetic and allegorical style which he took from Brecht. This vision, when turned onto 1940s South London, somewhere round the Walworth Road or maybe Coldharbour Lane—it is a little bit vague—gives a new kind of surreal gloss to standard British realism. It differentiates the film from the Carol Reed or Sidney Gilliatt films which the English critics loved, but proves very congenial for the riff-raff spiv film which the critics hated.

In fact, the next important spiv picture, Alberto Cavalcanti's *They Made Me a Fugitive*, made at Hammersmith for Warner Brothers and released in 1946, pushed expressionism even further than Odets. Like *Waterloo Road*, *They Made Me a Fugitive* also has a man-on-the-run theme, much more centrally, in fact, than its predecessor. The hero of the film, Morgan, played by Trevor Howard, is a black marketeer imprisoned in Dartmoor at the start of the film, having been framed for the killing of a policeman by his boss, Narcissus. (As recounted earlier, Narcissus (or 'Narcy') is a sadistic racketeer with headquarters located in an East End funeral parlour. Black market goods are transported in coffins accompanied by mourners in full regalia. 'Narcy' suggests 'nasty', 'nark' and 'narcotics'—Narcy having a line in what he calls 'sherbet'.) Morgan then escapes and is framed for a second murder, this time by a blind woman who had befriended him and given him a change of clothes, before she kills her drunken husband and blames it on Morgan, now wearing the dead man's suit. Morgan is now pursued both by the police and by Narcy, who wants to eliminate him before he can cause any trouble.

Enough plot! The main point to repeat is that the spiv character is split in two—Narcy is depraved and vicious, while Morgan, who is a demobbed ex-serviceman unable to find a job on civvy street, is an escapee from the spiv underworld, wrongfully accused and hunted, a man who has realized rather too late that Narcy is not just devoted to stealing and supplying harmless black market goods but is the kingpin of a ruthlessly terroristic criminal gang. Thus one member of the gang can win our sympathy while the other can be a monster. The man-on-the-run story, told from the point of view of the persecuted innocent, is one designed to win sympathy for the hero, however bad things may look, as we know from so many Hitchcock films. This works both for the AWOL husband in *Waterloo Road* and for the framed ex-serviceman in *They Made Me a Fugitive*, with its echoes of Warners' 1932 *I Am a Fugitive from a Chain Gang*.

The next major film in the British spiv cycle, Robert Hamer's *It Always Rains On Sundays*, made for Ealing in 1947, was a film which, like *Waterloo Road*, blended the crime film with a more typical Ealing depiction of a working-class community, featuring the criminal's wife, played by Googie Withers, as the central character. Once again, however, it was a man-on-the-run film, ending this time with a night-time chase through a railway marshalling yard. In 1948, the Boulting Brothers' *Brighton Rock*, based on Graham Greene's book, starred Richard Attenborough as the psychotic young criminal, and Edmond Gréville's *Noose*, another Hollywood production, followed the story of an American fashion journalist who recasts herself as a crime investigator to break up a vicious smuggling gang, bringing in such scarce commodities as watches and perfume from Amsterdam. Through her boyfriend who is a sports reporter, she gets help from the community, in the shape of boxers from the Old Kent Road, Covent Garden barrow-boys, Billingsgate market porters and Chelsea cabmen! In the end, they combine to overthrow the mafia-style king of the Soho black market, played by Joseph Calleia, who like all the other villains is especially cruel to women.

It is significant that at this point in the story, right at the end of the forties, as the British film industry faltered and the genre began what turned out to be its undeserved decline, Edmond Gréville's *Noose* featured two imported American stars—Joseph Calleia as a gangster and Carole Landis as a fashion reporter obsessed with Christian Dior's New Look, which signalled an end to wartime austerity—playing opposite Nigel Patrick as the charismatic spiv. Like Odets's *None but the Lonely Heart*, *Noose* was based on an original text by Richard Llewellyn, this time a stage play rather than a novel, and, like *They Made Me a Fugitive*, it was a Warners production, presumably made in England for the sake of authenticity, given that Llewellyn was bankable in Hollywood. Moreover, the director, Edmond Gréville, was French (like Marc Allegret, who directed another key British film of the time, the costume melodrama *Blanche Fury*, which had been released the previous year).

Then, in 1949, come what must be the high-points of the genre: Carol Reed's *The Third Man* (Korda and Selznick)—a spiv film transposed from London to post-war Vienna, with Orson Welles playing the fugitive black marketeer, another beguiling and fascistic rake—followed by Jules Dassin's even more extraordinary bombed-out cityscape, *Night and the City*, with Richard Widmark as Fabian, a club tout who has a tragic fantasy of controlling London's wrestling arenas, trying to survive in a bleak, British post-war underworld as he is hunted down, like Morgan, by gangs he has crossed. Arguably, Reed's *Odd Man Out*, made in 1947, could also be considered a spiv film, or at least a riff-raff realism film, with its IRA bank-robber-on-the-run as tragic hero. Dearden's *The Blue Lamp*, for Ealing, with Dirk Bogarde as the psychotic young criminal, provides a final variation on the model created by Granger, Griffith Jones and Attenborough. If Dearden's 1943 *The Bells Go Down*, with its vignette of a petty black marketeer, is considered the immediate forerunner of the spiv film, then *The Blue Lamp* would make an appropriate postscript, as the crime cycle mutates into a police cycle, with *Dixon of Dock Green*, *Zed Cars*, etc., coming down the line.

As it reached its close, the spiv genre had returned again to Hollywood, where it began. The two final films of the cycle, both released in 1950, were Jules Dassin's *Night and the City* and Carol Reed's *The Third Man*, with Orson Welles as the classic black market spiv-racketeer, Harry Lime—which was, of course, a David Selznick production. *The Third Man*, shot in the rubble of post-war Vienna, carried the interweaving of realism and melodrama to an unforgettable finale in the Viennese sewers, ending with Lime's fingers desperately quivering through the grating which blocks his exit to the street and freedom. It is a scene which recapitulates a whole series of set-piece finales in which the spiv finally dies, melodramatically and often semi-suicidally. Watching *The Third Man*, my mind went back to Narcy plunging off the roof of the Valhalla into the grimy alley below and to the convict on the run in *It Always Rains On Sunday*, throwing himself down onto the track as a goods train rumbles towards him through the dark, deserted marshalling yard. The forces of order are triumphant, of course, but our sympathies go to the doomed and defeated villain—even to Narcy, if only for his stubborn refusal to show a single spark of goodness, even as his rotten life ebbs away in the rain.

The endings of spiv films are often where melodrama decisively triumphs over realism, where British cinema unashamedly enters the eerie and fascinating realm of noir, the world of violence, darkness and death which Hollywood exploited so memorably at the very same time. It seems somehow appropriate that the cycle should begin and end with Hollywood, start with Odets and finish with Welles. It is true to say that four or even five of the six great spiv films had foreign directors— Odets for *None but the Lonely Heart*, Gréville for *Noose*, Dassin for *Night and the City* and Cavalcanti (the great Brazilian director) for his wonderful *They Made Me a Fugitive*. The fifth would be Robert Hamer's marvellously dreary and depressing *It Always Rains on Sunday* and the sixth, of course, Carol Reed's internationalized *The Third Man*, a Selznick co-production. In fact, I would like to go further and argue that the best films about any country are frequently made by foreigners, film-makers who tend to look askance and from an unusual angle. It is worth pointing out too that the Cavalcanti and Gréville films were both lit and shot by Otto Heller, the Reed films by Robert Krasker and the Dassin by Max Greene, born Mutz Greenbaum, all immigrants from Germany. (Douglas Slocombe was the cinematographer for *It Always Rains On Sunday*, Arthur Crabtree for *Waterloo Road*.)

If we look at a somewhat later period, the sixties, we find the same phenomenon—the most extraordinary films about England were made by Kubrick, Lester, Losey, Polanski, and Antonioni. In the thirties there were Dupont, Clair, Czinner and Korda. More recently Terry Gilliam's *Brazil* gave us an unforgettable vision of the Thatcher years. Hollywood cinema, of course, has always been cosmopolitan, offering us cinematic representations of America by Polanski and Antonioni (again) as well as by Hitchcock, Lang, Wilder, Ophuls and so many, many others, down to Ridley Scott. Outsiders—and I might include 'internal outsiders' in this category—often see things about a country which insiders miss or discount or repress. They make strange, as the Russian writer Victor Shklovsky would have put it (and he wrote one of the best books about

Berlin).[8] Insiders are not necessarily the best judges of their own society or the best able to represent it. National culture and national self-expression, as we all know, tend to be self-serving and mythologizing (all the more acutely so, perhaps, if, as with the thirties costume picture, foreigners prove to be even better at mythologizing than the locals, driving them on to ever-greater feats of self-deception). In fact, I would like to go still further: national culture, by definition, is mythologizing, self-serving and, at the same time, self-mutilating, designed as it is to focus a group identity by creating shibboleths and stereotypes, however 'cool'. This is well demonstrated, of course, in books like Benedict Anderson's classic study of the idea of the nation as an 'imagined community', by Eric Hobsbawm's work on 'the invention of tradition', by Robert Hewison's study of 'the heritage industry', and Ashis Nandy's dissection of the destructive reverse effects of the Indian empire on domestic British culture.[9]

Finally, I want to develop the argument about the aesthetics of film a little further. I believe it is important to ask ourselves what the strengths of British cinema really are, how we should evaluate British cinema from an artistic standpoint. It is universally accepted that the German and Russian film industries of the silent period produced waves of great films and great directors—Lang, Murnau, Pabst, Eisenstein, Vertov, Dovzhenko. French cinema of the thirties gave us Clair, Carné and Renoir. Italy, in the forties, produced Neo-Realism—Rossellini, Visconti and Fellini, soon to be followed by Antonioni. In the fifties, the French New Wave appeared—Godard, Truffaut, Resnais—and dominated the sixties, to be followed by a series of New Waves from other countries around the world. All this without even mentioning Hollywood! How does British cinema fit into this broader scheme of things? It is clear why British scholars should be interested in British film. But why should anybody else? What makes it of special interest? Why should students in Paris or Los Angeles be interested in British film?

As I read through copious new accounts of British studios or genres or periods or representations of gender or national identity, I must confess I began to wonder where aesthetics fits into the agenda of research and rediscovery. Perhaps the point has come when we need to step back for a moment and make some broad judgements about British cinema, to look at it again as an art-form, as Alan Lovell implied. Which are the films that really count, the films we wouldn't mind seeing again and again? What kind of a canon do we want to construct? Of course, the whole idea of a canon is contentious in itself, but film historians inevitably start to create a new canon simply by researching some areas more deeply than others, writing about some films with more care and enthusiasm than others. Gradually, the cinema described begins to take on a new shape as Powell and Pressburger become pivotal rather than Lean and Coward, as Gainsborough films become written about as much as Ealing, as the films of political exiles are resituated in their British context, as sixties kitchen-sink realism is looked at again with all the benefits of hindsight.

So I would like to end by claiming a key place in the pantheon of British cinema for the riff-raff realism of the spiv cycle. Surely any list of great British films has to include titles like *They Made Me a Fugitive*, *It Always Rains On Sunday*, *Odd Man Out*, *The Third Man*, *Night and the City*—not to mention *Waterloo Road*, *Brighton Rock* or *Noose*, all of which are certainly major works. Isn't this because the spiv cycle allowed directors to combine realism with melodrama, restraint with excess, to use Alan Lovell's terms—put another way, to explore the darker, more sinister side of Britishness without losing touch with the lived experience of the street and the community? And, I might add, didn't they perhaps lay the foundations for films like *The Servant* and *Performance* in the sixties, with their own image of the working-class rake and the charismatic man on the run? *Performance* even reduplicates the wounded-back-tending scene from *They Made Me a Fugitive*. What a double bill! In the final analysis, the case I want to make for the spiv film isn't a social, cultural or historical case. It is an aesthetic case. The British cinema that interests me is a cinema which produces great films, films which are masterpieces.

PART III

Themes and Styles

14

ARCHITECTURE AND FILM:
PLACES AND NON-PLACES

Architecture in film is never just itself. It is always a simulacrum of somewhere else, a symbolic representation of some other place—even the Rome of Rossellini's *Rome, Open City* and the Paris of Godard's *A Bout de Souffle* stand in for the selective cinema-specific Rome and Paris of Neo-Realism and the French New Wave respectively. Rossellini's Rome is a very different city from that of Wyler's *Roman Holiday*. However much Godard may have adored Minnelli, his Paris is not the same Paris in which Gene Kelly danced with Leslie Caron. Carol Reed's sinister Vienna in *The Third Man* is a very different city from the nostalgic Vienna of Max Ophuls's *La Ronde* and *Letter from an Unknown Woman* (with its very different picture of the Prater pleasure gardens). Similarly, the Los Angeles of *LA Confidential* is not the same as the Los Angeles of *Clueless*. The city that we see need not even be the cinematic city that it purports to be. To the student of architecture in the cinema, Helsinki, for example, calls to mind Warren Beatty's film *Reds*, in which Helsinki doubled for Petersburg and the architectural environment of the quite different city in which the Bolsheviks seized power. This is not simply a question of location versus studio set; it is more that the city of one director is a different place from the city of another director, and cinema architecture reflects that difference.

Recently I read a little book called *Non-Places—Introduction to an Anthropology of Supermodernity*, written by Marc Augé, who, it seems, is a

French ethnographer who has become especially interested in the concept of 'space', especially contemporary space—the space of non-symbolized travel and mobility.[1] He contrasts the idea of space—which you travel through—with the idea of 'place', which, in his mind, implies a certain stability and a set of historic associations and meanings, both private and public. Space, on the other hand, is punctuated by 'non-places'—apparent places which are really meaningless way-stations through which we travel. His examples include such typical non-places as airport lounges, service stations, supermarkets, leisure parks, hotels, clinics, conference centres and auditoria. This paradoxical world of jarringly juxtaposed places and non-places is grimly and grippingly evoked by *Blade Runner*.

Non-places, Augé comments, tend to be saturated with signage and texts (instructions, injunctions, information, etc.) as well as places where easy-listening music is played. While I was reading this book—in Los Angeles, the place where I was then living, before I embarked on the long journey to London—I began to wonder whether cinemas were non-places of the kind Augé describes. Certainly, the lobbies of large multi-screen cinemas are non-places and, arguably, the cinema auditorium itself is a non-place up to the moment when the film begins. Typically, there is easy-listening music, a plethora of signage in the form of posters and trailers, directions which way to go, injunctions to keep the hall clean, and so on. The situation when the film itself begins is somewhat different—we are transported into another space, a space which seems, in some ways, to be that of a 'place', in others that of a 'non-place'. It is a space which is both lived in and the site of fantasy, a kind of fantasy travel, a series of way-stations to which we have no real connection.

Back in the 1930s, Walter Benjamin already drew an analogy between cinema and architecture—in his now-classic essay on 'The Work of Art in the Age of Mechanical Reproduction'.[2] Benjamin argued that cinema and architecture were both art-forms which, while superficially visual, were in fact appropriated and apprehended by touch—they were primarily 'tactile' arts, as opposed to painting. In fact, Benjamin was not entirely happy with the word 'tactile'—what he wanted to argue was that cinema and architecture both required a kind of kinaesthetic habit-formation, the acquisition of a habitual mode of moving through space in order to understand and inhabit it unconsciously. Watching a film,

Benjamin believed, was much like moving through a building or a built environment. It required a sense of direction, an attentiveness to signs, symbols and meanings, an awareness of the purposes for which a place was intended and how it could be most efficiently used.

In this sense, architecture and cinema both provide sets of places and spaces which the user must learn how to travel through—a kind of knowledge which, in our culture, is acquired from a very early age. Augé himself notes that places too can be travelled through, as well as empty spaces and non-places—but the ways in which we traverse meaningful places are themselves meaning-laden. For Augé three things primarily differentiate places from non-places. He writes that, 'If a place can be defined as relational, historical and concerned with identity, then a space which cannot be defined as relational, or historical, or concerned with identity will be a non-place.' To define these terms, Augé returns to his experience as an anthropologist. 'Relational' space refers to bounded space which is laid out symbolically, so that each region of the space (or position within it) has a symbolic relation to others. 'Historical' space refers to space which has stable and meaningful historic associations. Space 'concerned with identity' refers to space which is personalized, with which an individual feels a strong personal or social relationship. Such bounded spaces are regarded by Augé as 'places' rather than 'non-places'.

Such places are, as Benjamin suggests, used spaces, lived in, densely inhabited, ingrained with meaning. Both Augé and Benjamin describe positively these spaces in which we move about, which are dynamic spaces rather than static, to which our relationship is kinetic rather than contemplative. We move within such spaces, we have an interactive relationship with them. At the opposite end of the spectrum are tourist sites, which we apprehend visually, from a spatial or psychological distance, looking at them, experiencing them in one gulp, rather than living in them. For Benjamin, cinema itself was divided into two types of film—one which demanded detached visual contemplation, which was essentially 'theatrical', which reproduced the static frame of the painting or proscenium; the other a cinema of montage which created a mobile space within which events were constantly reframed, extended and accelerated, approached and distanced.

We could make the same kind of distinction within architecture.

There are buildings which we feel are designed to be looked at and briefly visited; others which we feel are designed to be lived in and used as ongoing elements in our lives. This distinction is brought out very sharply in Denise Scott Brown and Robert Venturi's classic book on *Learning From Las Vegas*. Essentially Scott Brown and Venturi are celebrating the architecture of non-places—architecture which provides a basic 'shed' for transient use and a decorated façade as a roadside attraction. Like the non-places which Augé describes, Las Vegas is saturated with signage and symbolic elements directed towards the impersonal passer-by, driving down the Strip.

Scott Brown and Venturi vividly evoke an architecture of pastiche— 'Miami Moroccan, International Jet Set Style; Art Moderne, Hollywood Orgasmic, Organic Behind; Yamasaki Bernini cum Roman Orgiastic; Niemeyer Moorish; Moorish Tudor (Arabian Knights); Bauhaus Hawaiian'—and then they go on to quote Morris Lapidus, 'People are looking for illusion; they don't want the world's realities. And, I asked, where do I find this world of illusion? Where are their tastes formulated? Do they study it in school? Do they go to museums? Do they travel in Europe? Only one place—the movies. They go to the movies. The hell with everything else.' So which cinema are we talking about—Morris Lapidus's or Walter Benjamin's? And which architecture—the architecture celebrated in *Learning From Las Vegas*, or some other kind of architecture, symbolically meaningful in a very different kind of way?[3]

Let's begin to answer these questions by looking more closely at the cinema and its use of space, trying, perhaps optimistically, to be a little bit more precise than Walter Benjamin, who dealt, on this subject, in rather broad generalities. First, an essential distinction: space in the cinema is of two quite different types. There is the space created by the production designer, which is essentially a static space, and there is the second space created by the cinematographer and editor, which is essentially a dynamic space, which moves us about within the static space of the set or the location. The first corresponds to the space of an architect (many production designers were trained as architects); the second corresponds to the space of the story-teller, with its manipulation of point-of-view and its fascination with movement and action. This second space is essentially a narrative space.

Cinema is suspended between these two types of attitude—the construction of a place to be looked at and the construction of a mode of looking, a mode whose dynamics are determined by the need to tell a story. Movie set design tends to run along a spectrum from one end of the scale to the other—from movies whose design is essentially meant to impress the spectator visually to those whose design is subordinated to the narrative and the dramaturgy. This distinction is visible in the kind of sketches designers make in preparation for set-building. On the one hand there are those which storyboard the whole film, pre-determining camera positions and, as an additional benefit, saving money by envisaging a fragmentary set which only need contain the limited amount which the camera will see and no more. At the other extreme, there are sets which subordinate narrative to spectacle and seek to impose themselves on the viewer by their own size, visual splendour and sophistication.

A number of successful designers, when asked what kind of set is best, reply that it is the one which the spectator hardly notices, the one which is unobtrusive, which does not draw attention to itself, which is unnoticed by the spectator. One English designer defined the perfect set as the one where the spectator says, 'Sorry, old man, I didn't notice the settings.' Or, in the words of Léon Barsacq, décor should simply be 'a discreet, ever-present character, the director's most faithful accomplice'.[4] In contrast, the sets of *Intolerance* or *The Thief of Baghdad*, *Metropolis* or *Things to Come* or *A Matter of Life and Death*—or more recently, *Blade Runner* or *Brazil*—dominate the experience of watching the film, shift the balance decisively towards spectacle. In fact, the distinction between the two approaches precisely mirrors a distinction within cinema itself between narrative and spectacle. This distinction runs parallel to the mythic contrast between the two legendary founders of cinema—Lumière (realism) and Méliès (fantasy)—and it is reflected in substantive differences between different film genres. Spectacular sets, for instance, are particularly typical of the Biblical Epic, the Musical Comedy, the Science Fiction movie and the exotic Costume Drama.

When Scott Brown and Venturi, or Morris Lapidus, invoke Hollywood in relation to Las Vegas, it is these genres of grand spectacle to which they are implicitly referring us, not the Hollywood of dramatic narrative. Yet, when we think about the accepted masterpieces of cinema, we find quite a different kind of film, with a very particular attention to place, to a unique environment which we associate with a particular story and particular characters—the streets of Rome in Rossellini's *Rome, Open City* or those of Paris in Godard's *Breathless*, Xanadu in *Citizen Kane*, La Colinière in *Rules of the Game*, the Odessa Steps in *Battleship Potemkin*, the garbage dump in *Dodeskaden*, the town jail in *Rio Bravo*, the Bates motel in Hitchcock's *Psycho*, the saloon in John Ford's *My Darling Clementine*, Rick's place in *Casablanca*, Vienna's in *Johnny Guitar*, Mother Gin Sling's in *The Shanghai Gesture*, the convent in *Black Narcissus*, the railway station buffet in *Brief Encounter* or the sewers in *The Third Man*.

These are all places which are habitats in the sense I described above—spaces which are lived in and used by the characters with whom they are associated. Often they are the settings for disaster and breakdown. In Xanadu, Kane destroys his wife's bedroom; in La Colinière chaos breaks out among the house-guests; the motel in *Psycho* is the scene of a terrible crime. In these situations the drama of the film pivots on a breach in the symbolic order and the layers of meaning which have been carefully built up throughout the film. At the same time, the architecture of the sets is carefully designed both to dramatize and to be unobvious. These films all involved close collaboration between director, writer and set-designer—in order to ensure a reciprocal narrativization of décor and visualization of story-telling.

In contrast, books about production design and art direction tend to emphasize the visual and spectacular aspects of film sets. Partly this is because they follow conventional architectural history in their concentration on visual style rather than use or meaning, a tendency accentuated by the role given to production sketches, photographs and frame enlargements as full-page illustrations. For example, there is a considerable body of useful writing on 'art déco' and 'moderne' sets from the twenties and thirties which follows this pattern. Some of it, however, goes outside the field of stylistic influences and aberrations to discuss the social meaning of moderne. Howard Mandelbaum and Eric Myers, for example, point out that the use of moderne is clustered in certain types of setting—nightclubs, ocean liners, the bedrooms and bathrooms of 'sophisticated' women and the penthouse offices of industrial moguls: the leisure haunts of the idle rich, extravaganzas which project moderne into a world of fantastic stylistic exaggeration, a kind of super-moderne.[5] Stylistic modernity in set architecture is thus associated dramatically with excessive wealth, leisure, power and sexuality, the scandalous life-styles of the rich and famous. Cedric Gibbons, head of design at MGM, confirmed this trend by building his own Los Angeles home in a spectacular version of streamlined moderne.[6]

The correlation between modern architecture and corporate power was reinforced in Hollywood by Carl Laemmle's choice of Richard Neutra to design Universal-International's own corporate headquarters on Hollywood Boulevard in 1933. Neutra went on to design homes for two of Hollywood's most art-oriented directors, Josef von Sternberg and Albert Lewin. He is also believed to have served, along with Frank Lloyd Wright, as one of the models for the hero of *The Fountainhead*, directed by King Vidor, one of the very few Hollywood movies which is actually about architecture.[7] (Ayn Rand, the writer of the novel on which the film was based, herself bought Neutra's Sternberg house after the Second World War, when Sternberg was forced to sell it.) Frank Lloyd Wright himself was offered the job of designing *The Fountainhead* but was rejected after he asked for too much money (a quarter of a million dollars). Instead, the job went to an untried designer, Edward Carrere, who, in effect, pastiched Wright's work, with, according to at least one commentator, 'a hint of Aalto'.[8]

Ayn Rand's novel itself caricatured modern architecture while, at the same time, making it a vehicle for her own right-wing libertarian reverence for uncompromising individualism combined with corporate power. Carrere's designs were denounced in the architectural press simply as 'travesty' and 'perversion'. Carrere systematically exaggerated Wright's penchant for cantilevers, revelling in gravity-defying slabs and balconies and, in an over-the-top version of Wright's celebrated house, Fallingwater, piling cantilevers on top of cantilevers. Carrere's designs basically go for visual extravaganza, stressing the colossal and fantastic elements in modern architecture. Although *The Fountainhead* is set in the 1940s, it is somehow reminiscent of a biblical or science-fiction epic. It belongs with films like *Land of the Pharaohs*, portraits of megalomania, rather than films about architecture. Roark, the heroic central character, is simply a twentieth-century version of Vashtar, the master architect of the pyramids, created by Howard Hawks and William Faulkner.[9]

Another fascinating pastiche of Wright's Fallingwater can be found in Hitchcock's *North by Northwest*, designed by Robert Boyle, Hitchcock's favourite collaborator. Boyle's first job was to design *Saboteur* for Hitchcock, and he subsequently worked on *Shadow of a Doubt*, *North by Northwest*, *The Birds* and *Marnie*. Hitchcock demanded detailed storyboards from designers. He himself had begun in the 1920s as an art director and had quickly learned that by designing the set he could control not only the visual look of the film but also its dramatic development. After Hitchcock had approved Boyle's storyboards, it was simply a question of constructing them—not always a simple task. In *North by Northwest*, Boyle chose Fallingwater as the model for the villain's house near Mount Rushmore, where Roger Thornhill, played by Cary Grant, will finally thwart the evil plans of Philip Vandamm (James Mason) and rescue the woman he loves. The villain, true to form, is a rich and sophisticated art collector.

Boyle frankly puts dramatic and narrative considerations before the visual. 'I knew we had to have a house where Cary Grant would be in a precarious position if he was discovered; he had no way out. It also had to be in a position where he could see everything in the house: he had to see her bedroom, he had to see the living room, he had to see the balcony over the living room, and he had to be able to get down and get away.'[10] The attraction of Fallingwater, in the first instance, was that the cantilever would put the hero in a dangerous and precarious situation and Wright's use of glass would allow full visibility into the building from outside. Boyle, however, was particularly fascinated by a specific feature of Fallingwater: 'It had to be a kind of jungle gym for Cary Grant. The *Fallingwater* house, which Frank Lloyd Wright designed, was partly cantilevered, but that wasn't what interested me; it was the stonework in the *Fallingwater* house, which was horizontal striated stone. That was perfect for somebody to get a handhold and climb up; that's why I selected it. I was really influenced by the handholds.'

I would like to dwell for a moment on these handholds. In an essay entitled 'The Owner Makes His Mark', published in a book on suburban homes called *Dunroamin*, the English architect Ian Bentley provides a typology of 'planes of choice' in architecture.[11] He is talking specifically about the 'responsiveness' (his word) of architecture to its users' wishes, the amount of what he calls 'choice' which the building, specifically a typical suburban home, offers to those who inhabit it. Ian Bentley points out that there are three distinct levels at which users and their environments interact: those of physical form, use and meaning. The basic structure of a building is usually fixed and cannot be changed by its user except in superficial ways. Users rarely change even secondary or tertiary features, such as front porches or fireplaces. Even so, basic structures may still offer a wide range of responsiveness in terms of the different ways in which a house can be used and can be assigned personal meanings.

The second level, that of use, involves the users' choices as to the way in which different rooms are allotted different functions and the kind of functional fittings and furnishings with which they are filled, ranging from kitchen units to bedside lamps. The third level, that of meaning, typically involves the colour the walls are painted, the style of curtains or chairs, the design of household items or the accumulation of odds and ends on the mantelpiece. Bentley points out how, when we get to the personalization of bay-windows (these are suburban homes) versus, say, fireplaces, we are already dealing with different zones of meaning. The window is the outlet to the world beyond the house, the world of neighbours and passers-by. The fireplace, on the other hand, is traditionally the focus of the private world of the family itself (at least, before the challenge of the television set). Thus the user is actually living in three separate houses—a physical house with a certain profile and shape and certain fixed characteristics, a functional house organized within that shape for a range of different practical activities, and a symbolic house which is an expression of the cultural and ideological attitudes and tastes of its users.

It is important to bear these distinctions in mind when we look at the historic role of architecture in the cinema. Essentially, film architecture has been designed primarily to reflect the activities and attitudes of its users—the dramatic characters whose lives are depicted in the film. It is narrativized and dramatized architecture. Typically, in the great majority of films, designers begin with the second level, the level of use—what kind of architecture is needed functionally in terms of the story. Thus Fallingwater provided a model for Robert Boyle because it functioned like a jungle-gym and had plenty of handholds. On a second level, sets carry symbolic meanings which are extensions of the characters who inhabit them, just as the choice of furniture or pictures reflects on the character of a home's inhabitants in real life. On the third level, there is the fabric and visual form of the building. This too, of course, reflects on the identity of its users—it indicates whether they are rich or poor, for example. But, in certain situations, it also offers an opportunity for the designer, in Lawrence Paull's words, to make the architecture the 'star' of the film, as in *Caligari* or *Blade Runner*, to design for spectacle.[12]

Most studies of film architecture at which I have looked seem to gravitate unreflectively towards the small group of films which feature architecture as 'star'. Dietrich Neumann's book *Film Architecture*, published in 1996, provides a good example. From the silent period, it features a series of German expressionist films (*Caligari*, *Metropolis*, etc.) as well as *L'Inhumaine* (Mallet-Stevens) and *Aelita* (Alexandra Exter). Murnau's *Sunrise* introduces us to the Hollywood of the studio epoch—*Just Imagine*, *The Black Cat*, *Things to Come* (made in England), *Lost Horizon*, *The Fountainhead*. Contemporary film begins with Jacques Tati and concludes with *Blade Runner*, *Batman* and *Dick Tracy*. As you can see, the list is dominated, first by German Expressionism, then by Hollywood science fiction. Two of the films—*The Black Cat* and *The Fountainhead*—are actually about mad architects. In Edgar G. Ulmer's *The Black Cat*, the architect (maliciously called Poelzig) displays the bodies of his murdered mistresses in an ultra-modern building, built on a craggy hill above a sinister cemetery. On the symbolic level, Ulmer's film can certainly be seen as an implicit critique of modernism, an extreme case of the dystopian vision of modernity which also characterizes most of the science-fiction films on the list.

However, Jacques Tati is the director-designer whose films stand out in this group, in the sense that they are explicitly intended and pretended as critiques of modern architecture, from the contemporary user's point of view, on the functional level. Tati's comedy (like that of Buster Keaton or Charlie Chaplin or, in a way, *Just Imagine*, a futuristic satire made in the early 1930s) comes from showing what can go wrong in modern buildings, presenting their apparent superfunctionalism as a mask for their actual non-functionality. What comes across from Neumann's selection of great 'Film Architecture' is that it is clustered in the genres of dystopian science fiction, horror and crazy comedy.[13] Architecture as star represents criminal lunacy, pathetic farce or untrammelled despotism. With this in mind, it seems strange that architects themselves should be attracted by this vision of their art, even if it makes them the centre of attention!

In this context, it is interesting to note that Frank Lloyd Wright seems to be the architect who has exerted the most influence on film designers. I have already discussed Wright as the model for the criminal egomaniac in *The Fountainhead* and Fallingwater as the model for the evil villain's home in *North by Northwest*. *Blade Runner* uses Frank Lloyd Wright's Ennis Brown house as a crucial reference in its dystopian vision of LA as city of the future dominated by a Mayan-revival mega-structure. The lamasery in Frank Capra's *Lost Horizon*, another fantastic dystopia, appears to be modelled on Wright's Imperial Hotel in Tokyo—and also seems eerily to prefigure his much later Marin County Courthouse. Partly, of course, this was simply because Wright was the most prominent modern architect in America—Tati picks on Le Corbusier, Terry Gilliam chose Ricardo Bofill's complex at Marne La Vallée as the model for his villains' headquarters. But there is no doubt that it also reflects on the megalomania of the Mile-High Tower and Wright's grandiose plan for Broadacre City.

Given Wright's prominence, it is worth looking closely at the work of the one Hollywood director who actually worked with Frank Lloyd Wright as a young apprentice—Nicholas Ray. Ray, I believe, internalized the patriarchal image of Wright as tempestuous sage, along with his other heroes, Robinson Jeffers and Thomas Wolfe. His career and his persona reflect Wright the man rather than his individual films. His only direct comment on Wright's influence was that the architect's liking for long, low, horizontal buildings may have helped him to work successfully in CinemaScope, which most Hollywood directors at that time detested. But I believe that Ray also drew from Wright in his obsession with the idea of 'home' as the major theme of film after film. Ray's typical heroes and heroines are fugitives, itinerants, nomads, unable to settle down, or, like the pseudo-family in *Rebel without a Cause*, runaways who have rejected their natural home and try to set up a new imaginary one. In Ray's great early film *In a Lonely Place*, home is where you are most alone; in his mid-career masterpiece *Johnny Guitar*, the home you fantasized returning to is the place where you can only say, 'I'm a stranger here, myself.' Ray walked out of Taliesin and when he returned to Wisconsin to play the role of Wright as aged guru and teacher, surrounded by adoring youth, the project he embarked on was titled *We Can't Go Home Again*.[14]

With Ray, it is the symbolic meanings of home that are important, rather than glorification of the architecture itself. The most memorable 'architectural' location in his films is Austin and Ashley's moderne Planetarium, the scene of Sal Mineo's death at the end of *Rebel without a Cause*; but the key to Nicholas Ray lies in the trailer in *The Lusty Men*, the igloo in *Savage Innocents*, the hideaway shack in *They Live by Night*, or the gypsy encampment in *Hot Blood*. These are all types of building in which the symbolic level far outweighs the architectural. They are ephemeral or mobile structures which are consequently extremely responsive to the users' wishes, they are narrowly functional, and they symbolize the nomadic life-style of their occupants, an antinomic value to the fixed residence of the conventional citizen.

Motels are particularly interesting architectural items from this point of view. They play a central role in such classic films as Orson Welles's *Touch of Evil*, Alfred Hitchcock's *Psycho* and Henry Hathaway's *Niagara*. Venturi and Scott Brown spend very little time discussing the motel, although it clearly provides a classic case of roadside architecture. Las Vegas, however, with its high-style building, derives from 'Googie' coffee-shop design, mutating into theme park postmodern, whereas motels, as a general category, have remained boring and ordinary. The motel developed out of the tourist campsite via the motor court, before stabilizing as the motel in the immediate post-war period. Essentially motels came to consist of rows of functional cabins, which sought to give a minimal impression of homey lived-in domesticity. Although amounting to little more than a bedroom with a bathroom attached, they place considerable emphasis on symbolic furnishing, as Chester Liebs points out in *Main Street to Miracle Mile*, his classic book on 'American Roadside

Architecture'—heavy chenille bedspreads, an oak writing desk with a blotter, wall-to-wall carpeting, prints hung on the walls, closets lined with quilted satin paper, soap and shampoo, etc.[15] The emphasis is on providing an adequate set of functional articles (bed, closet, bathroom) which are replete with symbolic meaning.

The motel in *Psycho* was designed by Robert Clatworthy, who also designed the equally sinister motel in *Touch of Evil*. In both films, of course, a lone woman, played in both cases by Janet Leigh, is attacked— and in *Psycho* she is murdered. (In *Touch of Evil*, her room is over-run by a gang and she is abused before being injected with drugs and framed as a heroin user.) It seems generally agreed that Hitchcock had seen *Touch of Evil* before he embarked on *Psycho*. Hitchcock, however, is interested precisely in the banality of the Bates motel, which he offsets in two ways—first by filling the office with stuffed birds, second by insisting that the bathroom, the murder scene, should be gleaming white in contrast to the generally dark tones of the rest of the film. The stuffed birds have both a plot logic—they introduce the topic of taxidermy, thus preparing the ground for the final revelation that Norman Bates has preserved his own mother's body—and a symbolic function. Birds in Hitchcock are always prying, with beady eyes and Norman, of course, is a voyeur. The gleaming white of the bathroom, on the other hand, is used to highlight the contrast between light and darkness, the cleanliness of the shower and the filth of the swamp into which the body is thrown, the white shine of the tiles and the matt black of the blood. In *Psycho*, as in the great majority of films, it is the use to which a space is put that primarily determines its meaning. In film architecture, as we have seen, use and meaning rather than form are given priority, except in a specialized group of high-style movies. Even the prevalence of moderne in thirties Hollywood sets is tied to the cultural and social associations of modern architecture, rather than to its visual appearance, although the white–black contrast associated with modern architecture also suited black-and-white film. Hitchcock paid particular attention to the design of the bathroom in *Psycho* because it was where the murder took place. The most important sets or locations are those in which the most important dramatic action takes place, and the look of a classic film, both in general and in detail, is designed to reinforce the film's narrative logic.

Constructing a film narrative, I would argue, involves constructing a mental map. As we watch a film we create an internal diagram of the relationships between the different places which structure its development and the different trajectories the characters follow within and between those places. In their pioneering book *Mental Maps*, Peter Gould and Rodney White point out that our representations of place are mapped through underlying concepts such as district, path, centre, edge, intersection and landmark.[16] In a film, each character follows a series of paths which intersect with the paths followed by other characters, and the spectator classifies different locations in terms of their spatial, social and psychological relationships. The same is true of buildings. When the detective Arbogast enters the Bates house, a 'California gingerbread' house, in Hitchcock's words, his path crosses a border as he attempts to reach the centre of a 'district', where he feels he will find the key to his investigation. In going upstairs he crosses a second symbolic border and thus seals his own fate. Stairs are both landmarks within a house and paths which connect two regions. In many films they are the principal landmark in the house, placed in the well directly opposite the front door, from which the other rooms all radiate. In fact, they are also the centre of the house. In hotels and lodging houses, staircases form the central pathway on which characters encounter each other.

In film after film, crucial dramatic events take place on a staircase—classic examples can be found in *Citizen Kane*, *Battleship Potemkin*, *Odd Man Out*, *Letter from an Unknown Woman*, *Rio Bravo*, and, in Hitchcock films alone, *Psycho*, *Shadow of a Doubt*, *Rebecca*, *Spellbound*, *The Man Who Knew Too Much* and *Vertigo*. The house in which Joseph Losey's *The Servant* takes place was explicitly designed around its central staircase. According to its designer, Richard MacDonald, '[Losey's] central metaphor for *The Servant* was that the house was a snail. It had a central staircase that went through all three stories. It all sort of went convoluting into the kitchen.'[17] At both ends, according to Losey himself, it ended in a trap. Losey's biographer, David Caute, describes it as follows, 'Losey constantly tortured the staircase into new perspectives, angles, shadows, vantage-points, power points—a motionless object which was never at rest; the mute orchestration of the human quartet, its banisters lovingly polished by Barrett, the coiling snail linking the separate rooms, each of them a place of hierarchy, privilege or sexual subversion.'[18] The staircase is the prototypical feature of the house as prototypical place.

Both Augé and Venturi, in very different ways, point out that it is non-places which tend to be designed for immediate visual prominence and appeal, for speed-reading. They presume spectators who are potentially travelling past and whose attention has to be seized if they are to stop, have a closer look and perhaps make use of a space, potentially even transform it into a place. It may be that cinema is now entering a new phase in which the subordination of architecture to narrative will increasingly give way to its use as eye-catching spectacle, like an eighteenth-century folly. It has frequently been pointed out that films more and more resemble the rides in theme parks and that there is a growing symbiosis between the two entertainment forms. If this is indeed the case, then cinema is destined to become an art devoted to creating non-places for touristic consumption, rather than places for dramatic consumption. As 'high-style' spreads outside its traditional genres, cinema will finally have become a spectacular rather than a narrative medium.

The true meaning of tourism, Marc Augé argues, lies in its de-socializing abolition of place. Our touristic fascination with non-places throws us back into solitude. Even when travelling in a group, the relation we have with a non-place is never a social relation, but an individual and anonymous one. Augé points out that non-places are typically contractual—we acquire a ticket to enter an airport departure lounge or to view a famous monument. In the same way, we require a ticket to enter the cinema. The logic of this process, of course, leads us once again towards Las Vegas, where the contract is veiled by the mythology of luck, but the serial anonymity reaches an unusually level of intensity. We can now see a new trend beginning in both Vegas and LA, in both architecture and cinema, as Caesar's Palace gives way to the simulation of Paris and the screen is dominated by the futuristic high-tech spectacle of *The Matrix* or *The Phantom Menace*.[19]

There is a sense in which our fascination with a fantasy architecture of the future is more than simply a question of aesthetic taste. It seems to reflect a much deeper cultural change in Western society, the consolidation of the Society of the Spectacle about which Guy Debord warned us thirty years ago.[20] It was in the late sixties that cinema too began to change direction. The decisive films, of course, were *2001*, followed soon afterwards by *Star Wars*, and the beginning of a new trend in science-fantasy film, which recapitulated many of the themes of *Metropolis*, now re-released with a Giorgio Moroder score and pastiched in a Madonna video. As we enter a society dominated by spatial dislocation of many different kinds, we begin to turn towards films which seem premoni-tory—films such as *Blade Runner* or *Brazil*. At the same time, speculative theories about the 'End of History' and 'Posthistoire' have encouraged us both to discard the idea of history as meaningful narrative and to encourage dystopian irony.[21]

Globalization seems to have moved us away from a time-based towards a space-based culture, in which we can be constantly kept in touch with simultaneous events and sights from across the globe, while our sense of history as a meaningful succession of events is correspondingly eroded. This cultural change seems also to involve a move away from a tactile to an optical apprehension of the world, to a fascination with seeing at a distance, with access to an elsewhere, rather than learning to inhabit a space, physically integrating oneself into it, as Benjamin required of us. As Harold Innis argued, this is a culture which values mobility above memory. Or, to put it another way, a culture which values spec-tacle above narrative, which sees architecture in terms of public façades and views, rather than private spaces to be used and given symbolic meaning.

To me, the most fascinating films in their use of space are those made in a single set or place—Hitchcock's *Rope* or *Rear Window*, Carné's *Le Jour se Lève*, Fassbinder's *The Bitter Tears of Petra Von Kant*, Michael Snow's *Wavelength*. In these films we become gradually familiar with a place, building up our own set of memories, associations and expecta-tions, creating our own symbolizations, our own mental maps. But exotic spectacle and dystopian fantasy seem to be on the verge of winning. After all, as Augé concludes, 'In one form or another, ranging from the misery of refugee camps to the cosseted luxury of five-star hotels, some experi-ence of non-place is today an essential component of all social existence.' The cinema, it seems, is registering this dominant experience of non-place by foregrounding the visual rather than the tactile, in Walter

Benjamin's terms. In the age of digital reproduction, we seem to be creating a new kind of cinema with a new role for architecture and set design. Not surprisingly, this is an architecture of monuments, space stations and tourist attractions.

15

THE CANON

I became interested in the canon for two main reasons:

1. I began to wonder whether the debate about the canon which was taking place in other disciplines impinged in any important way on film studies. But what is the 'canon' in film studies? What would it mean, for instance, to 'open it up' when it seems so shadowy and amorphous? Are there really parallels between Literature, stretching back, it is said, to Homer and beyond, and our neonate Cinema, whose first centennial we have finally celebrated and left behind.

2. In rereading the history of aesthetics, which had always been the mainspring of my work, I began to wonder about the history of taste. 'Taste' was a concept central, for instance, to the aesthetic of Kant, but has somehow fallen by the wayside. What happened to it? Is it really unnecessary?

Attacks on the 'canon' are usually attacks on a sedimented regime of taste perceived as an 'absolutism'. Standards of taste in this kind of 'absolutist' regime are typically presented as 'objective', either because they are said to be guaranteed outright by the inherent 'laws' of art or, more cautiously, because they have passed the 'test of time' and thus are seen to reflect a filtering and convergence of values, as nearly as possible, towards the ideal of the 'objective'.

On the other hand, though opposed to this kind of 'objectivism', I remain deeply sceptical about 'relativistic' theories of taste, which tend to deny any intersubjective sense to words like 'good' or 'better' (let alone 'best'), despite the fact that both producers and consumers of art constantly use an unreflective discourse of 'taste' and 'value'. Film-makers decide that this take or this edit is the 'best', they try to make their film as 'good' as possible. Film spectators discuss among themselves how 'good' this or that film is, say at a festival, and point out what was 'wrong' with work they did not appreciate. Just subjective opinions?

Certainly, as a film-maker, I am aware that a complex 'debate' goes on around the making of any film, as decisions are taken in which different people, with different degrees of vehemence and from different positions of power, express preferences based both on their sense of taste and on a 'deeper' sense of what is aesthetically right or wrong. There is an assumption both of shared 'values' which make intersubjective communication and dialogue possible and of divergences within that framework. If the divergences become too acute, the framework dissolves and the film-making process becomes a nightmare.

As a consumer, I am a child of 'auteurism'. I was introduced, in a serious way, to the cinema while I was a student, and became involved as a script-writer soon after I left university. This was just at the time when the French New Wave burst on the world, and I became an avid reader of *Cahiers du Cinéma* and frequenter of backstreet repertory film theatres to familiarize myself with a backlog of Hollywood pictures recommended by *Cahiers* critics I ticked them off in Coursodon and Boisset's *Twenty Years of American Cinema* when I had seen them.[1]

Looking back on those years, I can now see that 'auteurism' was the last major and explicit attempt to rewrite the film canon. Rather than simply a theory of 'authorship' per se, it involved championing a specific set of film-makers. These were the 'auteurs' celebrated in critical articles and named, in hierarchical order, in the *Cahiers* 'Top Ten Lists', in *Movie* magazine's histogram of British and American directors, and in Andrew Sarris's Pantheon (two versions, with promotions and demotions which I carefully studied).[2] Lists seem trivial, but in fact they are crucial symptomatic indices of underlying struggles over taste, evaluation and the construction of a canon.

It could even be argued, I think, that the 'auteurist' revolution or paradigm shift was the last of a series of twentieth-century critical revolutions in the name of 'modernism' and against the *ancien régime* of artistic values. These were the revolutions which began in the nineteenth century—Thoré's rediscovery of Vermeer, the broader Pre-Raphaelite re-evaluation of the Renaissance, Mary Cassatt's championship of El Greco—and culminated in the twentieth century in Breton's list of surrealist predecessors, T. S. Eliot's reappraisal of the metaphysical poets or Le Corbusier's return to 'Classicism'.

This would suggest that changes in the canon are often linked to changes in production. As the *Cahiers* critics saw it, the overthrow of the existing regime of taste was a precondition for the triumph of new film-makers with new films, demanding to be judged on a different scale of values. This is also the case, for instance, with Sitney's construction of a canon for experimental film (through Anthology Film Archive and through his critical writings) which seeks to locate contemporary film-makers within both the modernist tradition and a literary tradition going back to the romantic poets.[3] This said, perhaps another revolution of the canon depends on another revolution in film-making.

In general, only during periods of challenge is the canon actually made explicit. This is true even of Literature, where 'Great Books' courses are the exception rather than the rule, and attention is focused on them precisely when the underlying system of values they represent is under threat. Often enough, it is my impression that they themselves are the sedimented relics of some long past struggle when the current regime was itself instituted. In reality, they probably do not reflect the point that the regime has now reached, which remains, in any case, amorphous and still in process, constantly under revision and adjustment.

The implicit canon is in constant flux. Marginal adjustments are being made all the time and even its central pillars are not necessarily fixed in concrete. It is a work of bricolage. New elements are assembled and outmoded areas are tacitly discarded. It is being patched up and pushed in one direction or another, through a complex process of cultural negotiation among a motley set of cultural gate-keepers, ourselves included. These gate-keepers both influence opinion and make practical decisions.

The key players can be summarily listed as follows.

First come archives and cinematheques. Archives decide which films to preserve and, through their film programming policy, which to screen. Preservation, of course, is the foundation of the whole enterprise of evaluation. While *films maudits* can survive for some time without anyone actually seeing them, in the end their reputation is bound to suffer. Moreover, we are more and more dependent on archives for the preservation of old films. Archive policy is particularly crucial in determining which films will survive from the silent period and even the 1930s and 1940s. It is archives, too, which decide in the first instance which 'rediscovered masterpieces' to launch on the world for critics and others to look at and consider.

One key indicative document here is the list of 'National Treasures' (selected American films) made annually by the Library of Congress. These lists are formally chosen by one person, the Librarian, on the basis of 'public opinion' and the preferences submitted by a committee made up of various Hollywood organizations, together with a few academics and critics. These annual lists seem to have been a response to the threat of colorization. Listed 'National Treasures' are supposed to be safe from abuse by distributors or exhibitors. This, of course, infringes on industry prerogatives, and, as a result, the project was vigorously contested by Jack Valenti, who nonetheless served on the Committee.

The lists themselves seem to be typical beltway hodgepodges, made up of representative films covering a number of different sectional interests or categories, with no single governing aesthetic. The first list, for instance, covers decades and genres, while the second covers modes and constituencies. The Library would thus be able to defend itself against any possible allegations of bias by pointing out how something of everything was represented. Nonetheless, it is meant to be the 'best' of everything and thus the list does indicate viable consensus candidates for canonization within some other, more coherent framework.

The '360° Pan' list of 'Treasures from the National Film Archive' in London is much more ambitious and programmatic. It covers 360 films chosen from the whole of world cinema, not just British or American cinema. In fact, it is deliberately intended to break out of the pattern whereby each archive collects only the films of its own country. The underlying idea, as I understand it, is that the 360 films selected and acquired should be publicly screened by the National Film Archive throughout each year (with five or six days off for holidays). Over a period of time the British Film Institute will also publish a series of books on each of the films. I am doing *Singin' in the Rain*.

This list was 'masterminded' by David Meeker, the Archive's Feature Film Officer, who constructed it in consultation with specialists of his choice in areas (such as 'animation', 'the cinema of China and Hong Kong', 'Finnish films', and so on) where he felt the need for advice. He followed three criteria:

1. To question the generally accepted view of 'classics' in the cinema and to retain only those titles that appear still to be relevant today (such as *Battleship Potemkin*, *Citizen Kane*, *La Règle du Jeu*).
2. To ensure that the world's leading film-makers are represented by at least one film each, and, in the case of established masters (Hitchcock, Ford, Ophuls, etc.), by as many films as is possible within such restricted parameters.
3. To insinuate into the project a number of titles which, in the UK, at least, have still to attain their deserved status.

Obviously, these are incendiary words. They contain a clear, revisionist drive. The 'generally accepted view of "classics"' is to be questioned, and less well-known, but more deserving, films are to be promoted instead. At the same time, however, the list is going to single out some directors as 'established masters' for preferential treatment. On my count, the list has about one-third American films (119), which must be a carefully considered proportion, and actually includes almost all the well-accepted 'classics' that I could think of, which is not all that surprising, considering its length.

However, most people I have talked to about the NFA list have been infuriated by it. Of course, there are a lot of choices that puzzled or offended me too. Why so many Chinese films and so few Indian or African or Latin American? Surely, this is the wrong choice for Marcel L'Herbier or for Sam Fuller? Whatever happened to Avram Room? More seriously, isn't the choice of British films completely wrong? On the other hand, doesn't this reflect not simply David Meeker's personal judgement, but the inadequate degree of attention that has been paid to writing the history of British film with an aesthetic dimension? It is clear that in dealing with American film, which has been raked through aesthetically a number of times, Meeker attempts to put together a mix of basic auteurism, pre-auteur 'standards' and quirky choices of his own.

I have dwelt on the role of archives at some length because I believe they have always played a key role in taste and canon formation and this is likely to increase in weight and scope as more and more films go out of commercial circulation. Looking back at the *Cahiers* revolution, it is clear how much this depended on the policies of Henri Langlois at the Paris Cinémathèque. In fact, when I first became a cinephile, I myself went to Paris and spent many happy and instructive hours in the Rue d'Ulm. Similarly, my own auteurist reappraisals of the sixties, during my 'Lee Russell' period, were largely dependent on retrospectives at the National Film Theatre. (Later the Edinburgh Film Festival played a similar role in promoting, for instance, through a retrospective, the critical boom in the films of Douglas Sirk, which later broadened out, in conjunction with feminist film study, into a boom in 'melodrama' as a genre.)

Second to the role of archives comes that of academics and critics—the overlapping categories of lecturers and scribblers. Academics play a key role not only by influencing young minds and writing books and articles, but also by choosing films for class screenings or, as in the case of New York University, drawing up required viewing lists which function something like foundation lists of 'great books' although without the same kind of authority, I think. In teaching a Ph.D. seminar on the idea of a canon (from which this chapter springs), I was struck that students, themselves future academics, critics and programmers, formed their own lists out of films first seen in three ways, in this order: class screenings, repertory cinemas or cinematheques, and video-cassette.

Critics also, of course, publish articles and books. They also make up the majority of 'Top Ten' and other similar lists, which academics feel a little embarrassed by. These lists, however, can have a considerable impact. I have already mentioned the *Cahiers* lists which I used to study avidly, both to measure my own judgements against and also as a source of films I should make an effort to see. These lists acted as 'markers' for the *politique*, challenging readers to agree with them or be prepared to argue back.

The *Sight and Sound* lists of 'Top Ten' films, drawn up every decade from 1952 to 1982, have served as a record and summation of international critical opinion, doubtless influencing not only their readers but also their contributors, who each go on to influence public taste in their own way for another ten years. Critics are also mainly responsible for opinion-forming 'buzz' or 'word of mouth', which reaches a peak at film festivals, a site of retrospectives as well as new releases, and the crucial circuit for an international exchange of views on what's good and what's bad, who's up and who's down. This 'buzz' in turn filters through to academics and archivists, as they strive to keep abreast of events.

Next, more problematic, perhaps, comes the role of film-makers. This is institutionalized at formal events like the Academy Awards, which present to the outside world the image of value to which the Hollywood industry aspires. As is well known, this itself involves an implicit trade-off between respect for the box-office, acknowledgement of professional standing, and aesthetic evaluation, all filtered through a sieve of unstated assumptions through which dramas, costume pictures and films with important themes pass more readily than horror movies or musicals. The Oscars, too, serve as a kind of caricature of mainstream, midcult values against which both mandarin and radical critics can react in constructing their own rival canons.

Film-makers also have their own informal view of their peers which in turn may feed through into critical discourse. This kind of view springs from the somewhat different way of looking at films that making them entails. It implies a particular sense of craft and a feeling for the ambitiousness or originality of other people's projects, as well as film-makers' wish to place their own work within a historical tradition or pay their debt to people who influenced them. The most obvious recent example of this is the role played by Coppola and Scorsese in the re-evaluation of Kurosawa or the rediscovery of Powell and Pressburger (mainly Powell).

In fact, there is a complex genealogy of influence and indebtedness which is left for critics and historians to unearth. Sometimes it is plain, on the record—like Bertolucci's love–hate relationship with Godard and

Pasolini or Lindsay Anderson's debt to John Ford and Humphrey Jennings. Sometimes it is more arcane, disguised as 'homage' or 'pastiche' or 'citation'. But the effect, as historians write about one director, explaining the subtext for some shot or sequence, is to draw attention to another. In this way, a kind of intra-filmic network of influences is inadvertently drawn up which makes the work of one film-maker seem crucial in understanding the work of another, who in turn . . . and so on.

Finally, of course, there is the audience. Here, I want to note in particular the role played by film-buffs and cultists. This is a special sub-group of spectators who feel especially enthusiastic about one genre, one director or even one favourite film. Not only are cultists organized, putting on their own screenings and events, but they exert pressure on exhibitors and critics through their dedication. In fact, many critics emerge out of the ranks of cultists. It could even be argued that the *Cahiers* critics were themselves cultists in origin, nurtured in the cine-clubs of the Left Bank which they attended in virtual gangs. Andrew Sarris, it is worth recalling, published a book called *Confessions of a Cultist*, and drew heavily in constructing his Pantheon on a cultist *sang pur*, Eugene Archer.[4]

Cultists play an apparently disproportionate role precisely because they care deeply (obsessively) about the films they love and constitute them spontaneously into a kind of 'cult canon'. The key transition occurs when they, so to speak, 'go public' and begin to argue the merits of their canon with outsiders instead of just celebrating them in semi-private cenacles. There are a number of cult films on the '360° Pan' list: not only *King Kong* and *Frankenstein*, but also the true cult classics, *The Most Dangerous Game* and *The Bride of Frankenstein*, as well as *Gun Crazy*, *Kiss Me Deadly* and *Peeping Tom*. Sometimes the line is hard to draw: are *The Wizard of Oz* and *Casablanca* cult classics or mainstream masterpieces? And are *Now Voyager* and *Mildred Pierce* feminist 'cult films' or counterparts and rivals to the auteurist 'classics' *Red River* and *The Searchers*?

The process of cultural negotiation among these many gate-keepers of taste results not only in the surface phenomena of lists and programmes, but also in the crystallization of an aesthetic paradigm at a deeper level. It is the task of theorists and historians to codify shifts of taste in terms of aesthetic theory and historical periodization. Thus when we look at the history of film taste we can see three contending phases of aesthetic theory-making. First, the 'Seventh Art' theories which grew up around the silent cinema and stressed *photogénie*, montage or filmic pantomime. These, in turn, were locked in to certain exemplary films: *Broken Blossoms*, *Potemkin*, *The Gold Rush*, which served as explicit lynch-pins in the implicit construction of a canon.

Silent film theory fought a long rearguard action through the thirties (vide Arnheim's notorious 'A New Laocoön') and was not really challenged until Bazin launched his counter-theory on the basis of *La Règle du Jeu*, *Citizen Kane* and Neo-Realism.[5] Bazin, however, was rapidly overtaken by his own heirs—the *Cahiers* group—who revised his interest in Renoir, Welles and Rossellini, updated it in favour of the 'late' films (*The River*, *Arkadin*, *Viaggio in Italia*) and introduced the auteurist canon pivoted around 'Hitchcocko-Hawksianism' (*Vertigo*, *Red River*). Auteurism was much more explicit in its canon-construction even than Bazin and set out to provide an entirely new and comprehensive mapping of Hollywood film, as well as a revision of European cinema. French 'Poetic Realism' of the thirties, for instance, was swept away.

However, the emergence of the French New Wave also had the effect of provoking a 'new wave' of taste, centred upon the aesthetic implied by the new 'art cinema' itself. Essentially, this was a non-Hollywood auteurism (often even counter-Hollywood), whose director auteurs were much more nearly equivalent to novelists, painters or composers in their aims and procedures. The key films here were *L'Avventura*, *Persona* and *8½*. This new paradigm reflected a shift from archive, cine-club and repertory theatre to festival and art-house as sites of viewing. The emphasis moved to 'new' and 'young' cinema, rather than historical research. Partly as a result of this, I think, this new wave of taste has never been seriously theorized, but has persisted as what might be called a 'common sense' of evaluation, a kind of 'modernist populism'.

These shifts in aesthetic paradigm imply and interlock with the work of film historians, especially in the way they detect turning-points and define periods. For instance, the whole conceptual ensemble of 'classical' cinema, 'classical' construction and 'classical' codes, used to characterize Hollywood film, has an 'aesthetic' subtext. What are the criteria appropriate to 'classical' cinema and are they different from those appropriate to 'non-classical' cinema? Does a positive evaluation of one rule out a positive evaluation of the other, or can we justify being eclectic? Where did 'classical' cinema begin and end—do we draw the line at the threshold of 'Griffithian' narrative construction (pre-Griffithian − pre-Raphaelite?) or at the coming of sound? What is the implication of terms like 'mannerist' or 'baroque' applied, say, to *Citizen Kane* or to *8½*? Are there common aesthetic criteria to be applied to each region of the Noel Burch anti-Hollywood triad: early, experimental and non-Western film?

If we study the actual lists which register the construction of a canon, a number of trends and tensions become apparent. I have looked at a wide variety of 'canonic indices'—listings in the index of once or currently well-regarded books, Museum of Modern Art programming lists, lists of 'cult classics' and the 100 best movies on video, archive selection and 'treasures' lists, student viewing lists, etc.—but in my remarks here I draw principally on critics' polls from 1952 to 1982, both because they more or less coincide with my own intuitions as to what the canon implicitly has been (despite my personal reservations), and also because they take place at intervals over time and thus give a clear sense of how tastes have changed. I have used my knowledge of other lists as supplementary evidence to check against critics' polls.

In both the 1952 *Sight and Sound* poll and the 1952 Belgian Cinémathèque poll, twenties silent films are strongly represented. *Gold Rush* (2, 2), *Potemkin* (4, 1), *Intolerance* (5, 9), *Greed* (7, 7), *Joan of Arc* (7, 13) and *Broken Blossoms* (21, 17) show up on both lists. Both lists also include *City Lights* (2, 4), *Le Million* (10, 4), *La Grande Illusion* (13, 4) and two forties films, *Bicycle Thieves* (1, 3) and *Brief Encounter* (10, 9). They choose different Flaherty films: *Louisiana Story* (5) and *Man of Aran* (9). However, there are also some significant divergences. Crucially, in the light of hindsight, the *Sight and Sound* poll has *La Règle du Jeu* at 10 and *Citizen Kane* at 13. Neither of these films makes the Brussels list.

In 1958 there was another Brussels poll, in conjunction with the Brussels World Fair, but based on a jury made up mainly of film-makers. A group of discontented critics voted for a 'Harry Langdon Prize' list and *Cahiers* also produced a polemical rival list. *Sight and Sound* followed in

1962. These lists make it obvious that something major is happening. The World Fair list runs as follows (with the 1952 Cinémathèque list position in brackets):

1. *Potemkin*   (1)
2. *Gold Rush*   (2)
3. *Bicycle Thieves*   (3)
4. *Joan of Arc*   (13) (*S & S* 7)
5. *La Grande Illusion* (4)
6. *Greed*   (7)
7. *Intolerance*   (9)
8. *Mother*   (–)
9. *Citizen Kane*   (–) (*S & S* 13)
10. *Earth*   (–) (*S & S* 19)

The 1958 list actually obliterates the thirties. Poetic Realism has gone. The list both adds to the number of silent classics and makes a single concession to 'modernity' by dropping *Brief Encounter* and substituting *Citizen Kane* alongside *Bicycle Thieves* and *La Grande Illusion*. The *Cahiers* list, in contrast, drops *Potemkin* from the first place and substitutes Murnau's *Sunrise* (cf. Bazin). This is followed by *La Règle du Jeu* (not *La Grande Illusion*), *Viaggio in Italia* (not *Bicycle Thieves*), *Ivan the Terrible* (not *Potemkin* again), *Birth of a Nation* (not *Intolerance*), *Mr Arkadin* (not even *Citizen Kane!*), *Ordet* (not *Joan of Arc*), *Ugetsu Monogatari*, *L'Atalante* (not more Russian silent classics) and *Wedding March* (not *Greed*). No. 11 is Hitchcock's *Under Capricorn* and 12 is *M. Verdoux* (not *Gold Rush*). What is strange about this list is that it more or less keeps the same directors, but simply changes the choice to a later work.

The *Sight and Sound* list four years later (1962) shows more clearly still the change that has been taking place. The New Wave, of course, has now appeared. *Citizen Kane* has gone right to the top of the poll, followed by *L'Avventura* and *La Règle du Jeu*. Then come *Greed*, holding firm, and *Ugetsu Monogatari*, another art film. Next, *Potemkin* and *Bicycle Thieves* (both slipping), along with *Ivan the Terrible*, followed by *La Terra Trema* and *L'Atalante*.

In this list not only is 'silent cinema' finally losing ground but the thirties are represented only by *Rules of the Game* and *L'Atalante*, which were post-war rediscoveries rather than films with continuing reputations. The neo-realists are still well represented, but they have been joined by Antonioni, as well as Mizoguchi. Above all, *Citizen Kane* and *La Règle du Jeu* have established themselves in the first three, where they will stay through 1972 and 1982 as acknowledged masterpieces.

The great change appears to take place during the sixties. In 1972, not one neo-realist film appears in the top twenty, and Stroheim's *Greed* has gone with them. *Potemkin* holds its place as the recognized cornerstone of silent film, and has been joined by Dreyer's *Joan of Arc* and *The General*, Keaton prospering as Chaplin declines. Keaton presumably appeared more 'modernist', closer to Beckett, while Chaplin's Victorian sentimentalism was finally catching up with him. Dreyer, it should be noted, was still working during the sixties and film-goers had been reminded of *Joan* in Godard's *Vivre sa Vie*.

European art film is now heavily represented. Fellini's *8½* and Bergman's *Persona* have moved ahead of *L'Avventura* and *Ugetsu Monogatari* respectively. *The Magnificent Ambersons* appears at no. 8, consolidating Welles's triumph, and *Wild Strawberries* at no. 10, consolidating the emergence of Bergman. Significantly, Hitchcock's *Vertigo* is at 12 and John Ford's *The Searchers* at 18. Welles and Renoir dominate the poll, followed by three silent movies and five recent art films. In the top ten, Welles and Keaton are the only American directors.

By 1982, however, *Singin' in the Rain* has appeared at no. 4, *Vertigo* at no. 7 and *The Searchers* at no. 10. There are six American films. The auteurist re-evaluation of Hollywood has finally arrived. *Potemkin* and *The General* are now the only remaining silent films. *8½* and *L'Avventura* are still there, though Bergman has vanished and *Ugetsu Monogatari* has been replaced by *The Seven Samurai*. In general, European art film can be seen as in retreat, giving ground to the new post-auteurist Hollywood choices.

The major trends in the *Sight and Sound* list during this thirty-year period can be summed up as follows:

1. Silent and early sound films gradually fall away. Eisenstein's *Potemkin* is the only silent film that survives from 1952 to 1982 (4, 6, 3, 6). It is eventually joined by Keaton's *The General* (–, 20, 8, 10).

2. Thirties film is all but eliminated. By 1982, *Rules of the Game* is the only 'formal' survivor. Carné, for example, is swept away by the post-war art film and Poetic Realism is all but forgotten.

3. Italian Neo-Realism survives into the sixties, but is then demoted very rapidly. As I remarked earlier, Stroheim's *Greed* goes with it. Once again, the beneficiaries are a second wave of more 'modernist' art films—$8\frac{1}{2}$, *Persona*, *Wild Strawberries*, etc.

4. The triumph of the festival 'art film' is not as solid as it first seems. *L'Avventura* falls from 2 to 5 to 7; *Ugetsu Monogatari* from 4 to 10 to –; $8\frac{1}{2}$ from 4 to 5. *Persona* and *Wild Strawberries* come and go. Only Kurosawa climbs up. *Ikiru* is 20 in 1962 and 12 in 1972. *Seven Samurai* leaps to third place in 1982. Interestingly, the French New Wave directors are not serious contenders.

5. *Citizen Kane* (13, 1, 1, 1) and *La Règle du Jeu* (10, 3, 2, 2) dominate the lists from 1962 onwards. They seem to replace Lean's *Brief Encounter* and Renoir's own *La Grande Illusion*.

6. Hollywood film does not dominate the polls (totals of 4, 2, 3 and 6). In the 1952 list, the American films are all by the great silent directors. Then comes Welles, with just Stroheim in 1962 and Keaton in 1972. Not till 1982 is the post-war American cinema represented: Donen–Kelly, Hitchcock, Ford.

The role played by *Citizen Kane* and *Rules of the Game* is particularly striking. Why did they rise so fast and then show such staying power? First, it should be said that they were supported both by *Cahiers du Cinéma* and by *Sight and Sound*. However, it is clear that they each occupied a particularly important place in André Bazin's view of the cinema. Along with the Italian neo-realist films, they were the chosen vehicles for his revived realist aesthetic and ontology of film. Both films too fitted with the rising ideology of the personal film-maker and both had a *film maudit* dimension. Renoir's film had been butchered and misunderstood. Welles was rejected and thrown out of Hollywood, at least according to the myth.

However, I think it is also crucial that both films are open to multiple and even contradictory readings and rereadings. Bazin, for instance, argued that *Kane* was a realist film. Welles's use of deep focus and the long take went against classical construction. Moreover, contrary to Sartre's view (Sartre was the first to introduce *Kane* to the French public, having seen it in America before it opened in Paris), it was on the side of freedom (depth of field; no manipulative editing) rather than fatality (flashback structure; story concluded, waiting only to be summed up). Nevertheless, Bazin seems to have had some doubts: for his own 1952 'Ten Best' list, he chooses Wyler's *The Little Foxes*, rather than *Kane*, as the exemplary film, alongside *Rules of the Game* and *Bicycle Thieves*.

Truffaut takes a very different line. He came to see the film as a masterpiece of artifice, full of tricks and devices. He places it in a tradition which derives from Murnau, not simply the Murnau of long takes and elaborate camera movements, but also the Murnau who built enormous *trompe-l'oeil* sets. For Rohmer, *Kane* was the film with which American cinema left its prehistory behind. He saw it as pointing forward towards the work of Mankiewicz (Joseph, not Herman) and introducing a new complexity of dramatic structure. Sarris later describes *Kane* as an 'American baroque' film, going beyond Hollywood Classicism into a realm of excess and extravagance.

Borges was fascinated by aspects of *Kane* which echoed his own work: the labyrinth without a centre, the play of mask and identity, the paradoxes of the detective story. I took a similar view in my 1975 'Introduction to *Citizen Kane*' where I saw the film as pointing forward towards *Last Year in Marienbad*.[6] More recently, Michael Denning has argued in 'Persistence of Vision' that *Kane* should be seen in relation to the Popular Front theatre movement from which Welles emerged.[7] Indeed, this line of thought suggests a Brechtian reading of *Kane*. Welles, after all, was the only American stage director Brecht admired and who he positively wanted to work with. Brecht was specially impressed by Welles's 1946 *Around the World in Eighty Days*.

The same kind of multiple readings can also be made of *Rules of the Game*. This too was a personal film emerging out of Renoir's involvement with Popular Front theatre. It reveals something of the same fascination with the modern media and the new type of hero associated with them (in fact, radio is diegetically inscribed within the film, rather than determining the shape of the soundtrack, as it does in *Kane*). Whereas Kane is associated with the press, Jurieu is a child of radio and aviation.

While Bazin could see *Rules of the Game* as a realist film, it is also possible to see it, as Truffaut saw *Kane*, as a work of extreme artifice, emerging from a theatrical tradition. Just as Welles places his modern hero in a Shakespearean or Conradian setting, so Renoir places his in a setting derived from Marivaux and de Musset. Both films mix genres— Welles: tragedy, bio-pic and detective story; Renoir: romantic comedy, tragedy and wild farce. Finally, both films were seen as 'breaking the rules' of narrative construction, although in very different directions.

Both films, in fact, were seen as signalling an end to the thirties and the beginning of a new epoch in the cinema—one which coincided, of course, with the defeat of fascism and the beginning of the new post-war historical epoch in Europe (and the end of the 'New Deal' period and a new world role in America). They represented the possibility of a new direction for cinema at a moment when new directions were called for. In this sense, they indeed form part of a more general shift in taste, along with Neo-Realism, as Bazin indicated. But whereas Neo-Realism was perceived as historically limited and, so to speak, 'monologic' in its basic aesthetic, *Kane* and *Rules of the Game* were more universal, open-ended and 'polylogic'.

Here their qualifications as *films maudits* were also important. They came to be seen, in a sense, as martyrs for the cause. Thus when European and American cinema were finally renewed, these two films were still looked back to as heroic ancestors, premonitory films whose promise only came to fruition years—indeed decades—later. At the same time, the films were sufficiently rich and open to be available to critics of different outlook, in different periods and in different cultural situations. As Frank Kermode argues in his book on *The Classic*, permanence (as a classic, within a canon) means that a work is 'timeless' not because its meaning or value is frozen permanently across time, but precisely because it proves itself susceptible to a range of different readings and evaluations across time (and across cultures as well).[8]

Thus the reasons why films enter the canon are usually complex. Why, for instance, *Vertigo* or *The Searchers*? Obviously their entry represents a revisionist look at Hollywood cinema, whose eventual triumph was undoubtedly connected with the efforts of, first, the French New Wave and, later, an 'American New Wave' (Scorsese, Coppola, Lucas) to emerge within their respective film industries. But *Vertigo* and *The Searchers* are also films which can be seen not simply in auteurist terms, but also with a modernist gloss. Unlike earlier genre thrillers or westerns, they display ambivalent ethics, 'dark' heroes, bleak endings, perverse and difficult relationships and psychological cruelty. Arguably, they are the two oddest films of two well-established directors. In this sense, both *Vertigo* and *The Searchers* can be seen as bringing together, on the one hand, a rehabilitation of the old masters and classic genres of Hollywood with, on the other, something more like the revenge of 'noir' or even existentialism.

The reputation of both films also reflects the *Cahiers* preference for late films, even 'testaments', as well as another important *Cahiers* tenet—a reversal of genre hierarchy (in contrast to the Oscars) associated also with a preference for wide screen, stars, colour, music and location over academy ratio, actors, black and white, silence and studio filming. Compared with, say, *Psycho* or *My Darling Clementine*, *Vertigo* and *The Searchers* are lush, landscape/cityscape pictures. When we look at the work of Scorsese, Coppola and Lucas, we can see the connection (despite Scorsese's excursus into black and white, or Coppola's infatuation with building the cityscape of Las Vegas in the studio). Once again, there is a complex *Nachträglichkeit* or 'retroactive causality' at work.

Finally, perhaps we can begin to ask what the future might hold in store. The most recent film on the 1982 *Sight and Sound* list was actually *8½*. It seems as if the canon had indeed begun to freeze. Since then, a look at a number of very different lists suggests that a new batch of American films are candidates for admission: *Bonnie and Clyde*, *2001*, *The Wild Bunch*, *Mean Streets* or *Taxi Driver* or *Raging Bull*, *Annie Hall*, *Chinatown*, *The Godfather* and *Blue Velvet*. All these films are in the top thirty of *Entertainment Weekly*'s 1990 '100 Best Movies on Video' list, along with *Citizen Kane* (2) and *Rules of the Game* (20 but, with *Seven Samurai* and *La Strada*, the only non-American film). Four of these films are on the NYU 'required viewing' list (along with *Nashville*) and three of them were the last films screened in UCLA's 'History of the American Motion Picture'. Seven of them are in the '360° Pan' list, which stops at 1979.

The other obvious possibility is the widening of the list to include global cinema, beyond Europe (mainly Russia, France and Italy), the

United States and Japan. This trend is clearly visible in the '360° Pan', though many may think it still inadequate. The NYU list includes Alea and Sembene. Similarly, historical research into early cinema will eventually feed through into the twenties and create a new revisionist canon. It already seems strange, for instance, that even a film like *Metropolis* fails to feature on any lists I have seen. Nothing much has happened in the evaluation of silent cinema since Bazin's readjustment in favour of Stroheim and Murnau, which then provoked a second readjustment within Stroheim's work towards *Foolish Wives* or *Queen Kelly*.

But, in the last analysis, we should probably look towards a much more fundamental shift in the underlying aesthetic paradigm, which has drifted more or less unchallenged since the early sixties. We might expect this to come from the direction of postmodernism, but here only *Blade Runner* has emerged as a serious marker. 'Postmodern' film theory still seems derivative and unclear about its aesthetic commitments. Or, as has so often happened in the past, we might expect yet another basic re-evaluation of Hollywood, either positive or negative, or recasting it in as yet unfamiliar light. This would mean, I think, looking away from the question of 'classical construction' which has dominated academic approaches to Hollywood in recent years, to odd and exceptional films which might begin to form a new pattern.

In any event, I do not believe the canon will disappear, however implicit it becomes. There are too many reasons why we have a canon. Basically, because priorities are set within practical limits of money, time and enthusiasm in every area from archives through universities to publishers and, in a community where there is some amount of intersubjective communication, these will tend to reinforce each other. It is for this reason that I think it is important to look carefully at how canons are constructed and what they indicate. Finally, I think aesthetics is central to film study and that since aesthetic inquiry necessarily involves judgements of quality, this must lead to debates over value and taste which will in turn lead to reassessments of the existing canon. I think the time has come for just such a debate.

TIME IN FILM AND
VIDEO ART

In their understanding of time, the artist's videotapes in 'Making Time'[1] are curiously reminiscent of some of the very first films made by the Lumière brothers at the end of the nineteenth century, films sometimes known as 'primitive'. Made before the appearance, development and triumph of editing or montage, these earliest films simply show one continuous action or event, which begins at the beginning of the film and ends as it ends. Even at the dawn of cinema, it is worth noting, the Lumière brothers seem to have taken care to time the action of their films so that their ending coincided with the end of the event filmed. Thus, in their famous *Workers Leaving the Factory*, the film begins with the factory gates opening, continues while more workers stream out and concludes with the gates being closed. Thus, in André Gaudreault's words, 'the film opens, presents one action through to its conclusion and then ends'. This is not exactly a narrative, because there is no causal chain involved, linking one event to another, but simply a single event, with no consequences except that all the participants have exited the frame by the end of the film, apart from a couple of onlookers who may be gate-keepers or something of that kind.

Some of these films are clearly staged for the camera (unlike the workers who would leave the factory whether there was a camera there or not), and thus begin to take on a dramatic quality which places them, perhaps, at the threshold of narrative. Thus, in *A Game of Cards*, our

234 THEMES AND STYLES

attention is monopolized by a waiter who is clearly over-performing for the camera, pointing hysterically at the cards, as Richard De Cordova describes it, and 'laughing as if in a fit'. This is not something he would reasonably be doing if there was no camera present. *Feeding the Baby* falls into the same category of film, showing the self-conscious reactions of onlookers as the baby is prodded into consuming its meal. Eventually the Lumière brothers made a film which is customarily considered as crossing the threshold into dramatic narrative—*L'Arroseur Arrosé*, which might be translated *The Waterer Watered*. This single-shot film shows a gardener spraying with a hose which a mischievous young lad then steps on, thereby stopping the flow of water, until the gardener looks down the nozzle in search of the blockage, whereupon the mischievous boy releases his foot and soaks the gardener, who pursues him off-screen in a rage. Many scholars of early cinema argue, however, that although this film shows us a story in dramatic form, it cannot yet be said to have told the story, to have narrated it. Telling, in their view, involves moving beyond the single-shot film to the edited film, within which the story is deliberately shaped, shot by shot, rather than simply recorded by the camera.

Many artists' videos, it seems, are atavistic works, deliberately return-ing to the single-shot technique which ruled at the very dawn of cinema, setting up a continuous action and then filming it within a given time-limit without any edits or even camera movements. In this respect, artists' videos simply followed in the footsteps of avant-garde film, which preceded video during the 1960s. In his book *Back and Forth: Early Cinema and the Avant-Garde*, Bart Testa discusses at length the fascination which avant-garde film-makers felt for the very first epoch of their art, deliberately echoing its simplicity and apparent naivety.[2] In Testa's words, avant-garde film-makers were 'fascinated with the origins of their art, however unattainable and mysterious these prove to be'. The crucial films for Testa are Ken Jacobs's *Tom, Tom, the Piper's Son*, made in 1969, and Ernie Gehr's *Eureka*, made in 1974. To make *Tom, Tom, the Piper's Son* Jacobs simply refilmed a 1905 film of the same title from the screen, closing in on particular areas or details with a wandering camera to create, in his own words, a 'dream within a dream', a subjective journey which reframes, recreates and reloops the original, seizing obsessively on a stray detail, refocusing and reframing it to bring out its mystery and beauty. In contrast, Ernie Gehr's *Eureka* elongates the film, a view from a trolley-ride in San Francisco in 1930, by freeze-framing every single frame so that the original effect of continuous movement is arrested and transformed into a discontinuous series of still images, a kind of freezing of Zeno's arrow of time, as Testa points out. In fact, both Jacobs's and Gehr's films elongate their original, by looping or by freeze-framing, both drawing attention to their own work of refilming and decelerating the original, slowing it down contemplatively.

We can find a similar effect, taken to more extreme lengths, in the films of Andy Warhol, such as *Sleep* (1963) or *Empire* (1964), each consisting of series of consecutive shots laid end to end, with total lengths of 5 hours 20 minutes (projected at below standard speed) and 8 hours 5 minutes respectively.[3] In *Sleep* and *Empire*, of course, action or even change of any kind is extremely minimal—indeed almost nothing happens although there are bouts of snoring in *Sleep* and the building lights are switched off and on to dramatic effect in *Empire*. *Sleep*, it should be added, was criticized at the time by Warhol's friend Taylor Mead, who dismissed it as a 'fraud' because it used repeated footage. Like Jacobs and Gehr, in fact, Warhol deliberately slowed his work down, influenced, it seems, by attending a concert organized by John Cage, featuring Eric Satie's piano piece *Vexations*, a work which lasted for 18 hours and 40 minutes, in which a single 80-second piece was repeated 840 times by different pianists. Warhol discussed the use of repetition with Cage following this concert, but never used repetition or indeed any kind of editing again after his experience with *Sleep*, explaining that he found it too 'tiring'. Perhaps an even more significant work by Warhol, however, was *Eat* (1964), a 39-minute film (at the slow projection speed of 16 frames per second) in which Warhol filmed Robert Indiana eating a mushroom, as instructed, as slowly as possible, managing to make it last for as long as 27 minutes, further extended by Warhol's choice of projection speed.

Eat is a crucial film in relation to the use of time in subsequent artists' videos because it combined a completely neutral film-making style with a deliberately time-based performance (eating a mushroom as slowly as possible). In contrast, the sleeping John Giorno or the Empire State

Building had nothing to do except sleep and be there, both unconscious activities. Indiana, on the other hand, received instructions which he was asked to follow consciously and deliberately. Task-based work of this kind eventually became a staple of artists' video work. It also bears some relation to the documentation of artists' performance on film which was already frequent in the early 1960s, although Indiana's performance took place simply in order for it to be filmed by Warhol, without any public existence of its own—enacted on a closed set, so to speak, with an eventual film screening as its only *raison d'être*.

A task-based performance, like Indiana's for Warhol, necessarily poses a new kind of problem for a film-maker or a video-maker. Put simply, it creates a new kind of suspense. Watching a film such as *Sleep*, we may wonder how long it will last before the sleeper awakes, what the duration of sleep will be, but we also know that this is an outcome over which the sleeper has no control. Robert Indiana, however, is consciously attempting to prolong the time-span of his performance and hence of Warhol's film. He is actively engaged in postponement and we thus become aware of him as a performer with two apparently contradictory goals—the primary task of eating a mushroom and the secondary (suspenseful) task of delaying completion of the first task for as long as possible. If we look at John Cage's work, we find a very similar programme within the field of music, another time-based art. While he was teaching at Black Mountain College, Cage gave just one lecture—a 'Defense of Satie'—in which he put the case for the importance of duration as a structuring idea in music, as a primary characteristic carrying more weight than that of harmony. 'With Beethoven', Cage noted, 'the parts of a composition were defined by means of harmony. With Satie and Webern they are defined by means of time lengths. The questions of structure is so basic, and it is so important to be in agreement about it, that one must now ask: Was Beethoven right or are Webern and Satie right?'[4] Cage had no doubts about the answer.

I answer immediately and unequivocally, Beethoven was in error, and his influence, which has been as extensive as it is lamentable, has been deadening to the art of music. Now on what basis can I pronounce such a heresy? It is very simple. If you consider that sound is characterized by its pitch, its loudness, its timbre, and its duration, and that silence, which is the opposite and, therefore, the necessary partner of sound, is characterized only by its duration, you will be drawn to the conclusion that of the four characteristics of the material of music, duration, that is time length, is the most fundamental.

Silence, Cage goes on to note, 'cannot be heard in terms of pitch or harmony. It is heard in terms of time length.' Cage added that 'before Beethoven wrote a composition, he planned its movement from one key to another—that is, he planned its harmonic structure. Before Satie wrote a piece, he planned the lengths of its phrases.' This, of course, is the same procedure that Warhol followed in his film-making. In a visual form such as film or video, as opposed to a musical form, the word 'harmonic' would find an equivalent in a word such as 'dramatic', just as 'melody' would find a rough equivalent in a term like 'narrative'. Thus Warhol planned the lengths of his shots before filming (each the length of a film roll) as opposed to a Hollywood film-maker who decided the lengths of shots in the editing, as a function of their narrative and dramatic value. Similarly, Warhol was concerned with the duration of actions rather than their dramatic quality or impact. This aesthetic, derived ultimately from Satie via Cage, was the one which finally fed through into the work of artist videomakers.

John Baldessari's tape in the 'Making Time' exhibition, for instance, is dominated by a ticking alarm clock set for twelve o'clock, establishing a limit on the ongoing activity of tuning glasses, its ticking providing an insistent rhythm, terminating in silence as the alarm finally stops ringing. Vito Acconci's tape displays a pointing arm—the artist's own arm presumably—showing the tremors, slight readjustments of posture, the wavering and deep breathing, the determined pointing and straightening of the head which signify a grim determination to keep the arm horizontal as long as the tape keeps running. In Bruce Nauman's tape, there is a rhythmic and then continuous drilling sound as the camera moves very slowly in towards an open mouth, before eventually stopping, starting and losing focus as the tape ends. Each of these tapes depicts an ongoing action with an increasingly insistent affirmation of the passage of time, shown by symptomatic actions or visible changes of state, concluding eventually, as the tape approaches its end, with the ongoing signs of an action itself approaching termination, due to completion of a schedule or simply loss of energy, until suspense is finally lifted as the tape runs out of time. These tapes are somehow about their own suspenseful descent towards inertia.

Film and video art, however, exhibit only a small fraction of the possible ways in which time can be used and understood. Time, which we tend to think about in purely linear terms, is in fact incredibly complex. In Roget's *Thesaurus*, for example, there are hundreds of time-related words listed under such semantically various headings as Neverness, Period, Indefinite Duration, Contingent Duration (provisionally, as long as it lasts, etc.), Long Duration, Transience, Endless Duration, Instantaneity, Priority, Posteriority, Present Time, Different Time (some other time, once upon a time, etc.), Synchronism, Futurity, Past Time, Newness, Oldness, Youth, Age, Earliness, Lateness, Timeliness, Untimeliness, Frequency, Infrequency, Regularity, Irregularity, Change, Permanence, Cessation, Continuance, Recurrence, Reversion, Relapse, Changeableness, Anticipation, Memory, Expectation, Preparation, Cause and Effect, Continuity, Discontinuity, Destiny and so on, running the whole gamut of temporality from Beginning to End.[5] In any consideration of video art or experimental film (which, to me, are strongly overlapping if not quite identical categories) the great majority of these terms seem relevant and applicable—there is even a sense of destiny in Acconci's holding his arm straight out in front of him for the continuing duration of his tape, a certain knowledge that the arm must eventually fall, combined with an uncertainty as to exactly when, whether before or after the tape comes to its anticipated end.

On the whole, however, we can simplify the issue of time by looking at the way in which it functions in literature, in speech and language. In verbal discourse, the development of time-related syntactic forms has clearly taken place as a function of the priorities we have given, over time, to clear and effective communication. This has influenced not only the semantics but also syntax, categories built into the formal structure of the language, into its 'grammar', rather than categories expressed in its vocabulary, in the meanings of individual words. The three most important of these time-related syntactic categories are tense, aspect and

TIME IN FILM AND VIDEO ART   239

modality. Indeed, scholars of linguistics have argued that these are the basic categories which all languages have in common and which are the first to develop when new languages are created—as when creole languages were created as a result of the movement of slaves or indentured labourers from different language communities into a new environment where they needed to create ways of communicating both with each other and with their masters. These languages—pidgins, creoles—provide the best evidence we have for theories about the origins of languages. They are more basic, they lack the complexity of more developed languages and thereby reveal more about the fundamental structures of communication—especially in their articulation of time.

First, tense. In any narrative, any telling of a story, whether as gossip or as literature, there is a need to distinguish between events in the past, present and future, and these distinctions of tense are staples of any language. In narrative cinema, they appear in the form of 'flashbacks' or, in the case of the future, 'flash-forwards'—flashback-like visions or dreams. These time-shifted sequences are embedded in the continuous present of a narrative, which can be marked as past, present or future in relation to the time in which the spectator watches the film, through costume, for instance, or through direct verbal information. Of course, as a film or video itself becomes an object from the past, this temporality is itself transformed, so that we get an effect of a 'past-within-the-past' or even, as in old science-fiction films, a 'future-in-the-past'. In fact, the range of the future tense, in a number of spoken languages, overlaps with that of modality, the aspect of language which conveys uncertainty as to reality—conditionals, subjunctives, optatives, all the forms which convey what may, could, might, should have happened or hopefully would happen if . . . right the way through to future events that simply 'must' happen, as if the 'if-ness' of the future could be unfailingly countermanded.

Besides 'tense' and 'modality', the third basic temporal category is that of 'aspect', which covers the status of events as just beginning, continuing, persisting and ending or having ended. It is precisely this spectrum of transition which we see in tapes like those of Acconci or Baldessari. In John Baldessari's tape the transitions between beginning, continuing, persisting and ending are clearly made visible by the on-screen alarm clock. In Shigeko Kubota's tape, there is a much more complex presentation of time—the artist's look is explicitly retrospective, looking back to an ending which is already in the past, the end of her father's life. It is a film about an ending which has already happened, but which in flashbacks to her father's death-bed is shown as still to come, anticipated and increasingly expected. It is a tape about recollection—looking back from the present on events in the past—and about mourning, which has its own complex temporal structure, a combination of remembrance with a sense of loss, of a time which has gone, never to be repeated. It is also a film about ending—about a life as it ends, preserved on tape and then included in a work of art which must itself come to its end.

The important point to note is that film and video, unlike painting or sculpture, are both explicitly time-based media. Often this is simply taken to mean that each work exhibits change through time and has a specific duration. In fact, however, the relationship of film and video to time is much more complex than that. It involves many different and complicated ways of presenting time, constructing time and thinking about time. In this respect, film and video function in very similar ways. At this point I want to make a polemical claim, perhaps one which is less controversial than I think—that the differences between film and video are contingent rather than essential, certainly as far as the art world is concerned. The difference between them is rather like the difference between drawing with a pencil and drawing with a pen or a stick of charcoal. These are all forms of drawing, although they use quite different craft tools or 'technologies'. Video replaced film for many artists around the end of the 1960s principally because it was easier to use, less complex technically. Among other things, it permitted artists to shoot works with a longer continuous duration than film, without the trouble of reel changes. Film and video have each developed their own traditions, and their forms of distribution and presentation are quite different, but these divergences are really of secondary importance, especially with the development of digital technology as an editing tool.

Video, like film, is a time-based medium using recorded light, primarily (although not exclusively) to represent the world in a 'realistic' manner and to display it on a screen. The quality of light on a television screen is different from that on a film screen just as the quality of ink on an etching is different from that on a lithograph. While we should acknowledge that there are some minor differences between the two media in their capacities for using time—for instance, in their ability to freeze time—we should accept that, on the whole, these are of minor significance. In fact, just as Cage noted about music, it is time that is the primary element in both kinds of work. Artists' video, however, tends to recognize the primacy of time as duration, whereas artists' work with film is more likely to fragment linear time and redistribute it in the interest of narrative complexity. In rejecting or minimizing cinematic narrativity video both pays tribute to the early years of film (and to their belated rediscovery in the 1960s) and confirms its structural affinity to modern music, to an alternative tradition based upon duration rather than upon story-telling and drama.

17

MISMATCHES (& *ACOUSMÈTRES*)

I

I first thought of writing about mismatches after watching James Benning's film *Utopia*, which I saw at a screening at the Art Institute in Pasadena. I have been following James Benning's films over the last three decades and, to my mind, he is one of the most important experimental film-makers, all of whose films are interesting in a number of different ways—topographic, stylistic, political, theoretical. Anyway, back to *Utopia*. The image track of this film consists of a series of quite long shots, very carefully framed, which Benning took on a journey through the desert in Southern California, near to the frontier with Mexico. Most of the shots are very still, usually with one focus of movement to hold the attention, often quite distant and even not quite recognizable. The soundtrack, on the other hand, is quite different. It consists of the dialogue, interviews and voice-over commentary from a documentary on the last days of Che Guevara, made by somebody else completely, which Jim Benning had simply pirated and attached to his own film, his own image track, although—on the face of it—his images had nothing whatever to do with Che Guevara. A mismatch, in fact. What struck me, however, was that I began to formulate connections in my mind, which sketched out a way of linking the images to the sounds, to the spoken text. I couldn't help noticing, for instance, that there was quite a lot of military presence and military activity out there in the desert. One shot, for instance, showed an endless train chugging through the wilderness, each flatbed loaded with heavy military equipment. Similarly, I began to speculate on the difference and similarity between the desert and the jungle—in which Che Guevara spent his last days. They are both a kind of wilderness, but one is, so to speak, transparent and the other opaque. I actually knew quite a lot about the last days of Che Guevara—I had seen both Leandro Katz's exhibition and his documentary about Che's last days. So, I knew in advance, more or less, what the soundtrack of *Utopia* would say as I watched Benning's film, and I could envisage what it must be showing—the jungle, the building where Che was held and killed—thus creating another strange mismatch, this time between the known but unseen and the unknown but seen. As a result of all this, I became interested in the history and theory of the mismatch, the artistic potential of disparity between image and sound.

2

Pursuing this theme, I remembered watching Woody Allen's *What's Up, Tiger Lily?*, a film in which he revoiced an action movie from Hong Kong, replacing the Chinese dialogue with American dialogue that completely altered the nature of the characters and the narrative, creating, in fact, a completely different film without changing the images at all, simply by substituting a different voice-track. Unlike Jim Benning's film, the new dialogue was actually spoken by the characters in the film and, because of our familiarity with revoicing, seemed quite plausible and certainly funny which was, after all, Woody Allen's principal concern. On the other hand, I knew all the time that there was another, completely different film lying hidden away beneath the surface patina of Allen's dialogue, one which I found myself guessing about even as I was following his version. A strangely schizophrenic experience—quite different from watching *Utopia* because it was a question of spoken dialogue rather than voice-over and because there was a certain plausibility in the mismatch, rather than a disconcerting arbitrariness.

3

Thinking about Woody Allen, I remembered once seeing a dubbed version of Godard's *Le Mépris* (*Contempt*), in which one of the characters, played by Georgia Moll, is an interpreter, a translator. She is necessary because the principal characters—Jack Palance, Fritz Lang, Michel Piccoli, Brigitte Bardot: producer, director, screen-writer, star—don't speak the same language or even the same language with the same accent, so that a translator is needed to enable them to communicate. One critic whose study of *Contempt* I read even suggests that Godard introduced the translator in order to pre-empt the actual extra-textual producers from dubbing the film. If so, he failed. In the film as Godard intended it, the soundtrack is strange, uncanny, because conversations between the principal characters take place between languages and through a third party. Conversations are filled with repetition (semantically, at the level of meaning) and consequently they slow down the tempo of the film. Dubbed, however, it is even stranger, because the translator is now a redundant character and the repetition is at the level of phonology— sentences are repeated in the same language in which they were originally spoken.

4

Godard, I knew, was much influenced by Jean Rouch, whose use of sound was itself very innovative. In *Chronicle of a Summer*, for instance, Rouch and Morin introduced their own voices into the soundtrack, questioning other people in the film, actually on screen, as Godard liked to do although he would speak to the actors from behind the camera, thus confusing on-screen and off-screen space, itself another kind of mismatch. In particular, Godard was strongly influenced, I remembered reading, by Rouch's film *Jaguar*, about the travels of a migrant worker through what is now Ghana, then the Gold Coast. Rouch apparently asked his principal character, played by Damouré, to record his own commentary on what he saw on the screen when a near-final cut of the film was projected, drawing on his own memories and experience of events as well as the photographic record of them which he was watching. In an earlier film, *Moi, un Noir*, Rouch had filmed Africans, this time in the Ivory Coast, acting out scenes in which they impersonated an American movie star—Edward G. Robinson, for example. There was something uncanny about this impersonation of one actor by another, particularly in such different circumstances. In *Jaguar* too there is something uncanny about a voice-over which seems to be being recorded while you are watching the film. Not exactly a mismatch, perhaps, but an unsettling conjunction of past and present: what has been recorded at some time in the past is being responded to as it is screened right now as if seen for the first time. I learned recently that when Rouch had finished his film *Hippopotamus Hunt*, he took it back to the village where it was shot, when the editing was finished, so that it could be screened for all those involved in the hunt. The villagers loved the film. They made him screen it for them seven times in succession. They only had one criticism: the music. It was quite wrong. Rouch was surprised. After all, he had recorded the music right there in the village. It was their music. 'Oh yes', they replied. 'We recognized it. But if you played it like that when you went hunting, the hippopotamus would take off in a hurry.'

5

Another uncanny moment occurs in Visconti's film *Bellissima*. In Italy films are often projected in the open air and, in one scene in the film, an interior scene, Italian film dialogue can be heard through an open window. One character listens and then remarks, 'Burt Lancaster!' Of course, it isn't Burt Lancaster. It is an Italian who has revoiced Burt Lancaster. However, in Italy, all major stars had their own revoicing specialist. Therefore the voice would sound the same—in Italian—in every film Lancaster made, thus preserving, so to speak, its 'authenticity'. It was the voice of Burt Lancaster, and recognizable as such, even though it was an Italian voice. It is the inverse of *Le Mépris*. In Godard's film the characters, including the translator, each speak in their own voice. In

Visconti's film the translator's own voice is recognized as that of a specific character. It is no longer his own voice. It's Burt Lancaster's.

6

This episode from *Bellissima* always reminds me of *Singin' in the Rain*, a film in which revoicing is an essential element of the plot. The success of a film, the success of the personal lives of characters in the film—success in general—depends on using one character to revoice another. Within the diegesis, within the imaginary world of the film, this duplicity has to be concealed, although, of course, it is revealed quite openly to the film's real-life viewers, to the audience. In the imaginary world of the film it is also revealed to the audience at the film's première, a revelation which serves as a dramatic device for what film scholars call the 'formation of the couple': Don Lockwood and Kathy Selden can now publicly reveal their love for each other and their names will be joined together on the film's publicity billboards. What the audience did not know, until the final credits, was that Jean Hagen, who plays the scheming and tone-deaf Lina Lamont, actually had a much better singing voice than Debbie Reynolds who plays Kathy Selden. Hagen's voice actually came out of Reynolds's mouth as *she* appeared to be dubbing Hagen's voice! Thus authenticity and inauthenticity were turned inside out. What was false turned out to be true and what was true turned out to be false. Mismatch was, so to speak, twisted into an eerie Moebius strip.

7

Revoicing can engender many strange paradoxes. In Buñuel's *That Obscure Object of Desire*, two separate actresses play the part of Conchita, one Spanish, the other French. Physically, they look different—faces, figures, acting styles. However, their clothes were similar and, more important, they were both dubbed by the same voice. A significant number of spectators believed they were the same person: one poll taken at a test screening at an American university showed that over two-thirds of the audience had never spotted the visual mismatch. In Jacques Demy's *The Umbrellas of Cherbourg*, the principal actors and actresses sing much of their dialogue, transposing themselves into the world of operetta. The singing voices, of course, are those of professional singers. Rather more surprisingly, the voices of the singers were also dubbed on to the actresses when they were speaking ordinary dialogue in order to maintain the same timbre and 'sound' in speech and in song. In Alain Resnais's *The Same Old Song*, the characters burst into song with a voice which is obviously not their own but the voice of the famous popular singer whose hit song is coming out of their mouths, the voice of Josephine Baker, Charles Trenet, Georges Brassens, Serge Gainsbourg or whoever originally made the song recognizable, singable and repeatable by almost anyone.

8

The Same Old Song is dedicated to Dennis Potter, whose own plays for television pioneered the dramatic trick of characters breaking into someone else's song, best known through *Pennies from Heaven*, transposed into a Hollywood film by Herbert Ross. In his last work for television, *Karaoke*, Potter went even further, having the main character, a version of himself played by Albert Finney, imagining that other characters, other people in the street or in a restaurant—the Pelican, for example— are singing songs and speaking dialogue from his own, as yet unreleased, television drama. Mismatch has now entered the world of pathology, of aural or acoustic hallucination, a kind of rancid *Alice in Wonderland* world.

9

Another unreliable soundtrack is to be found in Alain Robbe-Grillet's *The Man Who Lies*, the story of a man whose every word is suspect as an untruth. It is like an extreme version of his script for *Last Year in Marienbad*, in which language creates a world of uncertainty and enigma.

It is a mild form of mismatch, perhaps, but one that left its mark, I feel sure, on Marguerite Duras who later made two different films with an identical soundtrack, the same non-synch off-screen voices we heard in *India Song* reappearing in *Son Nom de Venise*.

10

In Christian Marclay's work soundtracks are separated from the image tracks with which they originally belonged and take on a life of their own. In *Vertigo (Soundtrack for an Exhibition)*, Marclay takes the soundtrack of Hitchcock's *Vertigo* and reorganizes it to create a kind of sampled soundscape, which we recognize as being drawn from *Vertigo*, with sounds associated with certain sequences and images, but which creates a very different version of the film in our imaginations, due both to the fragility of our memories and to the difference that the artist's use of superimposition, spacing and ordering has made to the original.

11

Another artist who has ventured into the world of film is Tacita Dean whose installation *Footsteps* is a homage to the work of 'footsteps' artists (now known increasingly as Foley artists in Britain, in deference to American terminology). The Foley artist resounds or renoises, rather than revoices—like the coconut clasher who created galloping horses in the golden years of radio. Through the use of 'footsteps' it is possible to summon up an imaginary film in the mind's eye, a sequence of actions which exists only in artificial but evocative sounds.

12

Julie Becker is an artist working with video, whose tape piece *Suburban Legend* reproduces the visuals of *The Wizard of Oz*, the great Hollywood musical, but with the original soundtrack replaced by Pink Floyd's *Dark*

Side of the Moon. Suburban Legend is a kind of case study of the folk belief that the Pink Floyd album was inspired by or has some kind of occult relationship to *The Wizard of Oz*. In the case of the artist's brother and his stoned friends, this was thought to be due to some kind of 'karmic occurrence'. Notice, they said, that the *Dark Side of the Moon* album cover has a big rainbow on it. In her 'Notes to be taken into consideration while viewing', Julie Becker points out that the words 'Balanced on the biggest wave' appear just as Dorothy is in danger of losing her own balance. 'Hear the softly spoken magic spell' is heard just as she leaves Professor Marvel's 'magic' wagon. 'And I am not frightened of dying' occurs as the tornado heads towards the farmhouse where Dorothy has taken shelter. 'I think I need a Lear jet' coincides with the appearance of the good witch Glinda in her magic bubble! 'And in the end' is heard as the Red Witch is crushed beneath the falling farmhouse and her feet curl up and disappear in a slithering movement. Julie Becker lists seventy-four such coincidences, moments when there seems to be some kind of occult connection between sound and image, at least to the stoned or obsessive viewer. My favourite note reads 'During this scene the Cowardly Lion receives his badge of courage. Sounds as if helicopters and war planes are flying overhead.' Julie Becker confesses that 'after about an hour' her attention began to waver and she lost her interest in noticing coincidences. I lost mine a lot earlier, after wondering about a strange ch-ch-ing sound in Munchkinland, without being able to come up with any good explanation for it . . .

13

Pierre Bismuth is a sound artist best known, perhaps, for his tape of a verbal description of the soundtrack of Antonioni's *The Passenger*, made in the absence of the image—just headphones with the soundtrack and a microphone into which the verbal description is spoken. It is an eerie experience listening to the tape, especially for me as a co-writer of the original screenplay, together with Mark Peploe. Not exactly a mismatch but certainly a different film.

14

Still on an autobiographical note I'm afraid, I feel bound to mention Yvonne Rainer's *Journeys from Berlin*, made in London in 1971, in which my son Chad, then still at infant school, plays a psychoanalyst, with Annette Michelson as the analysand. He breaks the silence by barking like a dog, thereby piling one improbability on another. The patient responds by remarking that she had room for one elective, so she signed up for a course with Bob Hope. 'His first line was so ridiculous that I walked out.' Soon afterwards, the child analyst is edited out and replaced by an adult analyst, before returning again after another, later cut to pick up a telephone and shout 'Yes?' into it in an angry voice, then disappear again. This whole scene is interrupted by long silences, the phone ringing, birdwings fluttering. At one point, the analysand talks, her lips move, but with no sound coming out, no audible sound at least. Speech that can be seen but not heard.

15

In the film *Penthesilea*, which I made with Laura Mulvey in the early 1970s, there is a long sequence in which I walk through a house talking about Kleist, whose great play on the subject of *Penthesilea, Queen of the Amazons*, written in 1820, had inspired our film. As I walk through the spacious rooms, a kind of greenhouse area full of plants, I am speaking my lines, stopping every now and again to look surreptitiously at a prompt card which has been placed on my itinerary in advance. The camera meanwhile heads off course, so that only my voice-off can be heard, while the lens discovers for itself a series of cards whose text I have either already spoken or have not yet reached. The result is a mismatch between the written and the spoken sequence of my text, a kind of counterpoint between sight and sound, seeing and hearing.

16

The idea of a counterpoint between sound and image was borrowed from Sergei Eisenstein, the moving spirit behind the statement on counterpoint that he signed and published, together with Vsevolod Pudovkin and Eisenstein's co-worker Grigori Alexandrov, in August 1928. In this manifesto they argued that:

> ONLY A CONTRAPUNTAL USE of sound in relation to the visual montage will afford a new potentiality of montage development and perfection. THE FIRST EXPERIMENTAL WORK WITH SOUND MUST BE DIRECTED ALONG THE LINE OF ITS DISTINCT NON-SYNCHRONIZATION WITH THE VISUAL IMAGES. And only such an attack will give the necessary palpability which will later lead to the creation of an ORCHESTRAL COUNTERPOINT of visual and aural images.[1]

In the end, nothing really came of this brave manifesto. (Eisenstein switched his attention to the 'synchronization of the senses'. Alexandrov became the leading Soviet director of jazz musicals, much appreciated by Stalin.)

17

The 1928 manifesto was written in the spirit of the silent avant-garde, an attempt to ward off the talkie's power to destroy the universal visual art of silent cinema. I was reminded of how *Ballet Mécanique*, the precursor of Eisenstein and Meisel's co-operation on *Battleship Potemkin*, was never fully realized and was made as a silent film rather than an audio-visual film as originally intended. The idea for the film came from the composer Georges Antheil who had been experimenting with 'machine music'. Antheil was introduced to the painter Fernand Léger, who had money and ideas, and to Man Ray's friend Dudley Murphy, who had experience and technical skills. Antheil himself then failed to complete the music for the film on time and abandoned his part in the project—although he later had a great success (or *succès de scandale*, at least) when he performed the music as a concert piece, complete with pianola, xylophones, wind machine, airplane propellor and siren. Towards the end of his life Murphy became a pioneer of soundies, short films for jukeboxes, predecessors of MTV, but neither he nor Léger ever put Antheil's soundtrack on to the film, as originally intended. It's strange watching the film knowing that it was originally made to accompany a soundtrack that isn't there and knowing enough about the soundtrack, in its finished form, to be able to imagine it.

18

Chris Marker's *Silent Movie*, a film-based art installation, was made in 1995 for the Wexner Centre, in Columbus, Ohio, to celebrate one hundred years of film. Four monitors each show a twenty-minute film, a montage of silent pictures, on the themes of *The Journey*, *The Face*, *The Gesture* and *The Waltz*. Each was accompanied by a soundtrack made by Marker, who knew that silent film was rarely silent: piano pieces from composers ranging from Scarlatti and Scriabin to Scott Joplin and Nino Rota. A fifth monitor showed a series of caption subtitles drawn from silent films, but, as Marker points out, giving unexpected meaning to the montaged images displayed alongside—*She cried over the lynx . . . So you're talking, but your mind is somewhere else . . . Listen to the wind . . . I'm listening . . . Did you hear an owl singin'?*

19

The transition from silence to speech was a difficult one for most silent directors. Chaplin restrained himself from speaking for years, resisting until the last ditch, first singing on screen in a meaningless, invented language, a would-be Esperanto, and then, in *The Great Dictator*, impersonating Hitler's *tone of voice* in nonsense words.

20

Hitchcock, however, leapt into the fray with experimental sound effects, predecessors, we might say, of his later pioneering work with theremin and electronic sound. Many years, later, in *Psycho*, he experimented with voice-off, with the voice of a mother who turns out eventually to be dead, stuffed by her demented son. Her voice is a kind of ventriloquism, spoken from somewhere else but attached to her dummy-like body. In the end, the voice transfers its attachment to Norman, himself inert now, a kind of dummy. Its source remains undisclosed.

21

The wizard's voice in *The Wizard of Oz* is different, I think, contrary to Michel Chion.[2] The source is undisclosed, hidden, but it is the voice of Oz. It is a TV or radio voice, transmitted.

22

To return to Hitchcock for a moment, some people know of Douglas Gordon's *24 Hour Psycho*, in which Hitchcock's film is replicated and slowed down to last for a whole day, but probably fewer are aware of *Close Your Eyes*, inspired, strangely enough, by John Boulting's 1940s film of *Brighton Rock*. On the gallery wall a text reads 'Close Your Eyes. Open Your Mouth'. Scattered around the floor are twelve speakers and a web of cables, each saying 'I love you', a single line from Boulting's film, but one that caught Gordon's attention.

23

Most theorists of radio sound assume that it creates a kind of 'cinema in the head' (Alexander Kluge's phrase, I believe). But writing 'In Praise of

Blindness' Rudolf Arnheim argued that 'the wireless artist must develop a mastery of the limitations of the aural', discouraging visualization.[3] Things should stay hidden! We should never pull back the curtain. Buñuel's script-writer, Michel Carrière, had the same attitude. One day, after the release of *Belle de Jour*, he was telephoned by a stranger who claimed that he knew the source of the indefinable sound coming out of a small box which is brought into a brothel by a Korean visitor, a sound which perturbs all the ladies except for Séverine, the film's heroine, who leads the Korean, with his mysterious box, into the bedroom. The stranger explained to Carrière that he knew from the sound what was in the box: a particular kind of beetle which, tethered on a fine gold chain, was used by Laotian women to increase their sexual pleasure. Carrière regretted that he ever heard the story. He preferred the undefinable to the all-too-specific, however charming and unanticipated. Michel Chion refers to the unseen, unknown source of a sound as the *acousmètre*, a word he borrowed from his teacher, Pierre Schaeffer, the pioneer of electronic music. The *acousmètre* should stay unexplained, unrevealed, unmatched.

24

I want to end by proposing a little film in honour of the mismatch. I would simply add the spoken text of this chapter, speeded up, of course, to the image track of *Ballet Mécanique*. It should be translated into Cantonese too, in homage to Woody Allen. And in homage to Jerry Lewis, it should surely end with the credit: 'Main Title Song by Marcel Marceau'.

BACK TO THE FUTURE

Digital technology will change the cinema, of course, but to understand the nature of that change it is necessary to look at the cinema both within its long-term historical context and in relation to its traditional structures of production, distribution and exhibition, each of which will be affected in a different way by the wave of technological change currently sweeping across the world. As a guide to thinking about the historical pattern of change within the media, the effects of new technology and the dangers of prophecy, I looked first at Daniel Czitrom's book *Media and the American Mind from Morse to McLuhan*, Armand Mattelart's *The Invention of Communication*, Michio Kaku's *Visions* and Joseph H. Corn's anthology, *Imagining Tomorrow: History, Technology and the American Future*.[1] I realize that three out of these four books focus specifically on the United States, but there is, after all, no denying the fact that America is the major player both in the global media and in the global entertainment industry, as well as in the development and global spread of digital technology. (Armand Mattelart's book, however, was first published in Paris as *L'Invention de la Communication*.)

First Czitrom's book. Czitrom's book, published in 1982, begins with the invention of the telegraph and goes on to discuss both the cinema and television, concluding with thoughts on cable television and the newly invented video disc. He also mentions the home computer as a technology which could enable domestic production of digital videos. On the whole, he sees new technological advances as encouraging negative tendencies—banalization, commodity fetishism, 'the urge towards global hegemony', the 'hidden political and social agendas' which always accompany technological change. At the same time he still holds out some hope for the 'utopian urges' which typically accompany new technological developments. However, the chapter which interested me the most is the one devoted to the work of Harold Innis and Marshall McLuhan. To many observers, McLuhan's idea of the 'global village' seems to have been borne out even more strikingly by the World Wide Web than it was by global television, as he had originally prophesied. On the other hand, its utopian promise is clearly open to question.

In this context, I found the work of Harold Innis much more relevant than that of his follower McLuhan, although it is much less well known. Innis was born in Canada in 1894 and pursued an academic career as an economic historian. As such, he became increasingly fascinated by the ways in which communication technologies determined both political and economic systems. His first work in the field of communication studies was an article on 'The Newspaper in Economic Development', published in 1942.[2] The newspaper, Innis noted, was made possible by the prior invention of the telegraph—which increased the supply of news as well as rationalizing and accelerating the process of news-gathering—and, shortly afterwards, the power press, which increased the overall capacity of newspapers and especially their capacity as a medium for advertising. The newspaper industry, in fact, became a pioneer in the techniques of mass production, mass distribution and mass marketing—establishing a model which was followed later by radio, television and, today, digital media. Even more important, however, was Innis's observation that the newspaper changed our concepts of both time and space, through its emphasis on immediacy and speed.

Innis went on to view the rise and fall of civilizations and the cultural changes within individual societies as driven primarily by the predominant means of communication. Historically, media that emphasized time naturally tended to be durable in character (parchment, clay, stone) and to favour decentralization and hierarchical types of institution, whereas media that emphasized space favoured light materials (paper, papyrus) and tended to produce centralized institutions—speed of communications, Innis noted, tends to favour centralized power. Digital media, of course, favour space in their global reach, are extremely 'light' (in fact, insubstantial) and clearly work to the advantage of centralized power, allowing instant communication between centre and periphery. I am aware, of course, that this analysis flies in the face of a utopian model of digital communication (in the tradition of Kropotkin and Mumford) which sees digital media as inherently decentralizing, as an arena for untrammelled dialogue and individual choice. While it is important to defend the utopian aspects of digital technology, we should nonetheless recognize, I think, that it is also a massive instrument of centralized power—political, economic and military.

Moreover, this centralization was foreseen from the beginning. As Michio Kaku describes in his chapter on 'The Intelligent Planet', the origins of the internet go back to 1977, when Zbigniew Brzezinski, President Carter's National Security adviser, ordered an immediate test evacuation of the White House, without any warning, as a preparation exercise to test response to unexpected nuclear attack. It took several hours for a helicopter to arrive, supposedly to whisk the President to a secure bunker. As a result, the Pentagon's Advanced Research Project Agency (ARPA) proposed a number of research projects—in the areas of Teleconferencing (assured contact between President, Vice-President, Chiefs of Staff, etc., dispersed for security reasons), Virtual Reality (flight simulators, etc., training pilots to fly in unanticipated adverse circumstances), Global Positioning System satellites (to create an effective missile strike capability), Electronic Mail (to ensure the post-war survival of an effective communications system, despite massive, continent-wide destruction). All these technologies were successfully developed in the United States—ARPANET, of course, mutated into the internet and World Wide Web—although many of them ended up feeding into diverse non-governmental areas—business conferences, amusement park rides, traffic flow management, distribution of pornography, etc. All these other uses, however, did not detract from the internet's military, intelligence and geo-political value, or from its eventual transmutation into a commercial market-place.

Innis, however, saw the history of communications, not simply in terms of speed and scope, important though these are, but also in terms which we might call 'semiotic'. Thus oral communication (and the culture associated with it) gave way to written modes of communication, eventually to printed communication, leading first to the book and then, as we have seen, to the newspaper, which naturally created a culture based on excitement, sensationalism and capriciousness, with a continuous turnover of temporally unrelated content. This trend, of course, continued further with the arrival first of radio, then of television. Broadcasting, as Czitrom, points out, is even more ephemeral than printing and publishing. In fact, Innis became increasingly pessimistic about the possibility of reversing the trend towards centralization and instantaneous communication—print, broadcast and eventually digital media.

How does the cinema fit into this narrative? The cinema, I would argue, has remained a largely time-bound medium, in contrast to journalism and television. Films take a surprisingly long time to manufacture, they are distributed to cinemas through what many might consider an antique transport system, and they are exhibited and consumed, not in private homes, like newspapers, radio, television and the internet, but in public cinemas, which are often elements set in a broader social space—a city street, a shopping centre, an entertainment district. Obviously, the question which now arises is whether the cinema industry will be absorbed, in due course, into the ever-expanding realm of digital media. Put another way, will the public continue to look for entertainment outside the home? Having survived the competition of radio and television, will the cinema survive the new impact of a new contender, a new form of home entertainment?

In the field of production, the cinema has clearly absorbed the opportunity offered by digital technology. The symbolic figure in this regard, of course, is George Lucas, who, very early on, saw the potential of digital technology for changing the spectator's experience of film-going, first through the use of digital visual effects and, second, through the innovative use of digital sound. Lucas's innovations eventually resulted in what is often called the 'ride' film—the creation, through film, of an experience analogous to that of a ride in an amusement park. The connection between films and 'rides' is a long-standing one—Alfred Hitchcock, for example, always remembered his own early experience with Hales' Tours, films made at the beginning of the century, in the prehistory of cinema, which simulated a train ride through the mountains or a tram ride through a city, distant precursors, not only of a film like Hitchcock's thriller *The Birds* (with its innovative use of electronic sound and special effects), but of a subsequent torrent of action adventure films, such as *Jurassic Park*, based on a fictional and digitally created world. Cinema is clearly destined to merge the traditional 'live action' film with the animation film—*Gertie the Dinosaur* as distant predecessor of *Jurassic Park*! Film directors and editors are already contemplating the prospect of creating actors' entire performances by manipulating the fully rotating simulacra of successful stars, stored within the computer as digitized data.

Distribution and exhibition will also be transformed by digital technology. Films will be streamed onto home computer screens, for example, as they already are on a small scale. But they can also be distributed through satellite or cell-phone technology, beamed directly into cinemas and exhibited digitally on the screen. To be honest, it isn't clear to me that there is an adequate economic rationale for this—the cost of trucking prints is not necessarily higher than that of transmitting them digitally, nor is it clear that digital images are necessarily superior to traditional Kodak film-stock. Moreover, it is important to remember that the cinema is an industry driven, over many decades, by a particular culture of celebrity—known traditionally as the 'star system'. It is not clear as yet how the public's response to digital simulacra would compare with its response to traditional screen performance by actors whose mass appeal is partly, if not largely, based on their live persona off-screen, as represented in personal appearances, as well as mediated through magazine and press coverage, television talk-shows, awards ceremonies, etc. . . . Of course, Mickey Mouse and Donald Duck were great stars, quite as famous and successful as Charlie Chaplin or Clark Gable, but their repertoire was severely limited—more or less restricted to programme-fillers and children's movies.

Cinema, at present, depends on a complex hierarchy of modes of exhibition—cinema screening, video-cassette, DVD, television screening, etc., with digital streaming to home computers lurking around the corner. It is clear too that 'new technology' companies are increasingly interested in merging the related worlds of television and digital media—hence, for instance, the America Online—Time-Warner-CNN merger, with its implicit prospect of bringing content, cable distribution and home entertainment into one package. It is not so clear, however, how this would affect the film industry, with its very different historic pattern of exhibition. There is an obvious family resemblance between a number of existing home entertainment media—press, radio, television, internet, etc.—but it is not at all clear how cinema would fit into this structure, except as a secondary form of exhibition, like the video-cassette market. Cinema survived the challenge of television and there seems no good reason why it shouldn't survive the challenge of the home computer too—television, after all, covers many more households than the internet.

In his book, *The Invention of Communication*, Armando Mattelart dates the beginning of marketing to the end of the nineteenth century. In 1901 the first experimental market research programme was launched in Chicago and in 1911 the first commercial company, Business Bourse, was incorporated. Soon target audiences were being identified and by the 1920s Arthur Nielsen was computing market share and others were developing quantitative measures to express the triadic relationship between media, product and consumer. The internet provides yet another environment for marketing, one which updates mail-order marketing and combines it with entertainment, as in music radio and television, and direct consumer-response, as in radio and television talk-shows. Radio and television are generally provided 'free' to the consumer and are financed through advertising revenue. Cinema, however, is financed through a pay-to-view system. Digital media, it seems, are still wavering between the two options. Consumers pay for their internet server on a user-fee basis, plus charges for telephone use which vary from cheap in the United States to expensive in other countries, but they may be charged electronically for some web-sites they visit, although many are financed through advertising. At the same time, they can purchase goods directly from online sites, as with mail-order marketing. Online multi-player games are also commercialized, it is important to note, and it has been suggested that the film industry will merge increasingly with the game industry, introducing avatars into the cinematic experience, along lines sketched in hypothetically by David Cronenberg.

Of course, many users still see the internet as primarily a venue for conversation or research, but these are simply specific choices within an ever-expanding repertoire of opportunities. Basically, the internet is an arena for making choices, which can include the digital equivalent of situationist *dérives* (random wanderings and encounters) as well as the equivalent of shopping sprees or entertainment opportunities. In this context, watching a particular film would be just one choice among a myriad others. In this sense, the internet is indeed like an imaginary space which can be accessed without ever leaving the confines of your actual home or (to a significant extent) your workplace. In fact, however, it is increasingly a space for marketing.

A recent issue of the magazine *Wired* was subtitled *Life After Holly-wood*, with a number of writers, including William Gibson, proclaiming the end of the traditional entertainment industry and exalting the idea of 'garage' movie making, like garage rock bands. It is a strange piece, ending up with the suggestion that digital 'sets' for digital films would be purchased from professional fabricators:

> Maybe a specialist market selling things like templates for an American suburb, or mall interiors, or car chases. These could be tweaked into more specific shape by the individual enthusiast. Some people might find that their most valuable asset is the set they've developed, which they can rent to others, to modify, layer over, cut, paste and sample.[3]

By the same logic, I suppose, you could develop digital characters and rent them out too. The basic idea is that of creativity as a kind of rewriting process, plagiarism with a personal twist—and an economic infrastructure. As Gibson's choice of words suggests, it is also inspired by the precedent of 'sampling' in the music industry—in fact, any film streamed onto a web-site would be available for sampling, just as downloaded music is.

Digital books are already published and purchased on the Web, so it is logical to think that digital films could be too. But, as things stand now, this involves a very marginal slice of the dotcom book market and I presume it would be much the same with films. The logical place for experimental and personal film, video or digital movie-making is in the art world—the gallery, the museum, the biennale. Increasingly the lines between film, video and art are being blurred. The differences between cinema, gallery and digital media are fundamentally differences of consumption rather than production. The same work can be shown in different kinds of venue but the way in which people look at it is different in each. In a cinema (or a specialized film venue) the spectator sits silently and watches all the way through continuously. In a gallery, spectators drift past, pausing, scanning casually, perhaps staying longer, rarely watching a work with concentrated attention all the way through, even though it is likely to be much shorter in its duration than a film shown in a cinema. Online, the spatial situation is unlike either film or video—the spectator is in close proximity to an image visible on demand, shown on a much smaller screen. Although the work may be exactly the same, the experience of watching it will be very different in each venue.

In his afterword to *Imagining Tomorrow*, Joseph H. Corn notes three principal effects of American technological utopianism—and when we talk about technological utopianism in its digital variant, it is really American utopianism that we are talking about. First, technological utopianism functions as an 'opiate of the masses'—substituting imaginary solutions based on the idea of a technological fix for engagement with the real issues. Thus, in Corn's example, modern glass-and-steel housing was seen as the answer to a housing crisis which really depended on problems arising from mortgage practices, land speculation, zoning restrictions or simply inadequate income. He concludes that 'to the extent that people believe in the myth of a future transformed and made better by things, support for real social change is undermined'. In today's context the internet can function as just such a transformative 'thing', distracting us from the real preconditions for change. Corn also points out how technological futurism, in the American context, fuels nationalism, creating an image of the nation based not on its past or its traditions but on its future prospects and, one might add, its spatial expansion through communication and travel networks. Third, futurism actually does serve to inspire new inventions, the brain-children not of rational, purposive thinkers but of dreamers and visionaries.

Perhaps it is just such a dreamer who will eventually find a way to harness the consumer mentality increasingly dominant in the World Wide Web to new forms of interactive art or to lure the internet-user out into creative digital environments, proto-Holodecks, probably to be found in museums, but also, I think, in theme parks and leisure centres. If so, it will not be the cinema that gains, but the art world and the world of tourist attractions, Disneyland and Las Vegas. The cinema will certainly become even more complex in its production process, more expensive, even further beyond the reach of ordinary people. It will continue to enhance its capacity for spectacle, thrill and sensation through digital means, while retaining the age-old armature of narrative, drama and scene-setting. Those who love cinema will go *back* to the future, back to experimental film, silent film, handmade animation, Super-8, celluloid. No doubt, new billionaires will buy their work and treasure it for its recreation of time past, its evocation of a society in which time passed so slowly and everything took a very long time indeed.

19

SPEED AND THE CINEMA

In 1959 the psychoanalyst Michael Balint published a book on the subject of *Thrills and Regression* which is of great interest not simply to Freudians but to film theorists and historians as well. Although Balint never mentions the cinema as such, his opening chapter on 'Funfairs and Thrills' covers a number of different varieties of thrill-laden activities, including those in which the thrill is directly experienced by participants and those in which thrills are experienced vicariously, as, for instance, at the circus where professionals entertain spectators with their thrilling feats on the tightrope and the trapeze or in the lions' den. Cinema is often discussed in relation to the theatre or the novel but its kinship to the circus is much less frequently admitted, even though we are all aware how important the vicarious enjoyment of thrills has been throughout the history of the cinema. From very early on, cinema exploited its capacity to create excitement. Even the very first films of the Lumière brothers had a thrilling effect on their audiences—we are all familiar with the many accounts of spectators cowering or fleeing the cinema as the train approached the station, threatening to run directly off the screen into the auditorium. Soon afterwards Georges Méliès was taking spectators on a rocket trip to the moon.

The very first category of thrill which Balint mentions is the class of those 'connected with *high speed*, as in all kinds of racing, horse riding and jumping, motor racing, skating, ski-ing, tobogganing, sailing, flying, etc.' Essentially, Balint sees thrills as structured in what he sometimes describes as three acts:

> (a) some amount of conscious fear, or at least an awareness of real external danger; (b) a voluntary and intentional exposing of oneself to this external danger and to the fear aroused by it; (c) while having the more or less confident hope that the fear can be tolerated and mastered, the danger will pass, and that one will be able to return unharmed to safety. This mixture of fear, pleasure, and confident hope in face of an external danger is what constitutes the fundamental element of all *thrills*.[1]

In the case of speed, of course, the danger consists of somehow losing control and crashing, or, in the particular case of a pursuit or chase, of being overtaken and captured or attacked. Often high speed is combined with the two other principal kinds of thrill which Balint mentions—the thrills connected with *'exposed situations'*, such as rock-climbing, deep-sea diving or lion-taming, and with *'unfamiliar* or even *completely new forms of satisfaction'*, such as new food, new clothes and 'new forms of "perverse" sexual activities'.

Speed is not simply thrilling in itself, once it has been sufficiently accelerated, but it also enables us to enter exposed and unfamiliar situations, far removed from the zones of safety and normality—to travel into space, for instance, beyond the frontiers of the known. Avid thrill-seekers, or 'philobats' as Balint calls them, are often involved in not simply dangerous but also highly competitive activities. Speed is closely connected to various forms of struggle or contest, ranging from races and, more threateningly, chases up to its decisive role in combat, where greater speed gives a clear advantage over an opponent. Balint notes that an 'element of aggressiveness is undoubtedly present in all philobatic activities' but thrills in themselves are not directed against an outside object, but valued for the subjective experience they bring to the thrill-seeker. In amusement parks and cinemas, violence is closely linked to thrill-seeking but the spectator's thrill is, so to speak, intransitive. Speed is enjoyed for its own sake, even though it may lead in the end to a second-order enjoyment of vicarious triumph over a villainous enemy. Thrills, Balint concludes, are essentially auto-erotic—they are ways of embarking on adventures which are fundamentally designed to give oneself pleasure just by the activity involved, so that any specific accomplishment which results, like crossing the finish line first or triumphing over an opponent, is really an added benefit, related to aggression rather than to philobatism as such.

In 1936, Alfred Hitchcock wrote a piece for *Picturegoer* titled 'Why "Thrillers" Thrive'. Hitchcock argued that shocks or thrills are necessary to us as human beings, that 'our nature is such that we must have these "shake-ups", or we grow sluggish and jellified; but, on the other hand, our civilization has so screened and sheltered us that it isn't practicable to experience sufficient thrills at first hand. So we have to experience them artificially, and the screen is the best medium for this.'[2] Hitchcock argues that in the theatre—or at the circus—the audience simply watches things happening, remote, impersonal and detached, whereas in the cinema 'we don't sit by as spectators; we participate'. Or at least, he might have said, the effective experience of participation is much stronger. Hitchcock goes on to cite a sequence in Howard Hughes's 1930 air combat film *Hell's Angels*,

> in which the British pilot decides to crash his plane into the envelope of the Zeppelin to destroy it, even though this means inevitable death to himself. We see his face—grim, tense, even horror-stricken—as his plane swoops down. Then we are transferred to the pilot's seat, and it is we who are hurtling to death at ninety miles an hour; and at the moment of impact—and blackout—a palpable shuddering runs through the audience. That is good cinema.

Hitchcock goes on to note that our enjoyment of the sequence as viewers is possible because 'in our subconscious we are aware that we are safe, sitting in a comfortable armchair, watching a screen'.[3] Moreover, Hitchcock added, we are also subconsciously aware that the pilot—or at least the actor who plays the role of pilot—is not really dead, any more than we are, that our vicarious thrill-seeking depends on the cinema's ability to trick us into identifying not simply with the feats of an acrobat or a gladiator but with a performance which is itself a construction, a 'trick' as Hitchcock liked to put it. Many years later, in 1949, Hitchcock wrote another piece, this time for *Good Housekeeping*, in which he discussed 'The Enjoyment of Fear'. The examples Hitchcock gives are those of enjoyable activities such as riding a roller-coaster, climbing a mountain, taking a midnight stroll through a graveyard, speedboat racing, steeplechasing, big-game hunting and so on. For that, Hitchcock says, 'is only the beginning. For every person who seeks fear in the real or personal sense, millions seek it vicariously, in the theatre and in the cinema.'[4] The audience experiences the same sensations as the real-world philobat ('the quickened pulse, the alternately dry and damp palm, etc.') but without, as Hitchcock puts it, 'paying the price'. In other words, the spectator's confident hope that the danger will pass is considerably stronger than that of the professional (a hope that Hitchcock was to shatter in *Psycho*, although there too the spectators were returned unharmed to safety).

It was at this point that Hitchcock introduced the distinction he often made subsequently, between *suspense* and *terror*. 'On the screen', according to Hitchcock, 'terror is induced by surprise; suspense by forewarning'. Suspense, like all thrills, depends on our anticipation of an impending threat, whether or not it is actually realized. The closer the threat, the greater the suspense. Thus Hitchcock's example is of the stroller in a dark street who hears footsteps behind. 'The walker stops, the footsteps are not heard; the pace is increased, so also the tempo of the thin sounds coming out of the night.' What interests me about this particular example is Hitchcock's allusion to 'tempo'. In 1950 Hitchcock gave an interview to the *New York Times* Magazine, which was titled 'Core of the Movie—the Chase'.[5] 'Well, essentially,' he observed, 'the chase is someone running towards a goal, often with the antiphonal motion of someone fleeing a pursuer.' Flight and pursuit. The chase, in fact, is intimately bound up with suspense. The closer the pursuer, the faster the tempo, the greater the suspense, the more powerful the thrill. Hitchcock goes on to discuss *Strangers on a Train*, 'the picture I am working on now', in which he was trying to exploit the dramatic possibilities of movement throughout the film, gradually building up the tempo until 'the final, physical chase, which must be short and breathtaking to avoid the error of anticlimax'.

In *Strangers on a Train*, Hitchcock was particularly proud of the sequence where the hero is playing tennis at Forest Hills while the villain plans his crime. Consequently the hero must play as hard and as fast as he can in order to win the match, get off the court, and overtake the villain. The villain, meantime, confident that his victim is tied to the tennis court, is taking his time and being very methodical. The camera cutting alternately from the frenzied hurry of the tennis player to the slow operation of his enemy, creates a kind of counterpoint between two kinds of movement.

Hitchcock describes his own expertise in constructing chase sequences as the result of combining what he had learned from literary sources, which fleshed out the basic chase motif with careful plotting and characterization, together with D. W. Griffith's pioneering cinematic use of the chase (in *Birth of a Nation*, *Intolerance*, *Way Down East* and *Orphans of the Storm*) as a physical event, typically a ride to the rescue, in which the spectator's reactions are manipulated by the technique of cross-cutting combined with an ever-accelerating tempo, while the spectator is kept aware of the dreadful threat which still hangs over the potential victim and the ever-shorter amount of time remaining. The closer the threat, of course, the greater the speed required of the rescuer and the more important it is for the potential victim to find ways of decelerating the approach of impending doom.

In the films Hitchcock mentions, Griffith drew on a tradition of races and chases which was almost as old as the cinema itself—Williamson's *Stop Thief!* and *Fire!* date from 1901, Edwin Porter's *Life of an American Fireman* was made in 1902, Cecil Hepworth's *Rescued by Rover* in 1905, although cross-cutting in the fully developed Griffith manner did not appear until 1908. From the very beginning cinema drew on the melodramatic theatre tradition of menace and jeopardy as twin engines of suspense. Griffith's contribution was to establish a style of film-making which accentuated the excitement of chase sequences through control over their tempo. In the second decade of the cinema, as Barry Salt notes, Griffith was already being criticized for the 'rush and turmoil' which characterized his films.[6] Salt believes this was due, partly at least, to Griffith's habit of under-cranking his films, shooting at fourteen frames per second or even lower so that the action appeared much faster than normal when it was projected. It is difficult, of course, to quantify the speed of film, beyond noting the now traditional norm of twenty-four frames per second in projection—the impression of speed is dependent on a number of disparate features. Under-cranking, slow motion, pixillation, jump-cuts, rapid camera movement, rapid tempo of editing, rapid movement within the frame, rapid delivery of dialogue, rapid narrative development—all of these can contribute to the impression of speed.

It is true to say, however, that film-makers have continuously sought methods of speeding up the cinematic experience, although the acceleration has not been entirely continuous. In his book *Film Style and Technology: History and Analysis*, Barry Salt reports on his detailed measurement of cutting rates throughout the history of the feature film. From 1912 to 1917 the longest average shot length (modal length) for a sample of American films was 7 seconds, from 1918 to 1929 it was 5 seconds, but after the coming of sound it lengthened considerably to 9 seconds, where it stayed until 1957. In the period between 1958 and 1963, however, it accelerated again to 6 seconds, where it stayed until 1981, when it accelerated even further, reaching 5 seconds again between 1982 and 1987. Salt's statistical analysis ends at this point, although he notes sourly that in the 1990s an increasing number of movies seem to be 'almost totally made up of tense action scenes', encompassing, I would presume, films such as *Speed* itself. (Hitchcock's films, it is worth remarking in parentheses, are notable for their early use of the 'shock cut', predecessor of the 'jump-cut', for their extremely high proportion of point-of-view shots and for a pronounced move towards shots of unusually long duration in the post-war period, culminating in his 1948 experimental masterpiece, *Rope*, which consists entirely of ten-minute takes laid end to end, in order to achieve a one-to-one ratio between film footage and dramatic action. By the end of the 1950s, however, Hitchcock's films were following the trend in reducing shot lengths again.)

Salt makes a number of other interesting points, observing, for example, that there is often a clear correlation between average shot length and directorial ambition. In this connection he cites the average shot lengths of 15 seconds for Jean-Luc Godard's *A Bout de Souffle* (*Breathless*) and of no less than 20 seconds for Joseph Losey's *The Servant*, as well as noting the predilection for long takes of Bob Rafelson, whom he characterizes as an American 'art film' director. At the extreme of this tendency to slow down the tempo he also notes Michelangelo Antonioni's use of *temps mort* (dead time). In Antonioni's 1960 *L'Avventura*, for instance, there were an unusual number of scenes which 'appear to have no obvious function in advancing the plot or illuminating the characters'. The extremes of deceleration, however, occur in avant-garde films. Warhol, like Hitchcock before him, strung unedited takes together with no compunction and his 1964 epic, *Empire*, consists of an eerie combination of ten-minute takes and *temps morts*, lasting for eight hours in all. Michael Snow's 1967 *Wavelength* is in effect a single continuous zoom shot which lasts for over three-quarters of an hour, and his *La Région Centrale*, filmed in 1971 in an uninhabited wilderness area in the north of Québec, continued for three hours with no cuts and no sign of human involvement except for glimpses of the film-maker's own shadow.

At the other extreme, experimental film-makers also produced films with unusually short shot lengths—Anthony Balch and William Burroughs's *Cut-Ups* in the 1960s or, even more radical, the flicker films of Paul Conrad and Paul Sharits, whose tempo is so accelerated that when exhibited in public they need to carry notices warning of the danger to viewers susceptible to epileptic episodes. Avant-garde film in the 1960s mounted a kind of pincer movement against the mainstream, accentuating both speed and slowness, trends which persisted in music video, on the one hand, and artists' films, on the other. The turn towards slowness which we see in the work of many avant-garde film-makers—absence of action, absence of editing, absence of camera movement—could best be interpreted as a reaction against the increasing speed of mainstream movies, whether it was intended or unintended. The *locus classicus* here was Snow's *Wavelength*, the film which, more than any other, opened the door to deceleration. Writing about *Wavelength* in 1982, Nicky Hamlyn made a distinction between what could be called 'interventionist' and 'alternative' films.[7] The 'interventionist' avant-garde retained a narrative format, albeit elliptical, and slowed it down by refunctioning conventional stylistic devices to delay the story rather than to hurry it along. The 'alternative' avant-garde, on the other hand, rejected conventional stylistic devices and looked for completely new ways of structuring a film, which might end up anywhere on the spectrum between ultra-fast and ultra-slow.

The avant-garde had traditionally favoured speed, ever since the futurists praised it as the core characteristic of the tempo of modern life. Speed became intimately bound up with the idea of modernity—the physical speed of express trains, racing cars, flying machines and the psychological speed of reaction time required by the modern city-dweller, confronted with a dynamic multiplicity of simultaneous events and impressions. René Clair's Dada film *Entr'acte*, made in 1924 as an entertainment to fill an intermission between two acts of the Swedish Ballet, was virtually an exercise in the use of speed. Clair gradually increased the tempo of a bourgeois funeral *cortège*, until the procession, including the substantial hearse, is moving at a gallop, finally transferring the momentum, by an editing trick, onto a roller-coaster, with the camera mounted in the front of a car, swooping at a giddying pace down into the abyss. In the Soviet Union, around the same time, Sergei Eisenstein developed his theories of montage, differentiating metric montage, with a strict mathematical basis, from rhythmic montage, in which the content of the action was an equal factor in determining a rhythm: 'Here the actual length does not coincide with the mathematically determined length of the piece according to a metric formula. Here its practical length derives from the specifics of the piece, and from its planned length according to the structure of the sequence.'[8]

In his most celebrated montage experiment, the Odessa Steps sequence in *Battleship Potemkin*, Eisenstein complicated the rhythm by alternating both between strict tempo (soldiers marching down the steps) and chaotic movement (the panic-stricken crowd) and, on the other hand, between an accelerating rhythm (the 'downward rushing movement of the soldiers') contrasted with the abrupt deceleration of the rhythm when a lone figure moves with 'slow solemnity' up the steps towards the advancing soldiers. After this 'caesura' (Eisenstein's term), the tempo is then accelerated even further as a baby's pram rolls out of control down the steps in front of them. Eisenstein speeds up both the action and the rhythm of the editing throughout the sequence, stabilizing it and slowing it down at poignant moments only in order to heighten the impression of speed when the rout of the protesting crowd continues unabated. Eisenstein's aim was to increase the pathos we feel for the victims by contrasting moments of solemnity and sudden slowness with the rapid onrush of the soldiers and the panic-stricken crowd. In *October*, made in 1927, two years later,

Eisenstein mimicked the tempo of a machine-gun firing at a crowd by accelerating the tempo of the editing, cutting back and forth between shots which were only two frames in length, a tiny fraction of a second, so that they looked like flickering superimpositions rather than separate shots.

Perhaps the most influential intervention of the avant-garde, however, was through Blaise Cendrars's editing of Abel Gance's 1922 film *La Roue*, especially his close-up montage sequence of train wheels, which became the model for many subsequent imitations. In this film, Cendrars and Gance already used a two-frame shot of the engine's furnace cut between shots of the rails and the locomotive cab, as well as another two-frame shot of the train's speedometer cut between two shots of the engine-driver. A close connection between the cinema and the locomotive had been established in the very earliest years of film with the Lumière brothers' *Train Entering the Station*, and it continued on through the so-called Hales' Tours, cinema exhibitions in which the viewer sat in a simulated train carriage to watch footage shot from a locomotive, until shots from speeding trains became a standard feature of the cinema, eventually giving way to shots from cars, motorbikes and, finally, space vehicles. The early avant-garde fascination with speed thoroughly infiltrated the mainstream cinema, while countervailing tendencies were marginalized into the art film and a subsidiary sector of the avant-garde. In fact, during the 1990s, even these surviving pockets of resistance have come under continuous threat as the culture of speed has accelerated its global expansion.

The case against speed was put with great clarity in the early 1950s by the great French critic André Bazin, in his essay on 'The Evolution of the Language of Cinema', in which he argued against montage and in favour of protracted shots which respected the spatio-temporal unity of events. Bazin welcomed the increased length of shots which characterized the first decades of sound film. For him, the villains of cinema history, albeit great artists, were Griffith, Eisenstein and Gance. 'In *La Roue*', Bazin observed, 'Abel Gance created the illusion of the steadily increasing speed of a locomotive without actually using any images of speed (indeed the wheel could have been turning on one spot) simply by a multiplicity of shots of ever-decreasing length.'[9] The key word here is 'illusion': Bazin was arguing for a cinema that would respect reality, that would not fall back on the manipulative tricks in which Hitchcock delighted. Rather than Griffith, Eisenstein and Gance, Bazin's models were Stroheim, Murnau and Flaherty, silent film directors in whose films, according to Bazin, 'montage plays no part, unless it be the negative one of inevitable elimination where reality superabounds. The camera cannot see everything at once but it makes sure not to lose any part of what it chooses to see.' When Flaherty filmed Nanook hunting, Bazin added, what mattered to him was 'the actual length of the waiting period . . . the actual length of the hunt is the very substance of the image, its true object'. Flaherty filmed the hunt in one protracted set-up.

When Michael Snow made *Wavelength*, he inserted two significant narrative incidents into the otherwise neutral time-space of the loft in which he had set up his camera, where the spectrum of change is otherwise restricted to the slow advance of the camera zoom, random changes in the light and the endless *glissando* of the soundtrack. In one of the incidents a bookcase is carried into the room and deposited there. In the other a man walks in and collapses on the floor, apparently dead. I had always wondered about these incidents and I was delighted to discover that Snow had talked about them in an interview. 'The film events', he said, 'are not hierarchical, but are chosen from a kind of scale of mobility that runs from pure light events, the various perceptions of the room, to the images of moving human beings. The inert: the bookcase that gets carried in, the corpse, as seen, dying being a passage from activity to object. Inertia.'[10] An important element of Snow's project, it seems, was that of breaking down the distinction between action and object, by paying attention to the bottom end of the scale of mobility rather than the top end, the zone of slowness where mobility runs up against inertia. I was struck by the way in which Snow's ecstatic voyage towards inertia by the slowing down of time echoed Roland Barthes's remarks on the hyperbolization of mobility by what he called, in the mid-1950s '*le jet-man*'. 'The pilot-hero', he noted, 'was made unique by a whole mythology of speed as an experience, of space devoured, of intoxicating motion. The *jet-man*, on the other hand, is defined by a coenaesthesis of motionlessness ("*at 2000 km per hour, in level flight, no impression of speed at all*"), as if the extravagance of his vocation precisely consisted in *overtaking* motion, in going faster than speed.'[11] Or, as we might put it, in reaching inertia through hyper-acceleration.

In this context, it is worth recalling a well-known story about George Lucas. When Mark Hamill, who played Luke Skywalker in *Star Wars* was asked about Lucas's direction of actors, he replied, 'His biggest direction to me was, "Faster, more intense".' The *Star Wars* series, of course, is all about action. Hollywood consistently shows philobats in rapid action on the screen to an audience of chair-bound ocnophils, viewers who, in Michael Balint's words, 'prefer to clutch at something firm when their security is in danger', and are 'only at ease in the state of stable security'.

NOTES

I AN ALPHABET OF CINEMA

1. This chapter was originally given as the Serge Daney memorial lecture at the Rotterdam International Film Festival, February 1998 and was first published in *New Left Review* no. 12 (November–December 2001). Born in 1944, Daney began his film-theorist career as a teenager in the darkness of the Cinémathèque in the Rue d'Ulm: 'I hated, in theatre, the social ritual, the assigning of seats in advance, the need to dress up, the parade of the bourgeoisie. In cinema—the permanent cinema—there is a black space that is fundamental, infinitely more mysterious.' He was a driving force within *Cahiers du Cinéma* throughout its many transmutations, from the early Hitchcocko–Hawksian years to the Maoist turn, the 'savage application' of Althusser and Lacan, the late seventies' rediscovery of cinephilia; editing the journal from 1973 to 1981. During the eighties he produced searing analyses of postmodern TV in the pages of *Libération*; and excoriated the mediatized Gulf War. Daney described himself as a *passeur*, a smuggler, border-crosser, go-between; and—homage to the creative role of oedipal hatreds—a *ciné-fils*. In 1991 he founded the review, *Trafic*. He died of Aids in June 1991.
2. Serge Daney, *Persévérance* (Paris: POL, 1994).
3. Susan Sontag, 'The Decay of Cinema', *New York Times* Magazine (25 February 1996), p. 60.

4. Jean-Pierre Coursodon and Yves Boisset, *20 Ans de Cinéma Américain, 1940–1960* (Paris: Éditions CIP, 1961).
5. Rem Koolhaas, *Delirious New York: A Retroactive Manifesto for Manhattan* (Academy Editions, 1978).
6. Andre Bazin, *What is Cinema?* trans. and ed. Hugh Gray (Berkeley: University of California Press, 1967).
7. Laura Mulvey, 'Visual Pleasure and Narrative Cinema', *Screen* vol. 16, no. 3, (1975), pp. 6–18.

2 GUERRILLA CONDITIONS: THE CINEMA OF WILLIAM SEWARD BURROUGHS

1. This chapter was first published in *Pix* magazine. In addition to the works cited in subsequent notes, I consulted the following books in writing this chapter: Anthony Balch, Interview, *Cinema Rising*, no. 1, London, April 1972; William S. Burroughs, *Electronic Revolution* (West Germany, Expanded Media Editions, 1970), and *Blade Runner (a movie)* (Berkeley: Blue Wind Press, 1979); Stephen C. Foster, *Lettrisme: Into the Present* (Iowa City: University of Iowa Museum of Art, 1983); Brion Gysin, *RE/SEARCH*, No. 4/5 (Writings and Interviews), San Francisco, 1982; Barry Miles, *William Burroughs: El Hombre Invisible* (London: Virgin Books, 1992); Barry Miles, *Paul McCartney: Many Years From Now* (London: Secker and Warburg, 1997); Ted Morgan, *Literary Outlaw: The Life and Times of William S. Burroughs* (London: Pimlico, 1991); and Jack Sargeant, *The Naked Lens: An Illustrated History of Beat Cinema* (London: Creation Books, 1997).
2. William S. Burroughs, *The Letters of William S. Burroughs, 1945 to 1959* (London: Picador, 1993).
3. William S. Burroughs, *The Soft Machine* (Paris: Olympia Press, 1961); *The Ticket that Exploded* (Paris: Olympia Press, 1962); *Nova Express* (New York: Grove Press, 1964). William S. Burroughs, *Time* (New York: 'C' Press, 1965).
4. Jennie Skerl, *William S. Burroughs* (Boston: Twayne, 1985).
5. Burroughs, *The Ticket that Exploded*, p. 151.
6. William S. Burroughs, 'Interview: The Art of Fiction XXXVI', *Paris Review*, no. 35 (Fall 1965), p. 1.

7. 'An Interview with Brion Gysin on the Films *Towers Open Fire* and *Cut Ups* (Paris, October, 1983)', *Cantrill's Filmnotes*, no. 43/44 (February 1984), pp. 38–42; p. 42.
8. Jeff Nuttall, *Bomb Culture* (London: MacGibbon and Kee, 1968), p. 155.
9. William S. Burroughs and Brion Gysin, *The Exterminator* (San Francisco: Auerhahn Press, 1960).
10. Ian Sommerville, 'Mr and Mrs D', *Gnaoua*, no. 1 (Spring 1964), p. 17.
11. Robert A. Sobieszek, *Ports of Entry: William Burroughs* (Los Angeles: LACMA, 1966).
12. Burroughs, *Time* (this text has no page numbers).

3   VIKING EGGELING

1. This chapter was first published in *Pix* magazine.
2. Wassily Kandinsky, 'On the Question of Form', in Wassily Kandinsky and Franz Marc (eds), *Blaue Reiter Almanac* (New York: Da Capo, 1974), pp. 147–87.
3. Ferruccio Busoni, *Sketch of a New Esthetic of Music*, trans. Theodore Baker (New York: Schirmer, 1911).
4. Louise O'Konor, *Viking Eggeling 1880–1925: Artist and Filmmaker, Life and Work* (Stockholm: Almquist and Wiksell, 1971).
5. Viking Eggeling and Hans Richter, *Universelle Sprache* (Germany, 1919).
6. Guillaume Apollinaire, *Apollinaire on Art: Essays and Reviews 1902–1918*, ed. L. C. Breunig (New York: Viking Press, 1972).
7. Kandinsky, 'On the Question of Form'.
8. Hugo Ball, *Flight out of Time* (New York: Viking Press, 1974/1996).

4   WHO THE HELL IS HOWARD HAWKS?

1. Barbara Leaming, *Katharine Hepburn* (London: Weidenfeld and Nicolson, 1995), p. 349.
2. For these diverse views of Hawks see the following: Richard Roud, *A Passion for Films: Henri Langlois and the Cinémathèque Française* (New York: Viking Press, 1983); Manny Farber, *Negative Space* (London: Studio

Vista, 1971); Jacques Rivette, 'The Genius of Howard Hawks', trans. Russell Campbell and Marvin Pister, in Jim Hillier (ed.), *Cahiers du Cinéma, the 1950s: Neorealism, Hollywood, New Wave* (Cambridge: Harvard University Press, 1985), pp. 126–131; Robin Wood, *Howard Hawks* (London: BFI, 1981); Peter Wollen, *Signs and Meaning in the Cinema* (London: Thames and Hudson/BFI, 1969); and Molly Haskell, *From Reverence to Rape* (New York: Holt, Rinehart, and Winston, 1974).

3. Cendrars is cited in 'The Modernity of Howard Hawks', *Cahiers du Cinéma*, no. 139 (January 1963); Jean-Georges Auriol, 'A Girl in Every Port', *La Revue du Cinéma*, December 1928. Both articles are reprinted in Jim Hillier and Peter Wollen (eds), *Howard Hawks, American Artist* (London: British Film Institute, 1996).

4. Roud, *A Passion for Films*.

5. Ibid.

6. Ibid., pp. 65–6.

7. Rivette, 'The Genius of Howard Hawks'. Maurice Schére, [Eric Rohmer], 'Les Maîtres de l'aventure' (on *The Big Sky*), *Cahiers du Cinéma*, no. 29 (December 1953); and '*Gentlemen Prefer Blondes*' (review), *Cahiers du Cinéma*, no. 38 (August–September 1954), pp. 41–5. André Bazin, 'How Could You Be a Hitchcocko-Hawksian?' in John Caughie (ed.) *Theories of Authorship: A Reader* (Boston: Routledge and Kegan Paul/BFI, 1981). Translation of 'Comment peut-on être Hitchcocko-Hawksien', *Cahiers du Cinéma*, no. 44 (February 1955), pp. 17–18. *Positif* editors, 'Quelques réalisateurs trop admirés', *Positif*, no. 11 (September–October 1954), pp. 49–59.

8. *Cahiers du Cinéma*, no. 56 (February 1956); reprinted in *La Politique des Auteurs* (Paris: Champ Libre, 1972).

9. Andrew Sarris, *You Ain't Heard Nothing Yet: The American Talking Film; History and Memory, 1927–1949* (New York: Oxford University Press, 1998), p. 264.

10. Peter Bogdanovich, *The Cinema of Howard Hawks* (New York: Museum of Modern Art, July 1962).

11. *Movie*, no. 5 (December 1962); Lee Russell, 'Howard Hawks', *New Left Review*, I/24 (March–April 1964), pp. 82–5.

12. Wollen, *Signs and Meaning in the Cinema*.

13. Rivette, 'The Genius of Howard Hawks', p. 126.

14. André Malraux, 'A Preface for Faulkner's *Sanctuary*', *Yale French Studies*,

no. 10 (Fall 1952), pp. 92–4; Jean-Paul Sartre, 'On *The Sound and the Fury*: Time in the Works of Faulkner', in Robert Penn Warren (ed.), *Faulkner: A Collection of Critical Essays* (Engelwood Cliffs: Prentice-Hall, 1966), pp. 87–93.

15. Lawrence Schwartz, *Creating Faulkner's Reputation: The Politics of Modern Literary Criticism* (Knoxville: University of Tennessee Press, 1990); Serge Guilbaut, *How New York Stole the Idea of Modern Art: Abstract Expressionism, Freedom and the Cold War* (Chicago: University of Chicago Press, 1983).

16. Henri Peyre, 'American Literature through French Eyes', *Virginia Quarterly Review*, no. 23 (Summer 1947), pp. 421–38, p. 427.

17. Claude-Edmonde Magny, *L'Age du Romain Américain* (Paris: Seuil, 1948).

5   HITCH: A TALE OF TWO CITIES (LONDON AND LOS ANGELES)

1. John Russell Taylor, *Hitch: The Life and Work of Alfred Hitchcock* (London: Faber and Faber, 1978).

2. Ibid., p. 276.

3. Alfred Hitchcock, 'Women Are a Nuisance', in Sidney Gottlieb (ed.), *Hitchcock on Hitchcock: Selected Writings and Interviews* (Berkeley: University of California Press, 1995), p. 80. Reprint of 'Alfred Hitchcock Tells a Woman that Women Are a Nuisance', *Film Weekly* no. 10 (20 September 1935).

4. Ibid.

5. Taylor, *Hitch*, p. 174.

6. Alfred Hitchcock, 'Close Your Eyes and Visualize', in Sidney Gottlieb (ed.), *Hitchcock on Hitchcock: Selected Writings and Interviews* (Berkeley: University of California Press, 1995), p. 246. Reprint of 'Close Your Eyes and Visualize', *Stage* (July 1936), pp. 52–3.

6   JLG

1. David Thomson, *Rosebud: The Story of Orson Welles* (New York: Knopf, 1997).

2. Roland Barthes, *Elements of Semiology* (London: Jonathan Cape, 1988).
3. Manny Farber, 'The Films of Jean-Luc Godard', *Artforum*, no. 7 (October 1968), pp. 58–61; p. 58.
4. Wheeler Winston Dixon, *The Films of Jean-Luc Godard* (Albany, NY: SUNY Press, 1997).
5. Colin MacCabe, 'Jean-Luc Godard: A Life in Seven Episodes (To Date)', in Raymond Bellour and Mary Lea Bandy (eds), *Jean-Luc Godard: Son + Image, 1974–1991* (New York: Abrams, 1992), pp. 13–21.
6. Kaja Silverman and Harun Farocki, *Speaking about Godard* (New York: NYU Press, 1998).
7. Fredric Jameson, *Signatures of the Visible* (New York: Routledge, 1992, p. 233).
8. Silverman and Farocki, *Speaking about Godard*, p. 82.
9. Ibid., p. 198.
10. Dixon, *The Films of Jean-Luc Godard*.
11. Michael Witt, 'The Death(s) of Cinema According to Godard', *Screen*, vol. 40, no. 3, Autumn 1999.
12. Jean-Luc Godard, 'Films d'un peu partout causant français'. Introductory address for a screening of *For Ever Mozart*, National Film Theatre, London, 1996.
13. Published as Michael Temple, 'The Nutty Professor: Teaching Film with Jean-Luc Godard', *Screen*, no. 40 (Summer 1999).
14. Jean-Luc Godard, in Jean Narboni and Tom Milne, (eds) *Godard on Godard: Critical Writings by Jean-Luc Godard* (New York: Da Capo, 1986), p. 173.

7   JEAN ROUCH

1. Richard Roud, *'A Passion for Films: Henri Langlois and the Cinémathèque Française* (New York: Viking Press, 1983).
2. Roud, *Passion for Films*, p. 14.
3. C. W. Thompson, *L'Autre et le Sacré: Surréalisme, Cinéma, Ethnologie* (Paris: Harmattan, 1995).
4. Erika Brady, *A Spiral Way: How the Phonograph Changed Ethnography* (Jackson: University Press of Mississippi, 1999), p. 31.
5. Ibid., p. 31, no. 13.
6. Jean-Luc Godard, 'B.B. of the Rhine', in Jean Narboni and Tom Milne

(eds), *Godard on Godard: Critical Writings by Jean-Luc Godard* (New York: Da Capo, 1986), p. 101.

8   FREUD AS ADVENTURER

1. S. Freud, 'A Disturbance of Memory on the Acropolis', *The Standard Edition of the Complete Psychological Works of Sigmund Freud* (London: Hogarth Press, 1964), XXIII p. 239.
2. Ibid., p. 243.
3. Ibid., pp. 246–7.
4. Jeffrey Moussaieff Masson (ed.), *The Complete Letters of Sigmund Freud to Wilhelm Fliess, 1887–1904* (Cambridge, Mass.: Harvard University Press, 1985).
5. Ibid., p. 194. The source of the Nile, at the Ripon Falls on Lake Victoria Nyanza, had been first 'discovered' by John Hanning Speke in the early morning of 3 August 1858. He announced this discovery in *Blackwood's Magazine* the following year and in 1863 he published his *Journal of the Source of the Nile*, but his claim was bitterly contested by a number of other geographers and explorers, led by Sir Richard Burton, Speke's former partner. The matter was due to be settled in September 1864 at the annual meeting of the British Association for the Advancement of Science, where Speke and Burton were both invited to present their rival points of view in a kind of 'Nile duel', as Burton put it. However, on the very day of the 'duel', Speke accidentally shot himself while out shooting partridges, and controversy smouldered on until Stanley's expedition of 1874–77 confirmed his claim. However, the Nile had still never been traversed continuously from mouth to source and, although 'Baker of the Nile' and Colonel Gordon came close to this achievement, the Mahdist rising and the fall of Khartoum in 1885 blocked all further access from the north. In April 1894 Uganda was subjugated by the British, and early in 1896 the British government appointed General Kitchener to lead an expedition south from Egypt to retake Omdurman and thus finally complete British control of the Nile from mouth to source, a goal eventually achieved by 1899, when, in Alan Moorehead's words, 'by a new system of railways and steamers, it was now possible for a traveller to make his unmolested way along the entire length of the

river' (*The White Nile* [New York: Harper, 1960]: the most informative study of this period of European exploration and imperial expansion). The main point I want to make is that the exploration and navigation of the Nile was still a topical issue at the very time Freud was writing.

6. Masson, *Complete Letters*, p. 219. This seems to be an allusion to Franklin's failure to find the Northwest Passage, and the wreck of the *Erebus* and the *Terror*. Freud later cited a dream by George Back, who took part in Franklin's first expedition, in *The Interpretation of Dreams*, *Standard Edition*, vol. IV, p. 132 (a footnote added in 1912).

7. Masson, *Complete Letters*, p. 323. Nansen's epic voyage in the *Fram*, an unsuccessful attempt to reach the North Pole by sea through the polar ice, took place in 1893 to 1896, and Nansen subsequently published his own account of the journey in 1906. Freud included Nansen's dreams in *The Interpretation of Dreams*, which also has a section on 'Explorers' Dreams', taken from Otto Nordenskjold, Mungo Park and others.

8. Masson, *Complete letters*, p. 353. Schliemann was first inspired to discover the ruins of Troy by a picture of Troy in flames in Ludwig Jerrer's *Illustrated History of the World*, a Christmas gift from his father when he was seven years old. From the moment he saw this engraving, he later claimed, he was determined to excavate the city. In 1870 he began digging at Hissarlik in Turkey, which he believed to be the true site of Troy, and in 1873 discovered what he called 'Priam's palace' and, soon afterwards, a treasure of gold, silver and copper objects (diadems, rings, goblets, vases, etc.). In 1881 he published his book, *Ilios*, describing his discoveries (Leipzig: Brockhaus).

9. Freud first alludes to this joke in his letter to Fliess of 3 January 1897, cited above (Masson, *Complete Letters*, p. 219). On 22 July 1899, he compares completing the third part of his dream book ('the metapsychological') to attaining 'Rome, Karlsbad', and he repeats the analogy, with increasing desperation, on 16 September 1899, 9 October 1899 and 22 February 1900 ('the stations at which one is thrown out are very numerous').

10. Masson, *Complete Letters* p. 398. In this letter Freud describes himself 'as in a continuous rage'. See also the letter of 14 April 1898 (ibid., p. 309) in which Freud describes a caving expedition in the Alps, where the guide amused him with his commentary. In one cave, he was 'full of humour. He was the discoverer of the cave, obviously a genius gone

wrong; constantly spoke of his death, his conflicts with the priests, and his conquests in these subterranean realms. When he said that he had already been in thirty-six "holes" in the Carso, I realized he was a neurotic and his conquistador exploits were an erotic equivalent.' Another cave reminded Freud of Tartarus: 'If Dante saw anything like this, he needed no great effort of imagination for his inferno.' With Freud in this cave was Dr Lueger, the anti-semitic 'master of Vienna' and mayor of the city, a suitably diabolical apparition.

11. Ibid., p. 412.
12. John Huston, *An Open Book* (New York: Knopf, 1980).
13. Ibid., p. 7.
14. Ibid., p. 17.
15. William Bolitho, *Twelve Against the Gods* (New York: Simon and Schuster, 1929).
16. John Huston, cited in Lawrence Grobel, *The Hustons* (New York: Avon Books, 1990), p. 126.
17. Bolitho, *Twelve Against the Gods*, Introduction.
18. 'If I cannot bend the higher powers, I will move the regions of Hell.' Masson, *Complete Letters*, p. 205, where Freud suggests the Virgil quote as the motto for the section on symptom formation in a projected book. He eventually used the quote on the title page of *The Interpretation of Dreams*.
19. Huston, *An Open Book*, p. 297.
20. Ibid., p. 294.
21. Peter Viertel, *Dangerous Friends* (New York: Doubleday), p. 40.
22. Jean-Paul Sartre, *Words* (New York: Vintage Books, 1981), p. 49.
23. Ibid., pp. 50–1.
24. Ibid., pp. 133–4.
25. Ibid., p. 147.
26. In Simone de Beauvoir, *Adieux* (New York: Pantheon Books, 1984), p. 132. Sartre notes that 'One of the heroic works that I wrote when I was eleven or twelve was Goetz von Berlichingen.' Huston mentions Sartre's play of *Goetz von Berlichingen* in *An Open Book*, where he calls it 'Lucifer'. Curiously enough, 'Lucifer' was also Sartre's first stab at a title for *Les Chemins de la Liberté*.
27. Sartre, *Words*, pp. 167–71.
28. Ibid., p. 209.

29. Ibid., p. 254.

30. Passage cut from *La Nausée*, cited in Simone de Beauvoir, *Memoirs of a Dutiful Daughter* (Cleveland and New York: World Publishing Co., 1989), p. 355. *La Nausée* originated in the 1920s as 'the factum on contingency' on which Sartre embarked, according to Raymond Aron, after taking Léon Brunschvicg's course on Nietzsche at the Ecole Normale Supérieure. The manuscript went through three complete drafts, with three different titles and innumerable cuts, changes and revisions before it was finally published as a novel in 1938.

31. De Beauvoir, *Adieux*, pp. 312–13.

32. Ibid., p. 323.

33. Ibid., p. 328.

34. Freud, *A Disturbance of Memory on the Acropolis*, p. 247.

35. Jean-Paul Sartre, *The Freud Scenario* (London: Verso, 1985), pp. 505, 539.

36. Ibid., pp. 537–8.

37. Janet Walker, 'Textual Trauma in *King's Row* and Freud', in Janet Bergstrom (ed.), *Endless Night: Cinema and Psychoanalysis, Parallel Histories* (Berkeley: University of California Press), pp. 171–87.

38. Jean-Paul Sartre, *Sartre on Theater* (New York: Pantheon Books, 1976), p. 262.

39. Sartre, *Words*, pp. 18–19.

40. Jean-Paul Sartre, *Lettres au Castor* (Paris: Gallimard, 1983), vol. 2, p. 538.

41. Masson, *Complete Letters*, p. 202.

42. Freud, *Standard Edition*, vol. IV, pp. 317–18.

43. Masson, *Complete Letters*, pp. 230–1.

44. Ibid., p, 60.

45. Ernest Jones, *The Life and Work of Sigmund Freud* (New York: Basic Books, 1953) I, 305.

46. Freud, *Standard Edition*, vol. I, p. 272.

47. Freud, *Standard Edition*, vol. VII, p. 202.

48. Freud, *Standard Edition*, vol. IV, pp. 299–301.

49. Masson, *Complete Letters*, p. 268.

50. Ibid.

51. For Orvieto, see especially Freud, *Standard Edition*, vols III, pp. 290–2, VI, pp. 2–4, 13, 34, and for Lake Trasimene, ibid., vol. IV, p. 196. In

The Interpretation of Dreams, Freud recalled how the childhood incident in which his father had failed to protest after he was ordered off the pavement and his fur hat was knocked off his head by an anti-semite struck him as 'unheroic conduct', which he contrasted mentally with 'the scene in which Hannibal's father, Hamilcar Barca, made his boy swear before the household altar to take vengeance on the Romans'. Lake Trasimene was the scene of Hannibal's greatest victory against the Romans, under Gaius Flaminius, in 217 BC, yet Hannibal never finally achieved his goal of conquering Rome. In a letter to Fliess on 3 December 1897, Freud noted that 'my longing for Rome is deeply neurotic. It is connected with my schoolboy hero-worship of the Semitic Hannibal and in fact this year [actually 1896, when he visited Orvieto— his own furthest point south] I have no more reached Rome than he did from Lake Trasimene.' In *The Interpretation of Dreams*, p. 194, Freud described how this journey 'took me past Lake Trasimene' and he 'sadly turned back when I was only fifty miles from Rome'. Freud recorded a series of four dreams about his own failure to reach Rome—in the first of these, interestingly enough, he dreamed that he was looking out of a railway carriage window at a view of the Tiber and the Ponte Sant'Angelo, the traditional point of entrance to the Vatican.

52. Freud, *The Psychogenesis of a Case of Homosexuality in a Woman*, Standard Edition, vol. XVIII, p. 152.
53. Sartre, *The Freud Scenario*, p. 273.
54. Ibid., pp. 278–81.
55. Ibid., p. 370.
56. Ibid., p. 373.
57. Ibid., p. 539.
58. Ibid., p. 382.
59. Robert Harvey, *Search for a Father* (Ann Arbor: University of Michigan, 1991).
60. Huston, *An Open Book*, p. 3.
61. Lawrence Grobel, *The Hustons* (New York: Avon Books, 1989), p. 292.
62. Ibid., p. 295.
63. Ibid., passim, especially pp. 552–3.

9   BLADE RUNNER

1. Mike Davis, *City of Quartz: Excavating the Future in Los Angeles* (New York: Verso, 1990).
2. John Friedmann, 'The World City Hypothesis', in Paul Knox and Peter Taylor (eds), *World Cities in a World-System* (Cambridge, UK: Cambridge University Press, 1995), pp. 317–31.
3. Manuel Castells, *The Informational City: Information Technology, Economic Restructuring, and the Urban–Regional Process* (Cambridge: Blackwell, 1989); Saskia Sassen, *The Global City: London, New York, Tokyo* (Princeton: Princeton University Press, 1991).
4. Marshall McLuhan, *Understanding Media: The Extensions of Man* (New York: Signet, 1964).
5. Sharon Zukin, *Loft Living: Culture and Capital in Urban Change* (Baltimore: Johns Hopkins University Press, 1982).
6. Giuliana Bruno, 'Ramble City: Postmodernism and *Blade Runner*', *October* no. 41 (1987), pp. 61–74.
7. Paul M. Sammon, *Future Noir: The Making of* Blade Runner (New York: Harper Prism, 1996), p. 110.
8. Alain Lipietz, 'Towards Global Fordism', *New Left Review*, no. 132 (March–April 1981).
9. Sammon, *Future Noir*, p. 174.
10. Guy Debord, *La Société du Spectacle* (Paris: Buchet-Chastel, 1967).
11. Manuel De Landa, *A Thousand Years of Non-Linear History* (New York: Zone, 2000).
12. Perry Anderson, *The Origins of Postmodernity* (London: Verso, 1998), passim.
13. Sammon, *Future Noir*, p. 115.

10   SPIES AND SPIVS: AN ANGLO–AUSTRIAN ENTANGLEMENT

1. Michael Korda, *Charmed Lives: A Family Romance* (New York: Random House, 1979).
2. Ibid.

3. Paul Tabori, *Epitaph for Europe* (London: Hodder and Stoughton, 1942).

4. Raynes Minns, *Bombers and Mash: The Domestic Front, 1939–45* (London: Virago, 1980), p. 160.

5. Michael Shelden, *Graham Greene: The Man Within* (London: Heinemann, 1994), p. 29.

6. Ibid., p. 34.

7. Norman Sherry, *The Life of Graham Greene: Volume Two: 1939–1955* (London: Jonathan Cape, 1994), p. 243.

8. Shelden, *Graham Greene*, p. 317.

9. Kim Philby, *My Silent War* (New York: Ballantine, 1983).

10. Paul Tabori, *Alexander Korda* (New York: Living Books, 1966), p. 268.

11. Inge Lehne, *Vienna, the Past in the Present: A Historical Survey* (Vienna: Österreichischer Bundesverlag, 1985), p. 162.

12. Jacques Sandulescu, *Hunger's Rogues: On the Black Market in Europe, 1948* (New York: Harcourt Brace Jovanovich, 1974).

13. Graham Greene, 'Tales from the Vienna Woods', in John Russell Taylor (ed.), *The Pleasure-Dome: Graham Greene, The Collected Film Criticism, 1935–40* (London: Secker and Warburg, 1972), p. 174.

14. Graham Greene, 'Pépe le Moko', in John Russell Taylor (ed.), *The Pleasure-Dome: Graham Greene, The Collected Film Criticism, 1935–40* (London: Secker and Warburg, 1972), pp. 144, 145.

15. Philby, *My Silent War*.

16. Ibid.

11   RULES OF THE GAME

1. Jean-Luc Godard, 'Films d'un peu partout causant français'. Introductory address for a screening of *For Ever Mozart*, National Film Theatre, London, 1996.

2. Rudolf Arnheim, 'A New Laocoön: Artistic Composites and the Talking Film' (1938), in *Film As Art* (London: Faber and Faber, 1983), pp. 199–230.

3. Stanley Cavell, *Pursuits of Happiness: The Hollywood Comedy of Remarriage* (Cambridge: Harvard University Press, 1981).

4. Andrew Sarris, *The American Cinema* (New York: Da Capo, 1996), p. 56.

5. Henry Green, *Party Going* (London: Hogarth, 1939).

6. T. S. Eliot, *The Idea of a Christian Society* (London: Faber, 1939).
7. Virginia Woolf, *Between the Acts* (London: Hogarth, 1941).

12   THE LAST NEW WAVE

1. This analysis of Thatcherism emerges from debates carried on by a number of authors. See especially: Andrew Gamble, *The Free Economy and the Strong State* (Basingstoke: Macmillan, 1988); Stuart Hill, *The Hard Road to Renewal* (London: Verso, 1988); Bob Jessop, Kevin Bonnett, Simon Bromley and Tom Ling, *Thatcherism* (London: Polity Press, 1988); Scott Newton and Dilwyn Porter, *Modernisation Frustrated* (London: Unwin Hyman, 1988); and Henk Overbeek, *Global Capitalism and National Decline: The Thatcher Decade in Perspective* (London: Unwin Hyman, 1990). For the general anti-Thatcherite cultural efflorescence under Thatcherism, see Robert Hewison, *Future Tense* (London: Methuen, 1990). Films coming from outside London, it should be noted, like Bill Forsyth's Scottish films or the Liverpudlian *Letter to Brezhnev*, seem strangely less bitter than the London films, although a vein of cynicism underlies the mood of astringent comedy and wry fantasy. Northern Ireland has been marginalized in the cinema, as in the political arena, although Alan Clarke's extraordinary television work there represented the most startling and successful convergence of political with formal preoccupations in any of the media.
2. These words are quoted without citation by Roy Armes, in *A Critical History of the British Cinema* (London: Secker and Warburg, 1979). They are requoted parodically in Peter Greenaway's *The Draughtsman's Contract*, with painting substituted for cinema. For another version, see also Truffaut's remark that there is 'something about England that's anti-cinematic', in François Truffaut, *Hitchcock* (London: Panther, 1969).
3. Jacques Belmains, *Jeune Cinéma Anglais* (Lyon: Premier Plan, no. 44, May 1967).
4. On the Angry Young Men and their impact on the cinema, see: Harry Ritchie, *Success Stories: Literature and the Media in England 1950–1959* (London: Faber and Faber, 1988) and Robert Hewison, *In Anger* (London: Weidenfeld and Nicolson, 1981). John Hill, *Sex, Class and Realism:*

British Cinema, 1956–63 (London: British Film Institute, 1986), provides a comprehensive survey of the movement in film.

5. François, Truffaut. 'A Certain Tendency of the French Cinema', *Movies and Methods*, vol. 1, ed. Bill Nichols. (Berkeley: University of California Press, 1976), pp. 224–237. Reprint of 'Une certaine tendance du cinema français'. *Cahiers du Cinéma,* no. 31 (January 1954), pp. 15–28.

6. See Robert Murphy, *Realism and Tinsel* (London: Routledge, 1989), which takes its title from Michael Balcon's pamphlet, 'Realism and Tinsel', based on a talk given to the Film Workers Association in Brighton in 1943. This is available in Monja Danischewsky (ed.), *Michael Balcon's 25 Years in Films* (London: World Film Publications, 1947). In his talk, Balcon especially stressed the contribution Grierson's unit had made as 'the men who kept realism going on the screen' and the potential for a new type of film bringing a realistic treatment to 'story elements' within the industry.

7. See Peter Wollen, 'Scenes from the Future: Komar & Melamid', in *Between Spring and Summer* (Tacoma, Wash., and Boston, Mass: Tacoma Art Museum and Institute of Contemporary Art, 1990).

8. For the post-war history of modernism in Britain, see Alan Sinfield, *Literature, Politics and Culture in Postwar Britain* (Oxford: Basil Blackwell, 1989). He is also very illuminating on the sexual and class politics of the Angry Young Men.

9. For *Close Up* and *Borderline*, see Roland Cosandey, 'Re-assessment of "Lost" Film', *AfterImage*, no. 12, Autumn 1985, which contains a full bibliography. See also Anne Friedberg, 'The Film Journal *Close Up*', doctoral thesis presented at NYU, 1983.

10. For the Film Society, see Jen Samson, 'The Film Society 1925–1939', in Charles Barr (ed.), *All Our Yesterdays* (London: British Film Institute, 1986).

11. For Humphrey Jennings, see Mary-Lou Jennings, *Humphrey Jennings* (London: British Film Institute, 1982).

12. Sir Alexander Korda can be seen as one of the roster of émigré knights described by Perry Anderson in 'Components of the National Culture', *New Left Review*, no. 50, July–August 1968, along with Sir Isaiah Berlin, Sir Ernst Gombrich, Sir Lewis Namier and Sir Karl Popper. Yet Korda, it should be noted, worked with the revolutionary Béla Kún regime in Hungary and was a refugee from counter-revolutionary dictator Admiral

Horthy. Later, however, he became an intimate and patron of Churchill and his circle.

13. For the music hall, pierhead and seaside tradition, best exemplified by George Formby, the ukelele-playing hero of the Beatles and Morrissey, see Murphy's chapter on 'The Spiv Cycle' in *Realism and Tinsel*.

14. For wartime and post-war romanticism, see especially: David Mellor, *A Paradise Lost* (London: Lund Humphries, 1987), and Robert Hewison, *Under Siege* (London: Weidenfeld and Nicolson, 1977).

15. The best brief treatment of the British struggle against the economic power of Hollywood, led by Harold Wilson, is in Murphy, *Realism and Tinsel*.

16. See *This is Tomorrow Today* (New York: P.S. 1, The Institute for Art and Urban Resources, 1987) and, for the subsequent shift in British popular culture, Dick Hebdige, *Hiding in the Light* (London: Comedia, 1988).

17. For a general treatment of the 1960s, see Robert Hewison, *Too Much* (London: Methuen, 1986).

18. The indispensable sources for Derek Jarman are his two books of journals, Derek Jarman, *Dancing Ledge* (London: Quartet, 1984), and Derek Jarman, *Modern Nature* (London: Century, 1991). See also the special number of *AfterImage*, 'Derek Jarman . . . Of Angels & Apocalypse', *AfterImage*, no. 12, Autumn 1985. I have also drawn from Derek Jarman, *Derek Jarman's Caravaggio* (London: Thames and Hudson, 1986), Derek Jarman, *The Last of England* (London: Constable, 1987), and Derek Jarman, *War Requiem* (London: Faber and Faber, 1989).

19. Michael Powell was inspired by Friedrich Feher's film *The Robber Symphony*, which is described by Graham Greene in his review in the *Spectator*, 24 May 1936, reprinted in Graham Greene, *The Pleasure-Dome* (Oxford: Oxford University Press, 1980).

20. For Greenaway, I have drawn mainly from Peter Greenaway, *Papers* (Paris: Dis Voir, 1990), which contains a selection of his artwork with his own commentary, and Peter Greenaway, *Fear of Drowning by Numbers* (Paris: Dis Voir, 1988. A number of Greenaway's scripts are also published.

21. For Kitaj, see Marco Livingstone, *R.B. Kitaj* (Oxford: Phaidon Press, 1985). Kitaj did actually introduce Kenneth Anger and Michael Powell to each other: 'I brought Anger and Powell together because they admired each other. They're both quite mysterious and since I introduced them, I painted them together in their disjunction.'

22. See Peter Greenaway, 'Meurtre dans un Jardin Anglais', *L'avant-scène cinéma*, no. 333, Paris, October 1984. The translation of Greenaway's remarks is my own.

23. For the Oulipo group of writers, see Warren F. Motte Jr. (ed.), *Oulipo* (Lincoln: University of Nebraska, 1986).

24. For new romanticism and Blitz culture, see Caroline Evans and Minna Thornton, *Women and Fashion: A New Look* (London: Quartet, 1989).

25. Derek Jarman was one of a number of gay film-makers who made films in Britain during the Thatcher years, including Terence Davies, Isaac Julien, John Maybury, Ron Peck and Cerith Wyn Evans.

26. See Gary Indiana's interview with Peter Greenaway, in *Interview*, on the occasion of the New York release of *The Cook, the Thief, his Wife and her Lover*.

27. Reliable sources are few for this period in British cinema. For the Black Workshops, see especially Mbye B. Cham and Claire Andrade-Watkins (eds), *Blackframes* (London: Celebration of Black Cinema Inc. and the MIT Press, 1988), and Coco Fusco, *Young British and Black. The Works of Sankofa and Black Audio Film Collective* (Buffalo, NY: Hallwalls/Contemporary Arts Center, 1988).

28. See D. N. Rodowick, *The Crisis of Political Modernism* (Urbana: University of Illinois Press, 1988).

13   RIFF-RAFF REALISM

1. Robert Murphy, *Realism and Tinsel: Cinema and Society in Britain, 1939–49* (London: Routledge, 1989).

2. Alan Lovell, 'British Cinema: The Unknown Cinema'. Address at a British Film Institute seminar, London, 1960.

3. Alan Lovell, 'The British Cinema: The Known Cinema?' Address to the Education Department at the British Film Institute, 1985.

4. Michael Balcon, 'Realism and Tinsel', Address at the Workers Film Association, 1943.

5. Raynes Minns, *Bombers and Mash: The Domestic Front, 1939–45* (London: Virago, 1980).

6. Ibid., p. 159.

7. Michael Balcon, 'Realism and Tinsel', (London: Workers Film Association, 1944).

8. Viktor Shklovsky and Richard Sheldon. *Zoo, or, Letters Not About Love* (Normal, Ill.: Dalkey, Archive Press, 2001).

9. Benedict Anderson, *Imagined Communities: Reflections on the Origin and Spread of Nationalism* (London: Verso, 1983); Eric Hobsbawm and T. O. Ranger, *The Invention of Tradition* (Cambridge: Cambridge University Press, 1983); Robert Hewison, *The Heritage Industry: Britain in a Climate of Decline* (London: Methuen London, 1987); Ashis Nandy, *The Intimate Enemy* (Delhi: Oxford University Press, 1983).

14   ARCHITECTURE AND FILM: PLACES AND NON-PLACES

1. Marc Augé, *Non-Places—Introduction to an Anthropology of Supermodernity* (London: Verso, 1995).

2. Walter Benjamin, 'The Work of Art in the Age of Mechanical Reproduction', in *Illuminations* (New York: Schocken Books, 1969).

3. Robert Venturi, Denise Scott Brown and Steven Izenour, *Learning From Las Vegas* (Cambridge, Mass.: MIT Press, 1977). The Lapidus quotation is taken from *Progressive Architecture*, September 1970.

4. Quoted in the chapter on 'Set Theory and Set Denotation' in Charles Affron and Mirella Jones Affron, *Sets in Motion: Art Direction and Film Narrative* (New Brunswick: Rutgers University Press, 1995). This is an unusually ambitious book which attempts to develop a theoretical approach to art direction.

5. Howard Mandelbaum and Eric Myers, *Screen Deco* (New York: St Martin's Press, 1985).

6. For the Cedric Gibbons home see Brendan Gill, 'Cedric Gibbons and Delores Del Rio', in *Architectural Digest*, Los Angeles, April 1992.

7. Ayn Rand, *The Fountainhead* (New York: Bobbs-Merrill, 1943).

8. For the architectural influences on Carrere's designs for *The Fountainhead*, see the 'Epilogue' in Donald Albrecht, *Designing Dreams: Modern Architecture in the Movies* (London: Thames and Hudson, 1986), and 'The Fountainhead' in Dietrich Neumann (ed.), *Film Architecture: From 'Metropolis' to 'Blade Runner'* (Munich: Prestel, 1996).

9. George Nelson, 'Mr Roark Goes to Hollywood', *Interiors*, April 1949, cited in Albrecht, *Designing Dreams*.

10. Robert Boyle interview in Vincent LoBrutto, *By Design: Interviews with Film Production Designers* (Westport, Conn.: Praeger, 1992). See also 'Lost Innocence: Art Direction and Alfred Hitchcock' in Robert S. Sennett, *Setting the Scene: the Great Hollywood Art Directors* (New York: Abrams, 1994). See also the quotation from Charles Affron's interview with Boyle, cited in 'Set as Punctuation' in Affron and Affron, *Sets in Motion*.

11. Ian Bentley, 'The Owner Makes His Mark', in Paul Oliver, Ian Davis and Ian Bentley, *Dunroamin: the Suburban Semi and its Enemies* (London: Pimlico, 1981).

12. Lawrence Paull interview in LoBrutto, *By Design*.

13. Neumann, *Film Architecture*.

14. Bernard Eisenschnitz and Nicholas Ray, *An American Journey* (London: Faber and Faber, 1993). See also my essay on Nicholas Ray· 'Never at Home', in *Sight and Sound*, London, May 1994.

15. Chester Liebs, *Main Street To Miracle Mile* (Boston: Little Brown, 1985).

16. Peter Gould and Rodney White, *Mental Maps* (Boston: Allen and Unwin, 1986). For a different view of 'psycho-space', see Anthony Vidler, 'The Explosion of Space: Architecture and the Filmic Imaginary', in Neumann, *Film Architecture*

17. David Caute, *Joseph Losey* (New York: Oxford University Press, 1994), p. 10.

18. Ibid. An extremely Bachelardian passage is Caute's vivid description of the qualities of 'psycho-space'.

19. Alan Hess, 'Las Vegas', in *Googie: Fifties Coffee Shop Architecture* (San Francisco: Chronicle Books, 1985).

20. Guy Debord, *La Société du Spectacle* (Paris: Buchet-Chastel, 1967). Debord's concept of 'spectacle' depends on a viewer/viewed separation which is both physical and mental.

21. For the intellectual history of the concepts 'End of History' and 'Posthistoire', see Perry Anderson, 'The Ends of History', in *A Zone of Engagement* (London: Verso, 1992).

15   THE CANON

1. Jean-Pierre Coursodon and Yves Boisset, *20 Ans de Cinéma Américain, 1940–1960*. Paris: Éditions CIP, 1961.
2. Andrew, Sarris 'The American Cinema', *Film Culture* (Spring 1963), pp. 1–29; and his *The American Cinema: Directors and Directions, 1929–1968* (New York: Da Capo, 1996).
3. P. Adams Sitney, *Visionary Film: The American Avant-Garde* (New York: Oxford, 1974).
4. Andrew Sarris, *Confessions of a Cultist: On the Cinema, 1955–1969* (New York: Simon and Schuster, 1970).
5. Rudolf Arnheim, 'A New Laocoön: Artistic Composites and the Talking Film' (1938) in *Film As Art* (London: Faber and Faber 1983), pp. 199–230.
6. Peter Wollen, 'Introduction to *Citizen Kane*', *Film Reader* 1 (1975), pp. 9–15.
7. Michael Denning, *The Cultural Front: The Laboring of American Culture in the Twentieth Century* (London: Verso, 1997).
8. Frank Kermode, *The Classic* (London: Faber, 1975).

16   TIME IN FILM AND VIDEO ART

1. 'Making Time: Considering Time as a Material in Contemporary Film and Video', Inaugural Exhibition at the Palm Beach Institute of Contemporary Art, March–May, 2000. Works consulted in writing this chapter include the following: Bernard Comrie, *Aspect* (Cambridge: Cambridge University Press, 1976); Regina Cornwell, *Films by American Artists* (London: Arts Council of Great Britain, 1981); Thomas Elsaesser (ed.), *Early Cinema* (London: BFI Publishing, 1990); Gérard Genette, *Narrative Discourse* (Ithaca, NY: Cornell University Press, 1980); Paul J. Hopper, *Tense-Aspect: Between Semantics and Pragmatics* (Amsterdam/ Philadelphia: John Benjamin, 1982).
2. Bart Testa, *Back and Forth: Early Cinema and the Avant-Garde* (Toronto: Art Gallery of Ontario, 1992).
3. On the films of Andy Warhol, I am indebted to Stephen Koch, *Stargazer:*

Andy Warhol's World and His Films (New York: Marion Boyars, 1985); Jon Stout (ed.), *The Films of Andy Warhol* (Los Angeles: Filmforum, 1994).

4. John Cage, 'Defense of Satie', in Richard Kostelanetz (ed.), *John Cage: An Anthology* (New York: Da Capo, 1991), pp. 77–84; p. 81.

5. Peter Mark Roget, *Roget's Thesaurus* (London: Longman, 1852, 1992).

17   MISMATCHES (& ACOUSMÈTRES)

1. Sergei Eisenstein, Vsevolod Pudovkin and Grigori Alexandrov, 'Statement on Sound', trans. Richard Taylor. In Richard Taylor and Ian Christie (eds), *The Film Factory: Russian and Soviet Cinema in Documents, 1896–1939* (Cambridge: Harvard University Press, 1988), pp. 234–5.

2. Michel Chion, paper presented to the School of Sound Conference, London, UK, April 2000.

3. Rudolf Arnheim, 'In Praise of Blindness', *Radiotext(e)* (New York: Semiotext(e), 1993).

18   BACK TO THE FUTURE

1. Daniel J. Czitrom, *Media and the American Mind: From Morse to McLuhan* (Chapel Hill: University of North Carolina Press, 1982); Armand Mattelart, *The Invention of Communication* (Minneapolis: University of Minnesota Press, 1996); Michio Kaku, *Visions: How Science Will Revolutionize the 21st Century* (New York: Anchor, 1997); Joseph H. Corn, *Imagining Tomorrow: History, Technology, and the American Future* (Cambridge, Mass.: MIT Press, 1986).

2. Harold Innis, 'The Newspaper in Economic Development', *Journal of Economic History* 2 (Supplemental Issue: 2nd Annual Meeting of the Economic History Association, Williamstown, Mass., 4–5 September 1942), pp. 1–33.

3. William Gibson, 'William Gibson's Filmless Festival', *Wired* 7.10 (October 1999), p. 228.

19   SPEED AND THE CINEMA

1. Michael Balint, *Thrills and Regression* (New York: International Universities Press, 1959), p. 23.
2. Alfred Hitchcock, 'Why "Thrillers" Thrive', in Sidney Gottlieb (ed.), *Hitchcock on Hitchcock: Selected Writings and Interviews* (Berkeley: University of California Press, 1995), p. 109. Reprint of 'Why "Thrillers" Thrive', *Picturegoer*, 18 January 1936, p. 15.
3. Ibid.
4. Alfred Hitchcock, 'The Enjoyment of Fear', in Sidney Gottlieb (ed.), *Hitchcock on Hitchcock: Selected Writings and Interviews* (Berkeley: University of California Press, 1995), p. 117. Reprint of 'The Enjoyment of Fear'. *Good Housekeeping*, no. 128 (February 1949), pp. 39, 241–3.
5. Alfred Hitchcock, 'Core of the Movie—the Chase (interview with David Brady)', *New York Times* Magazine (29 October 1950), pp. 22–3, 44–6.
6. Barry Salt, *Film Style and Technology: History and Analysis*, rev. edn (London: Starword, 1992).
7. Nicky Hamlyn, 'Seeing is Believing: *Wavelength* Reconsidered', *After-Image*, no. 11 (Winter 1982–83), p. 30.
8. Sergei Eisenstein, 'Rhythm', in *Eisenstein Volume 2: Toward a Theory of Montage*, ed. Michael Glenny and Richard Taylor (London: British Film Institute, 1991), p. 228.
9. André Bazin, 'The Evolution of the Language of Cinema', in his *What is Cinema?* trans. and ed. Hugh Gray (Berkeley: University of California Press, 1967), p. 25.
10. Scott MacDonald, 'Michael Snow (Interview)', *A Critical Cinema 2* (Berkeley: University of California Press, 1992), p. 64.
11. Roland Barthes, 'The Jet-man', in his *Mythologies* (New York: Hill and Wang, 1962), pp. 71–3.

FILM-MAKERS/DIRECTORS

FILMOGRAPHY

GENERAL INDEX